D0347461

Law for the Layperson

LAW FOR THE LAYPERSON:
AN ANNOTATED BIBLIOGRAPHY OF
SELF-HELP LAW BOOKS

SECOND EDITION

By
Jean Sinclair McKnight

Based on
Law for the Layman, by Frank G. Houdek

KF
1
.H68
1997

Fred B.
Rothman & Co.
Littleton, Colorado 80127
1997

Library of Congress Cataloging-in-Publication Data

McKnight, Jean Sinclair
    Law for the layperson : an annotated bibliography of self-help law
books. — 2nd ed. / by Jean Sinclair McKnight.
            p.   cm.
        Rev. ed. of : Law for the layman / Frank G. Houdek. 1991– .
        Includes bibliographical reference and index.
        ISBN 0-8377-0869-9 (soft cover : alk. paper)
        1. Law—United States—Popular works—Bibliography.   I. Houdek,
Frank G. Law for the layman.   II. Title.
KF1.H68   1997
016.34973—dc21   96-39509
                                                                       CIP

© 1997 Jean Sinclair McKnight
All rights reserved.

Printed in the United States of America

This book is dedicated to my mother, Jean Sinclair, and, of course, my incomparable and impossibly wonderful husband, Ed.

TABLE OF CONTENTS

    Listed below are the subject headings used in arranging the annotations for the bibliography. Headings marked with an asterisk (*) include items both general and *state specific*. *See* and *See also* references are also provided.

ACKNOWLEDGMENTS

Thanks to Frank Houdek for the opportunity to do this book, an update of his original *Law for the Layman*. Thanks also to Pam Graham, who subdued a sea of typos and an unruly database without complaint; to Ed Burhenn, intrepid interlibrary loan procurement guy, who repeatedly went above and beyond the call of duty to help (and with a smile, no less!); and to Kathy Garner and Laurel Wendt, who didn't say "I told you so" nearly as many times as they were entitled to. And finally, thanks to the many publishers who sent copies of their self-help publications for review, making this publication possible.

Introduction to the Second Edition
by Jean McKnight

I am pleased to take up this publication where Frank Houdek left off, and hope that it helps people find the information they need to bring us a little closer to the elusive goal of justice for all.

All of Frank's well-put introduction to the first edition applies to this edition as well, except that the publications listed here were published on or before March 1, 1996, and the publications prior to 1990 have been omitted as they are likely to be dangerously out of date. There are a few exceptions in areas where newer titles are not available, on the assumption that something old is better than nothing at all.

Jean McKnight
April 1, 1996

INTRODUCTION TO THE FIRST EDITION
BY FRANK HOUDEK

When I began my career in law libraries as a reference librarian at the Los Angeles County Law Library in 1975, the single most popular book in the collection was a paperback explaining how to get a divorce without a lawyer. Though I have not been employed at LACLL since 1979, nor served a California clientele in six years, I would guess that the current edition of this publication[1] is still the most frequently requested item in that and most other public law libraries in California. And it is very likely that similar publications from other jurisdictions enjoy the same level of popularity in other libraries around the country.

The high cost of legal assistance, efforts at streamlining legal procedures,[2] the inability of the organized bar to meet the legal needs of a sizable segment of the general populace (those too wealthy for legal aid but too poor to hire a private attorney) are just some of the factors which have contributed to the rise of self-representation. Whether an increase in the number and variety of "self-help" law books is another cause of this phenomenon or a response to it is really not relevant—the fact is that there are now literally hundreds of books, pamphlets, and articles which seek to help non-lawyers help themselves. They cover many subjects and give counsel on a wide variety of situations with legal ramifications. The problem for the ambitious "do-it-yourselfer" is not a paucity of materials which provide assistance, but rather choosing from among the many available items those which are best suited for the question at hand. This is often a confusing and time-consuming task.

1.   Sherman, Charles E. *How to Do Your Own Divorce in California.* 16th ed. Occidental, CA: Nolo Press, 1990.
2.   California's "no-fault" divorce law became effective in 1970. A simplified procedure for securing a summary dissolution of short-term marriages was enacted in 1978, effective January 1, 1979.

XV

This bibliography is designed to overcome that problem. The main section, a subject-arranged and annotated list of self-help law books, provides an immediate solution in two ways: (1) it identifies which items among thousands of law-related publications are written expressly with the non-lawyer in mind and (2) it further separates those by topic and jurisdiction so that the reader can choose which ones are likely to be most helpful. The annotations[3] provide additional assistance by more clearly describing the subject content and identifying specific features of each publication which might prove valuable depending on the particular needs of the individual. Such features might include sample forms, checklists of things to do, step-by-step procedures to follow, and nontechnical explanations of the applicable law.[4] Knowing what is available from each book may further clarify one's selection of materials to consult.

The plethora of self-help law books also presents a problem for the conscientious acquisitions librarian, whether situated in a law, public, or academic library setting, who often must juggle limited budget dollars against a seemingly never-ending flow of books in determining which items to purchase. The dilemma is compounded by the fact that since many self-help publishers are small, their materials are usually not available on approval and often are either quickly out of print, out of date, or both. This bibliography addresses these difficulties by trying to be as comprehensive as possible in its listing of publications which are currently available, by providing a Jurisdiction Index so that items of purely local interest are not overlooked, and by providing a Publisher List with address and phone number so that quick action to acquire items is facilitated.

Other aspects of the bibliography intended to simplify its use are the Author Index and the Title Index. The former lists in alphabetical order each author represented in the bibliography, with a reference to the title of the publication and the subject under which the complete description and an annotation can be found. This provides access when an author's name is known but one is unsure of where the item might have been included within

---

3. A few items are listed without annotations. These are works which were identified as being "self-help law books" but which were not available to the author for examination prior to publication of the bibliography. Annotations will be provided in future supplements.

4. The explanations of the law in such materials are usually limited to a discussion of general principles. Relevant statutes may be covered and, depending on the subject, applicable administrative regulations. However, analysis of specific court decisions is usually beyond the scope of most self-help law books.

the subject list. The latter lists in alphabetical order the title of each work listed in the bibliography and the subject where it can be found. Once again, this facilitates location of an item when only a title is known.

A word about the publications which are included in the bibliography. Almost every self-help law book warns its readers that timeliness is of the utmost importance and that reliance on outdated legal information can be extremely hazardous. This statement is certainly true and for this reason only the most recent publications[5] are listed. Within these time constraints, the attempt has been made to identify every "self-help" book related to sub-stantive law or legal procedures which is currently available.[6] It is clear, however, that such a task is not as straightforward as it might seem, since many books which might be of assistance to the non-lawyer are written with the lawyer in mind.[7] Drawing the line is not always easy but the tendency has been to err on the side of overinclusion rather than underinclusion. Still, there are certainly some items which have been overlooked—it is hoped that such materials will be located and included in the regular supplementation which is planned for the bibliography.

Frank Houdek
March 1991

5. Most of the items included in the bibliography have been published within the last three years. Older items have been included where there was nothing more recent available in the library for the particular subject or where the information contained therein continued to be relevant despite the time elapsed since publication. No item published prior to 1980 is included.

6. The cut-off date for inclusion, in as much as such an arbitrary time period can be maintained, was publication on or before March 1, 1991 [the second edition cut-off date was March 1, 1996—JM].

7. It is also clear that the converse is true—many "self-help" law books are potentially useful to the attorney as well, especially one who is faced with a problem in an area of the law with which he or she is unfamiliar. For this reason, attorneys as well as non-attorneys may profit by referring to this bibliography.

PART ONE
GENERAL/COMPREHENSIVE WORKS

American Bar Association. *The American Bar Association Family Legal Guide.* Chicago, IL: Times Books. Random House, 1994. 732p.

The forward to this book notes that a recent ABA survey revealed that "most lower and moderate income families' legal needs are related to basic, everyday issues of life: housing, personal finance, family and domestic concerns (such as divorce and child support), employment-related issues, personal injury, and community problems." This book separates the many areas of law into chapters that specifically deal with these types of issues. Written in a question-and-answer format, in very simple language. Each chapter gives phone numbers and ends with suggestions of where to go for further information. Includes a glossary and a detailed chapter on when and how to use a lawyer, with rather lawyerly explanations of what you can expect in the way of fees and fee structures.

Battle, Carl W. *Legal-Wise: Self-Help Legal Forms for Everyone.* 2nd ed. New York, NY: Allworth Press, 1991. 208p.

Basic forms for: preparing or probating a will; making a living will or living trust; making an organ donor pledge; assignments of personal rights; power of attorney; buying, selling, or leasing real estate; selling personal property; contracting for repairs of services; simple divorce or separation; name change; small claims court affidavit; releases; patents, trademarks, and copyrights; bankruptcy; IRS audits; and advice on when and how to retain an attorney. Explanations of pertinent concepts and pitfalls are included for each topic.

Christianson, Stephen G., Esq. *100 Ways to Avoid Common Legal Pitfalls Without a Lawyer.* Seacaucus, NJ: Carol Publishing, 1992. 294p.

For each of one hundred alphabetically arranged legal topics, ranging from abortion to zoning, the author offers a brief synopsis of the current state of

1

the law, and suggestions on how to deal with problems yourself or with non-lawyer help. Contact information for appropriate agencies is included. Only very basic information is given, no step-by-step instructions (although there are a few sample forms), just a good idea of where to start. Includes a 50-state directory to getting your legal questions answered at low or no cost.

Court TV and American Lawyer, editors. *Court TV's Cradle-to-Grave Legal Survival Guide: A Complete Resource For Any Question You Might Have About the Law.* 1st ed. Boston, MA: Little, Brown, 1995. 487p.

While the subtitles' claim that this book is a complete resource for any question you may have about the law it is, of course, a bit of an overstatement, this hefty guide does offer information on a wide array of legal issues of common interest. Written in a readable and sometimes humorous question-and-answer format. Includes the text of the U.S. Constitution.

Haas, Carol. *The Consumer Reports Law Book: Your Guide to Resolving Everyday Legal Problems.* Yonkers, NY: Consumer Reports Books, 1994. 484p.

Discusses legal issues which affect most people, offering enough information to help you recognize your legal rights and to get an idea of what options you have when your rights have been violated. Topics include: the family; planning your estate; contracts; wrongful injury; cars and driving; buying or renting a home; the workplace; consumer rights and obligations; how the legal system works; choosing and working with an attorney; and trials. Also includes: addresses and phone numbers for obtaining further information; the U.S. Constitution; a glossary; and sample letters.

Hauser, Thomas. *The Family Legal Companion.* New York, NY: Allworth Press, 1992. 256p.

Basic, brief information about everyday legal issues in a question-and-answer format. Covers wide range of topics such as: your job; landlords; pets; wills; travel; neighbors; and social security. Explanations are very short and general, and do not address variations in state laws. Offers good general information as a starting point for understanding basic legal issues, but not much help with any specific subject, as a great many topics are included. No forms or procedural help, with the exception of two pages of advice on negotiating small claims court.

In Trouble? 104 Legal Ways Out. Irvine, CA: LawPrep Press, 1991. 1 vol.

Know Your Rights, and How to Make Them Work for You. New York, NY: Reader's Digest, 1995. 1 vol.

Legal Breakdown: 40 Ways to Fix Our Legal System. Berkeley, CA: Nolo Press, 1990. 88p.

Departing from their usual "how-to" focus on a specific subject, various Nolo Press authors have come together in this publication to offer an eclectic mix of ideas on how to improve the legal system. They offer concrete proposals covering a wide range of areas and issues from "simplify legal paperwork" and "make the courthouse user-friendly" to "reform the child support system" and "require lawyer impact statement." Each idea is concisely presented in 2 to 3 pages containing background information, problem analysis, and a proposed solution (titled "what to do"). You may not agree with all the suggested reforms, but at least they serve to introduce the issues to public scrutiny.

Mierzwa, Joseph. *The 21st Century Family Legal Guide.* Highlands Ranch, CO: Prose Associates, 1994. 452p.

Answers common legal questions about such topics as: rights and freedoms; family law; home; car; job and credit; insurance; health care; retirement; governments benefits; taxes; estates; crimes; the judicial system; and lawyers. "While this book was not intended as a do-it-yourself guide, it has been written to help you keep legal fees to a minimum by giving you information you can use to ask the right questions when you do need a lawyer's help." Offers numerous references to sources of further information and advice on finding and dealing with a lawyer if you do decide to use one.

Milton, Jay with Ginita Wall. *Cover Your Assets: Lawsuit Protection; How to Safeguard Yourself, Your Family, and Your Business in the Litigation Jungle.* Austin, TX: Crown, 1995. 224p.

Schachner, Robert W. and Marvin Quittner. *How and When to Be Your Own Lawyer: A Step-by-Step Guide to Effectively Using the Legal System.* Garden City Park, NY: Avery Publishing Group, Inc., 1993. 416p.

How to decide whether you really need a lawyer, and how to best help your case with or without one. Concise explanations of how our legal system works and how to research, prepare and present your case, and how to appeal or collect a judgement after trial. Also discusses how to get what you deserve without going to court, by settling out of court or taking advantage of mediation or arbitration. Sample litigation forms (not ready to use) are included.

Sitarz, Dan. *The Complete Book of Personal Legal Forms.* 1st ed. Carbondale, IL: Nova Publishing Co. 1993. 248p.

Intended to provide a typical individual with "most of the legal documents necessary for day-to-day life." The author explains situations in which each form would be appropriate, and notes particular situations in which the aid of a lawyer is strongly recommended. Forms are written in the plainest possible language, and terms unfamiliar to most laypersons are defined. Includes forms dealing with: wills and trusts; personal property and real estate; powers of attorney; releases; financing and collection documents; marital settlement agreement; and other topics.

Sloan, Irving J. *More Everyday Legal Forms.* Dobbs Ferry, NY: Oceana Publications, 1992. 211p.

A large number of sample forms covering a wide variety of subjects are presented here. The forms include blanks to be filled in with appropriate information when used, but there are no explanatory comments to assist you in doing so. Nor are there annotations to help you decide if and how a form should be modified to meet the unique circumstances of each particular situation, although the introduction clearly warns the reader that modification is often necessary. Forms included cover such needs as: sale of a professional practice; bill of sale; installment note; business insurance; compromise and settlement; general release; warranty deed to convey real property; residential and commercial leases; landlord and tenant notices; wills; short-term trust; support agreements; living-together agreements; power of attorney; and retaining an attorney for a fixed fee.

Terry, Brent. *The Complete Idiot's Guide to Protecting Yourself from Everyday Legal Hassles.* Indianapolis, IN: Alpha Books, 1995. 309p.

Warda, Mark. *Simple Ways to Protect Yourself from Lawsuits: A Complete Guide to Asset Protection.* Clearwater, FL: Sphinx Publishing, 1996. 200p.

This book provides strategies you can use to protect your assets from lawsuits. It is divided into six parts: an overview of asset protection planning; shielding yourself against claims; protecting property in your name; taking property out of your name; when disaster strikes; and your immediate action plan. Also includes appendices of state and federal bankruptcy exemptions and state exemption comparisons, sources of further information, and selected forms. Forms are ready to use, but the author, notes that "for a [sic] extra level of protection (except on IRS forms) you can retype them on your computer or typewriter. If they were created by you they look less like a fraud on creditors than if they came from an asset protection book."

Warner, Ralph and Stephen Elias. *Fed Up with the Legal System: What's Wrong and How to Fix It.* 2nd ed. Berkeley, CA: Nolo Press, 1994. 200p.

Ralph Warner and Stephen Elias describe what they think is wrong with our legal system, and what we ought to do to fix it. They make a lot of sense! Do us all a favor and encourage your legislators to read this book.

You, Your Family & the Law: A Legal Guide for Today's Families. Washington, DC: HALT, 1993. 232p.

CALIFORNIA

Guerin, Lisa and Patti Gima. *Nolo's Pocket Guide to California Law.* 3rd ed. Berkeley, CA: Nolo Press, 1994. 208p.

A quick reference guide to California law covering legal issues "most likely to affect people in the ordinary course of their lives." Criminal law (except traffic violations) is not included. Some federal laws of common interest are included, such as some dealing with Social Security and bankruptcy. Topics are grouped alphabetically, with concise explanations. Each section of the book contains a list of additional resources on that topic. Each law mentioned is cited, so that you can look up the full text if you like. A section on finding the sources of those citations is also included.

Wallace, L. Jean. *What Every 18-Year-Old Needs to Know About California Law.* Austin, TX: University of Texas Press, 1994. 172p.

Intended to "help young adults avoid costly and frightening encounters with the law," this book provides information on laws to be aware of, plus guidance on which situations are serious enough to require a lawyer's assistance and which are not, and how to hire an attorney if you need to. Peppered throughout with "humorous" true stories to illustrate legal points.

TEXAS

Wallace, L. Jean. *What Every 18-Year-Old Needs to Know About Texas Law.* Austin, TX: University of Texas Press, 1994. 172p.

Intended to "help young adults avoid costly and frightening encounters with the law," this book provides guidance on exotic pitfalls of the law which an eighteen-year-old might easily be unaware of, such as the illegality of swearing in public in Texas. The book provides much such information on laws to be aware of, plus guidance on which situations are serious enough to require a lawyer's assistance and which are not. Peppered throughout with "humorous" true stories to illustrate legal points.

PART TWO
SPECIFIC SUBJECTS

ADA AND DISABILITY

Allen, Jeffrey G. *Complying With the ADA: A Small Business Guide to Hiring and Employing the Disabled.* New York, NY: John Wiley & Sons, 1993. 210p.

The book begins with the assertion that accessability is not only good for the disabled, but good for business as well. Part One deals with hiring issues, from recognizing who is regulated and protected by the ADA to understanding the scope and enforcement of the regulations. Methods and advantages of recruiting disabled workers are included. Recognizing and avoiding discrimination as defined by the act is stressed. Part Two deals with accommodating disabled employees, and the complicated question of what constitutes reasonable accommodation. Recognizing exactly where and for whom accommodations must be made is discussed, and tips for accommodating specific disabilities are included. Also includes information on tax incentives to encourage accommodation, and ADA accessibility guidelines for existing buildings and new construction and alteration.

Castellano, Lucinda A., Randy Chapman, and The Legal Center. *Prentice Hall ADA Compliance Advisor.* Englewood Cliffs, NJ: Prentice-Hall, 1993. 1 vol.

Leavy, Robert M. *The Rights of Mentally Disabled People.* Carbondale, IL: Southern Illinois University Press, 1996. 1 vol.

ADOPTION

California

Zagone, Frank and Mary Randolph. *How to Adopt Your Stepchild in California*. 4th ed. Berkeley, CA: Nolo Press, 1994. 192p.

Designed for simple, uncontested stepparent adoptions, this book provides practical and legal information to help the reader decide whether to adopt, information to determine if adoption is legally possible, and a step-by-step guide for petitioning the court for adoption. It explains the three types of stepparent adoption procedures in California: absent parent consents; absent parent can't be found (leading to an action based on failure to support the child, abandonment, or terminating parental rights); and absent parent won't consent. Sample forms are provided in the text with explanations as to how they should be filled out; tear-out forms for actual use are provided in the appendix.

Florida

Nickel, Gudrun M. *How to File an Adoption in Florida*. Clearwater, FL: Sphinx Publishing, 1993. 145p.

Explains how to file an adoption in Florida, with specific information on adopting stepchildren, non-stepchildren, adults, or intermediary pre-planned adoptions. With Florida Supreme Court-approved forms. Discusses confidentiality and the State Adoption Information Center. Includes text of selected statutes and adoption flowcharts to clarify the process.

AIDS

McCormack, Thomas P. *The AIDS Benefits Handbook*. New Haven, CT: Yale University Press, 1990. 257p.

Describes the benefits programs available to help AIDS victims, and how to cut through the red tape to get the help you are eligible for. Includes state-by-state lists of resources and suggestions for program improvements to pass on to elected officials and program administrators. Concise summaries of available programs show what benefits are offered, who is eligible, exactly where and how to apply, and how to appeal. Also includes a list of local AIDS support groups.

Ruebenstein, Martin. *The Rights of HIV-Positive People*. Carbondale, IL: Southern Illinois University Press, 1996. 1 vol.

ANIMALS

Randolph, Mary. *Dog Law*. 2nd ed. Berkeley, CA: Nolo Press, 1994. 336p.

Urbanization has greatly increased animal regulation, making legal questions concerning dogs a common occurrence (e.g., How many dogs can my neighbor keep? What can I do about a dog that barks all night? Am I liable if my dog bites a child who teases it?). This book attempts to answer many common questions relating to dogs, or shows how to find the answers. Topics covered include: landlords and dogs; buying and selling dogs; veterinarians; personal injury and property damage; disputes with neighbors; traveling with dogs; and vicious dogs. An appendix provides a list of state dog-bite statutes.

ARBITRATION AND MEDIATION

Freidman, Gary. *Taking Charge of Your Own Divorce: A Guide to Mediation*. New York, NY: Workman Publishers, 1993. 1 vol.

Lovenheim, Peter. *How to Mediate Your Dispute: Find a Solution You Can Live With Quickly and Cheaply Outside the Courtroom*. 1st ed. Berkeley, CA: Nolo Press, 1996. 325p.

The ultimate self-help, no-lawyer solution: mediation. Courts are increasingly requiring mediation for custody disputes, small claims, and civil suits, and many people are wisely turning to this quick and inexpensive method of resolving disputes of their own accord. The book shows how to handle a mediation from start to finish, including step-by-step instructions for choosing a good mediator and planning your strategy, and detailed advice on how to conduct yourself for a successful mediation. The emphasis of this book (and this approach) is on reaching a "win-win" agreement, where both sides come away with the best possible compromise, rather than the winner take all approach taken by the courts.

ARTISTS AND CRAFTSPEOPLE

Art, the Art of Community, and the Law: A Legal and Business Guide for Artists, Collectors, Gallery Owners, and Curators. Bellingham, WA: Self-Counsel Press, 1994. 202p.

Crawford, Tad. *Business and Legal Forms for Fine Artists.* New York, NY: Allworth Press, 1990. 144p.

Begins with a brief overview of the contracting process, such as oral and written contracts and the use of standard provisions, but for a more in-depth handbook on the legal issues faced by artists, readers are referred to the author's own *Legal Guide for the Visual Artists.* This publication is primarily devoted to actual forms used by artists, with a brief explanation and "Negotiation Checklist" accompanying each form. The latter is particularly helpful because it provides a thorough checklist to insure that all relevant items are provided for in the document. Samples are provided for such things as selling an artwork, commissioning an artwork, creating a limited edition, rental or exhibition of a work. Forms available on diskette for Mac or PC.

Crawford, Tad. *Business and Legal Forms for Illustrators.* New York, NY: Allworth Press, 1990. 160p.

Provides a complete set of forms to meet the majority of legal and business needs of a professional illustrator. A brief introduction to contracts and advice on standard provisions is provided. Negotiation checklists accompany each form to help the illustrator bargain successfully. Among the 17 forms included are agreements with agents, book publishers, collaborators, and galleries. A licensing agreement for spinoffs (e.g., posters, ceramics, novelties, etc.) is provided, as well as forms covering lectures, nondisclosure of ideas, and permission to use a copyrighted work. Specific suggestions on the use of each form are offered. Forms available on diskette for Mac or PC.

Crawford, Tad. *Legal Guide for the Visual Artist.* New York, NY: Allworth Press, 1990. 256p.

The purpose of this book is to introduce artists to the legal problems of both art in commerce and artists' rights. It covers a large variety of business and legal issues that any artist must confront at one time or another, including copyright and moral rights; sales by artist, gallery, or agent; taxation (including hobby losses); studios and leases; the artist as collector; estate planning; and artists and museums. Model contracts and other forms are interspersed throughout, although the reader may also want to refer to the same author's *Business and Legal Forms for Fine Artists* for a more thorough presentation on the use of such materials. An appendix includes a listing of organizations, agencies, and groups which provide assistance to artists.

Crawford, Tad. *Protecting Your Rights and Increasing Your Income: A Guide for Authors, Graphic Designers, Illustrators, and Photographers.* New York, NY: Allworth Press, 1990. Audio, 60 min.

Crawford, Tad and Eva Doman Bruck. *Business and Legal Forms for Graphic Designers.* New York, NY: Allworth Press, 1990. 244p.

This book provides forms, checklists, and negotiation tips for the graphic designer and design firm. The first group of forms relates to the organization and smooth functioning of the business aspects of a design studio and are arranged according to the typical chronology occurring in the course of business. Included are estimate and proposal forms, project status reports, payables index, artwork log, and collection letters. A second group focuses on contractual relationships outside the firm, such as agreements with illustrators, printers, agents, and manufacturers. A variety of release forms are provided. Notes accompanying each form explain the purpose of each provision and the checklists insure that all issues will be considered. Forms available on diskette in PageMaker format for Mac or PC.

DuBoff, Leonard D. *Business Forms and Contracts (in Plain English) for Craftspeople.* Portland, OR: Interweave Press, 1990. 128p.

Leland, Caryn R. *Licensing, Art and Design.* New York, NY: Allworth Press, 1990. 128p.

Describes how creators of art works and designs (e.g., graphic designers, architects, illustrators, etc.) can transform ideas and concepts into financial successes through the process of licensing. An overview of the business and legal aspects is provided, including a discussion of the rights of creators under the "law of ideas" and copyright, patent, and trademark laws. Agreements to use in the pre-licensing stage are presented, followed by a thorough analysis of the provisions of a licensing contract. Suggested model forms and a checklist for negotiating licensing agreements are provided. Use of a licensing agent is also considered.

Norwick, Kenneth P., Jerry Simon Chasen, and Henry B. Kaufman. *The Rights of Authors, Artists, and Other Creative People.* Carbondale, IL: Southern Illinois University Press, 1992. 1 vol.

Victoroff, Gregory T. (compiled and edited by). *The Visual Artist's Business and Legal Guide.* Englewood Cliffs, NJ: Prentice Hall, 1995. 338p.

Explains copyright law and other protections available to visual artists, contract law as applies to art sales and consignments, licensing, and dealing with agents, and suggestions and legal tips for promoting, exhibiting, and selling your work and avoiding art frauds. Final chapters deal with restrictions on artistic content and the economics of art, including collecting money that is due to you, grant writing, insurance, and when to mediate or hire a lawyer.

Wilson, Lee. *Make It Legal.* New York, NY: Allworth Press, 1990. 272p.

Primarily addressed to graphic designers and advertising agency creative staffs as a guide to the various areas of law which affect their professional activities on a daily basis. After a general overview, separate sections examine the basics of copyright law, trademark law, libel, privacy, and publicity law, and false advertising law. The book includes many anecdotes to illustrate how these laws interact with the world of advertising and to raise the consciousness of the reader about issues that need to be considered. Problem recognition and avoidance is emphasized. Copyright and trademark registration procedures are explained. Sample forms and the identification of additional resources are provided in the appendix.

ATTORNEY AND CLIENT

Baker, Stephen. *How to Survive a Lawyer.* Los Angeles, CA: Price/ Stern/Sloan, 1991. 1 vol.

Carroll, Nicholas. *Dancing with Lawyers: How to Take Charge and Get Results.* Lafayette, CA: Royce-Baker Publishing, 1992. 192p.

A guide for the client who wishes to supervise and control the relationship with an attorney, as opposed to the other way around. Advice is offered on how to locate the right lawyer for the particular job, how to negotiate fees, and how to insure that the lawyer does the work in a timely manner. Helpful descriptions of law firm operations are also included.

Hayes, J. Michael. *Help Your Lawyer Win Your Case.* Clearwater, FL: Sphinx Publishing, 1994. 176p.

The author points out that your lawsuit will proceed faster and cost less if you know what your attorney needs and are prepared to help him or her prepare the case. Offers suggestions on finding a good lawyer, what to say at the initial meeting with him or her, and negotiating the legal system. Includes checklists and information forms to help you prepare for a meeting with your lawyer.

Hedglon, Mead. *How to Get the Best Legal Help for Your Business (At the Lowest Possible Cost).* New York, NY: McGraw Hill, 1992. 296p.

According to the author, "the focus of this book is on obtaining an acceptable outcome in any legal matter at a reasonable cost." It is directed to the small business owner who must decide how to deal with the many legal needs which inevitably arise: Is a lawyer needed? Should in-house lawyers be used? Should outside counsel be consulted? How does one hire a trial attorney? What to do first when one is sued? These and other issues are thoroughly explained by the author in a readable style, made even easier to understand by the inclusion of examples and illustrations. Checklists of procedures are provided for each chapter, along with a variety of sample forms. Attorney-client relations are effectively dealt with in chapters on controlling legal costs through budgets, how to read a lawyer's bill, and using systems that keep the client in touch with the attorney.

Klein, Raymond. *Putting a Lid on Legal Fees: How to Deal Effectively with Lawyers.* Los Angeles, CA: Interlink Press, 1986. 189p.

Tips on selecting the right lawyer and keeping control of your costs. As the author notes, the lawyer is the expert, but you are the boss. Offers strategies for controlling a business' legal costs as well and an individual's, and explains how to take advantage of inexpensive alternatives to litigation. Includes: a preventative law checklist; rules to avoid excess fees in litigation;

a litigation plan and budget; sample fee agreements and billing formats; contract clauses to motivate out-of-court settlements; and a sample advertisement for a general counsel.

Leeds, Dorothy. *Smart Questions to Ask Your Lawyer.* New York, NY: Harper Paperbacks, 1992. 278p.

A book of questions you should ask your lawyer in various situations to assure that both you and your lawyer are aware of crucial issues. Also offers some assistance as to whether you may be able to get by without hiring a lawyer at all. Enables you to speak intelligently with your lawyer and recognize legal problems that you may be able to avoid. The book is divided into ten sections: dealing with choosing a lawyer; family law; real estate; contracts; starting your own business; lawsuits; criminal law; civil rights; bankruptcy and creditors rights; and attorney ethics and behavior.

Ostberg, Kay. *Using a Lawyer . . . and What to Do If Things Go Wrong: A Step-by-Step Guide.* Rev. ed. New York, NY: Random House, 1990. 146p.

Offered as a consumer guide for managing business dealings with a lawyer, this book has advice on how to avoid problems with lawyers and how to resolve them if preventive steps fail. It is organized chronologically, beginning with levels of client involvement, continuing to ways of finding, hiring, and working with a lawyer, and ending with methods of resolving disputes with a lawyer. Extensive appendices provide a model client-attorney agreement, a prepaid legal services plan contract, a graphic presentation of the stages of a lawsuit, a state-by-state list of programs for resolving disputes, a glossary, and a bibliography.

Ostberg, Kay and Theresa Meehan Rudy. *If You Want to Sue a Lawyer—A Directory of Legal Malpractice Attorneys.* Washington, DC: HALT, 1995. 130p.

Sigman, Robert. *Legal Malpractice.* Altamonte Springs, FL: Legovac, 1990. Audio

Starnes, Tanya. *Mad at Your Lawyer.* 1st ed. Berkeley, CA: Nolo Press, 1996. 220p.

How to deal with problems you have with a lawyer, with a focus on dealing with them before they become critical. Describes what you can reasonably expect from a lawyer and how to deal with the most common complaints against lawyers, up to and including filing suit against them. Emphases the importance of taking charge of your own case and keeping track of what your lawyer is doing—and billing you for. Also explains how lawyers bill, how to avoid and handle fee disputes successfully, and how to change lawyers if yours is not doing what you think he or she should, even if you are right in the middle of litigation.

BANKRUPTCY

Doran, Kenneth J. *Personal Bankruptcy and Debt Adjustment: The Fresh Start, A Step-by-Step Guide.* New York, NY: Random House, 1991. 1 vol.

Elias, Stephen, Albin Renauer, and Robin Leonard. *How to File for Bankruptcy.* 5th ed. Berkeley, CA: Nolo Press, 1995. 400p.

Explains routine procedures for Chapter 7 bankruptcy filings. Includes introductory chapters (e.g., an overview; should you file?), procedure chapters (e.g., filling in and filing forms, handling case in court), and reference chapters (e.g., secured debts, pensions and bankruptcy, non-dischargeable debts). Particularly useful are the "fast track" messages throughout the text which signal the reader as to materials that may be skipped depending on one's circumstances. The simplest situation can be handled by reading two chapters and referring to two appendices. Exemptions for each state are listed in the appendix, which also includes forms and worksheets.

Elias, Steve, Albin Renauer, Robin Leonard, and Lisa Goldoftas. *Nolo's Law Form Kit: Personal Bankruptcy.* 1st ed. Berkeley, CA: Nolo Press, 1993. 120p.

Haman, Edward A. *How to File Your Own Bankruptcy (Or How to Avoid It).* 1st ed. Clearwater, FL: Sphinx Publishing, 1990. 138p.

This book seeks to help individuals with financial problems analyze their situation and decide whether they should file for bankruptcy. If bankruptcy is chosen, either as a way of discharging debts or setting up a payment plan, it explains the procedures to follow in a concise, straightforward manner. Corporate, partnership, or business-related bankruptcies are specifically excluded from coverage. Part 1 explains the basics of bankruptcy law and procedure. Part 2 discusses whether you should file for bankruptcy, also explaining how to avoid bankruptcy and providing alternative approaches to dealing with financial setbacks. Part 3 covers preparation for bankruptcy (e.g., arranging finances, gathering information) and Part 4 instructs on bankruptcy procedures for both debt discharges (Chapter 7 bankruptcies) and payment plans (Chapter 13 bankruptcies). The appendices contain 22 reproducible forms and a listing of local exemptions alphabetically by state.

Koff, Gail J. *The Jacoby and Meyers Guide to Personal Bankruptcy.* New York, NY: Henry Holt, 1991. 1 vol.

Leonard, Robin. *Chapter 13 Bankruptcy.* 1st ed. Berkeley, CA: Nolo Press, 1994. 368p.

Reich, Lawrence R. and James P. Duffy. *You Can Go Bankrupt Without Going Broke: An Essential Guide to Personal Bankruptcy.* New York, NY: Pharos Books, 1992. 241p.

A straightforward guide to the large variety of issues confronting anyone in financial difficulty who is considering (or may wish to consider) bankruptcy as a possible solution. The text is sprinkled throughout with concrete examples, case histories, and checklists of questions to consider, all of which combine to clarify the subject for the lay reader. The various types of personal bankruptcy are explained as well as possible alternatives. Both the law and the procedures which are followed are thoroughly presented. Exemptions are examined on a state-by-state basis. How to select at attorney (and whether one is needed) is presented. Appendices include a glossary of terms, a list of federal bankruptcy exemptions, and many filled-in sample forms that can be used as examples.

Sigman, Robert. *Bankruptcy.* Altamonte Springs, FL: Legovac, 1990. Audio

Sitarz, Daniel. *Debt Free: The National Bankruptcy Kit.* Carbondale, IL: Nova Publishing Co., 1995. 256p.

All the forms and instructions you need to file Chapter 7 personal bankruptcy in any state; with questionnaires, checklists and sample forms to clarify what you need to do. Reflects the major changes in bankruptcy law that occurred in 1994. Explains how to retain the maximum allowable amount of property in each state.

Ullian, Leonard. *In Debt? Help Is on the Way: from Financial Distress to Financial Relief: A Consumer's Guide to Resolving Your Financial Problems, Understanding the Benefits of Personal Bankruptcy.* Needham, MA: Consumer Financial Solutions, 1991. 159p.

A clear and simple explanation of how bankruptcy can help people in financial trouble. This book is not intended as a do-it-yourself guide and forms are not included. The authors suggest you consult a bankruptcy attorney if you decide, having read their book, that bankruptcy could help you. Includes 20 pages of questions, answers and hypotheticals. Appendices include text of several relevant statutes and sample Chapter 7 and 13 discharge documents.

Ventura, John. *The Bankruptcy Kit.* Chicago, IL: Dearborn, 1996. 208p.

BUSINESS

Brown, W. Dean. *Incorporating in* _____. Knoxville, TN: Consumer Publishing Inc., 1991. 1 vol.

The *Incorporating in . . .* series explains the benefits of incorporation and the specific steps required to incorporate your business in the title state. Tax saving strategies are also discussed. The publisher offers a telephone help line (not toll free) to answer any further questions, although, of course, they cannot give legal or tax advice (that's called practicing without a license, and it's illegal). Each book includes forms and elaborately decorated stock certificates.

Daily, Frederick W. *Tax Savvy for Small Business.* 1st ed. Berkeley, CA: Nolo Press, 1995. 320p.

Damman, Gregory C. *How to Form and Operate a Limited Liability Company: A Do-It-Yourself Guide.* Bellingham, WA: Self-Counsel Press, 1995. 228p.

Explains the advantages and disadvantages of a limited liability company and what types of companies are eligible, with instructions for starting or converting an existing business. Also discusses important issues in conducting and managing a limited liability company and tax considerations. Contains various sample forms including: sample articles of organization forms for each state;

text of the Uniform Limited Liability Company Act; and a state-by-state directory of information about forming a limited liability company.

DuBoff, Leonard D. *The Law (In Plain English) for Small Businesses*. 2nd ed. Somerset, NJ: John Wiley & Sons, 1991. 240p.

Frasier, Lynn Ann. *The Small Business Legal Guide*. Naperville, IL: Sourcebooks, 1996. 159p.

How to set up a small business or purchase an existing business or franchise, comply with necessary statutes and regulations, take advantage of legal protections available to you (especially trademarks, patents, etc.), and recognize and prevent potential legal problems in all aspects of your business. Also offers non-legal advice on creating and maintaining a successful business. Sample IRS, UCC, organization, and name reservation forms are included.

Hancock, William A. *The Small Business Legal Advisor*. 2nd ed. Blue Ridge Summit, PA: TAB Books, 1992. 1 vol.

This book is intended to give small business owners the information they need to avoid expensive legal problems. It is not intended to take the place of a lawyer, but to "help you get the most value for your dollar from him or her," and the first chapter is dedicated to finding and using a good lawyer. Further chapters discuss: starting a business; buying a going business; franchising; employee hiring; compensation and benefits; unions; forms; warranties and credit; occupational safety and health; product liability; intellectual property (patents, copyrights, trademarks, trade names); insurance; and staying clear of white collar crime. The author advises readers to consult *The Small Business Tax Advisor*, *The Small Business Legal Advisor*, and *The Small Business Financial Advisor* for further information. The last chapter of the book, entitled "Another View," is an interview with a attorney about retainers and client involvement, and general trends in legal assistance for small businesses. No forms are included.

Hedglon, Mead. *How to Get the Best Legal Help for Your Business (At the Lowest Possible Cost)*. New York, NY: McGraw Hill, 1992. 296p.

According to the author, "[T]he focus of this book is on obtaining an acceptable outcome in any legal matter at a reasonable cost." It is directed to the small business owner who must decide how to deal with the many legal needs which inevitably arise: Is a lawyer needed? Should in-house lawyers be used? Should outside counsel be consulted? How does one hire a trial attorney? What to do first when one is sued? These and other issues are thoroughly explained by the author in a readable style, made even easier to understand by the inclusion of examples and illustrations. Checklists of procedures are provided for each chapter, along with a variety of sample forms. Attorney-client relations are effectively discussed in chapters on: controlling legal costs through budgets; how to read a lawyer's bill; and using systems that keep the client in touch with the attorney.

Kamoroff, Bernard, C.P.A. *Small Time Operator: How to Start Your Own Small Business, Keep Your Books, Pay Your Taxes & Stay Out of Trouble.* 20th ed. Laytonville, CA: Bell Springs Publishing, 1995. 1 vol.

Written by a financial advisor and accountant for small businesses, this book is a step-by-step guide to starting and operating a small business. It assists in the business' aspects of such an operation, also serving as a workbook that includes bookkeeping instructions and a complete set of sample ledgers. Section One "Getting Started"; Section Two "Bookkeeping"; Section Three "Growing Up"; and Section Four "Taxes." An appendix covering miscellaneous topics is included, followed by ledgers for income, year-end income summary, credit, expenditure, year-end expenditure summary, equipment, and payroll.

McGregor, Ronald J. *Buying a Business: A Step-by-Step Guide.* Traverse City, MI: Michigan Management Group, 1990. 112p.

Just as promised: A step-by-step guide to buying a business. Divided into five parts: locating a business for sale; analyzing the business; establishing an offering price; preparing the purchase offer; and closing the sale. Appendices include: forms for evaluating businesses, sites, and equipment/fixtures; a list of relevant publications available from federal agencies; an entrepreneur's guide to preparing a business plan; and "cardinal rules for the successful purchase of a business."

McKeever, Mike. *How to Write a Business Plan.* 4th ed. Berkeley, CA: Nolo Press, 1992. 272p.

Milano, Carol. *Hers: The Wise Woman's Guide to Starting a Business on $2,000 or Less.* New York, NY: Raincoast Books, Inc., 1991. 208p.

All about starting a business of your own, including deciding what sort of business to start. This isn't really a self-help legal book at all, but the publisher sent me a free copy, and it is really pretty good, so I slipped it in anyway, hoping it would be of use to some of you business-starting types. After you read this and decide to start your own business, you'll be able to use the other books to solve your newfound legal problems; so, in a way, it isn't totally unrelated.

Munna, Raymond J. *Legal Power for Small Business Owners and Managers.* Kenner, LA: A Granite Publishers, 1991. 309p.

Ray, James C. *The Most Valuable Business Forms You'll Ever Need.* Clearwater, FL: Sphinx Publishing, 1996. 144p.

Offers suggestions for making sure that all of your contracts are legal and to protect yourself from liability, and forms and instructions for 50 commonly needed contracts and documents, including: employment; confidentiality; non-competition and indemnification agreements; copyright assignment and license; partnership agreement; power of attorney; bill of sale; mortgage and lease agreements; demand for payment; mediation and arbitration agreements; relapse of judgement; affidavit; consignment; and many more.

Sanderson, Stephen L.P., editor. *Standard Legal Forms and Agreements for Small Business.* Bellingham, WA: Self-Counsel Press, 1990. 208p.

A book of forms for use in standard, unambiguous situations in both business and personal affairs. Primarily useful in simple, straightforward transactions rather than complex business settings. Forms are grouped by general subject such as: collections; credit/debit, leases; employment; and real estate. They are accompanied by notes which briefly explain the purpose and use of each form.

Sitarz, Daniel. *The Complete Book of Small Business Legal Forms.* 1st ed. Carbondale, IL: Nova Publishing Co., 1991. 248p.

Intended to provide "the typical small business with most of the legal documents necessary for day-to-day operations," including purchase, sales, credit, collection, employment, and real estate contracts, and sole proprietorship, partnership, or corporation documents. Contains 125 forms valid in all states and Washington DC, and is divided into 19 chapters covering various situations. Each form includes an explanation of relevant legal terms and conditions and the situation in which the form could be appropriately used. Language is as plain as possible and unavoidable legal terms are clearly defined where first used. The author points out that plain language is not only acceptable but preferable to legal jargon as it helps to avoid future misunderstanding. Forms are not designed to be torn out.

Sitarz, Daniel. *Simplified Small Business Accounting*. Carbondale, IL: Nova Publishing Co., 1995. 256p.

Designed to be used by small business owners with no accounting experience. Provides the forms (including tax forms) and instructions you need to do your own accounting. Questionnaires and checklists make it easier to keep track of the information you need. Explains why clear and consistent bookkeeping is vital and how you can manage it efficiently. Includes helpful calendars of accounting tasks and data sheets to prompt you to collect the information you need and submit paperwork for taxes, etc. in a timely manner.

Steingold, Fred. *The Legal Guide for Starting and Running a Small Business*. 2nd ed. Berkeley, CA: Nolo Press, 1995. 1 vol.

Discusses how to: structure your company to your best advantage; name your business and product; obtain the licenses and permits you need; buy a business or franchise. The book also covers: tax basics; leasing; employment issues; credit and debt collection; contracts; resolving legal disputes in or out of court; representing yourself in small claims court; choosing and dealing with a lawyer; and doing your own legal research. Information included is relevant in all states, but state specific information is not included. Appendices give addresses and phone numbers for state offices that provide help to small businesses and Federal Trade Commission offices. No forms.

Steingold, Fred. *Small Business Legal Pro*. Version 2.0. Berkeley, CA: Nolo Press, 1996. Computer software

Warner, Ralph and Joanne Greene. *How to Start Your Own Business: Small Business Law*. 1st ed. Berkeley, CA: Nolo Press, 1993. Audio

Alabama

Brown, W. Dean. *Incorporating in Alabama.* Knoxville, TN: Consumer Publishing Inc., 1991. 1 vol.

The *Incorporating in . . .* series explains the benefits of incorporation and the specific steps required to incorporate your business in the title state. Tax saving strategies are also discussed. The publisher offers a telephone help line (not toll free) to answer any further questions, although, of course, they cannot give legal or tax advice (that's called practicing without a license, and it's illegal). Each book includes forms and elaborately decorated stock certificates.

Shaw, Karen A., Michael D. Jenkins, and Anthony J. Walters. *Starting and Operating a Business in Alabama.* Grant's Pass, OR: Oasis Press, 1996. 1 vol.

The first chapter reviews basic considerations about going into business, including choosing the legal form and buying an existing business. General information for actually starting and staying in business is then offered, followed by a focus on the specific laws and practices of the state. The procedures and forms needed to start a business are provided and explained; checklists of regulatory requirements, tax-saving ideas, and names and addresses of organizations and government resources are also provided.

Stanko, Gary G. and Mark Warda. *How to Start a Business in Alabama.* Clearwater, FL: Sphinx Publishing, 1994. 120p.

This book provides information and ready-to-use forms to open your own business in Alabama. Chapters cover choosing the form of your business, registering your business' name and trademarks, contracts, insurance, obtaining licenses, complying with laws and regulations, and paying state and Federal taxes. Also includes a brief list of titles for further reading.

Alaska

Shaw, Karen A., Michael D. Jenkins, and Anthony J. Walters. *Starting and Operating a Business in Alaska.* Grant's Pass, OR: Oasis Press, 1996. 1 vol.

The first chapter reviews basic considerations about going into business, including choosing the legal form and buying an existing business. General information for actually starting and staying in business is then offered, followed by a focus on the specific laws and practices of the state. The procedures and forms needed to start a business are provided and explained; checklists of regulatory requirements, tax-saving ideas, and names and addresses of organizations and government resources are also provided.

Arizona

Brown, W. Dean. *Incorporating in Arizona*. Knoxville, TN: Consumer
     Publishing Inc., 1991. 1 vol.

The *Incorporating in* . . . series explains the benefits of incorporation and the specific steps required to incorporate your business in the title state. Tax saving strategies are also discussed. The publisher offers a telephone help line (not toll free) to answer any further questions, although, of course, they cannot give legal or tax advice (that's called practicing without a license, and it's illegal). Each book includes forms and elaborately decorated stock certificates.

Shaw, Karen A., Michael D. Jenkins, and Anthony J. Walters. *Starting
     and Operating a Business in Arizona*. Grant's Pass, OR: Oasis
     Press, 1996. 1 vol.

The first chapter reviews basic considerations about going into business, including choosing the legal form and buying an existing business. General information for actually starting and staying in business is then offered, followed by a focus on the specific laws and practices of the state. The procedures and forms needed to start a business are provided and explained; checklists of regulatory requirements, tax-saving ideas, and names and addresses of organizations and government resources are also provided.

Arkansas

Brown, W. Dean. *Incorporating in Arkansas*. Knoxville, TN: Consumer
     Publishing Inc., 1991. 1 vol.

The *Incorporating in* . . . series explains the benefits of incorporation and the specific steps required to incorporate your business in the title state. Tax saving strategies are also discussed. The publisher offers a telephone help line (not toll free) to answer any further questions, although, of course, they cannot give legal or tax advice (that's called practicing without a license, and it's illegal). Each book includes forms and elaborately decorated stock certificates.

Shaw, Karen A., Michael D. Jenkins, and Anthony J. Walters. *Starting and Operating a Business in Arkansas.* Grant's Pass, OR: Oasis Press, 1996. 1 vol.

The first chapter reviews basic considerations about going into business, including choosing the legal form and buying an existing business. General information for actually starting and staying in business is then offered, followed by a focus on the specific laws and practices of the state. The procedures and forms needed to start a business are provided and explained; checklists of regulatory requirements, tax-saving ideas, and names and addresses of organizations and government resources are also provided.

California

Brown, W. Dean. *Incorporating in California.* Knoxville, TN: Consumer Publishing Inc., 1991. 1 vol.

The *Incorporating in . . .* series explains the benefits of incorporation and the specific steps required to incorporate your business in the title state. Tax saving strategies are also discussed. The publisher offers a telephone help line (not toll free) to answer any further questions, although, of course, they cannot give legal or tax advice (that's called practicing without a license, and it's illegal). Each book includes forms and elaborately decorated stock certificates.

Shaw, Karen A., Michael D. Jenkins, and Anthony J. Walters. *Starting and Operating a Business in California.* Grant's Pass, OR: Oasis Press, 1996. 1 vol.

The first chapter reviews basic considerations about going into business, including choosing the legal form and buying an existing business. General information for actually starting and staying in business is then offered, followed by a focus on the specific laws and practices of the state. The procedures and forms needed to start a business are provided and explained; checklists of regulatory requirements, tax-saving ideas, and names and addresses of organizations and government resources are also provided.

Colorado

Brown, W. Dean. *Incorporating in Colorado.* Knoxville, TN: Consumer Publishing Inc., 1991. 1 vol.

The *Incorporating in . . .* series explains the benefits of incorporation and the specific steps required to incorporate your business in the title state. Tax saving strategies are also discussed. The publisher offers a telephone help line (not toll free) to answer any further questions, although, of course, they cannot give legal or tax advice (that's called practicing without a license, and it's illegal). Each book includes forms and elaborately decorated stock certificates.

Shaw, Karen A., Michael D. Jenkins, and Anthony J. Walters. *Starting and Operating a Business in Colorado.* Grant's Pass, OR: Oasis Press, 1996. 1 vol.

The first chapter reviews basic considerations about going into business, including choosing the legal form and buying an existing business. General information for actually starting and staying in business is then offered, followed by a focus on the specific laws and practices of the state. The procedures and forms needed to start a business are provided and explained; checklists of regulatory requirements, tax-saving ideas, and names and addresses of organizations and government resources are also provided.

Connecticut

Brown, W. Dean. *Incorporating in Connecticut.* Knoxville, TN: Consumer Publishing Inc., 1991. 1 vol.

The *Incorporating in . . .* series explains the benefits of incorporation and the specific steps required to incorporate your business in the title state. Tax saving strategies are also discussed. The publisher offers a telephone help line (not toll free) to answer any further questions, although, of course, they cannot give legal or tax advice (that's called practicing without a license, and it's illegal). Each book includes forms and elaborately decorated stock certificates.

Shaw, Karen A., Michael D. Jenkins, and Anthony J. Walters. *Starting and Operating a Business in Connecticut.* Grant's Pass, OR: Oasis Press, 1996. 1 vol.

The first chapter reviews basic considerations about going into business, including choosing the legal form and buying an existing business. General information for actually starting and staying in business is then offered, followed by a focus on the specific laws and practices of the state. The procedures and forms needed to start a business are provided and explained; checklists of regulatory requirements, tax-saving ideas, and names and addresses of organizations and government resources are also provided.

26

Delaware

Shaw, Karen A., Michael D. Jenkins, and Anthony J. Walters. *Starting and Operating a Business in Delaware.* Grant's Pass, OR: Oasis Press, 1996. 1 vol.

The first chapter reviews basic considerations about going into business, including choosing the legal form and buying an existing business. General information for actually starting and staying in business is then offered, followed by a focus on the specific laws and practices of the state. The procedures and forms needed to start a business are provided and explained; checklists of regulatory requirements, tax-saving ideas, and names and addresses of organizations and government resources are also provided.

Florida

Brown, W. Dean. *Incorporating in Florida.* Knoxville, TN: Consumer Publishing Inc., 1991. 1 vol.

The *Incorporating in* . . . series explains the benefits of incorporation and the specific steps required to incorporate your business in the title state. Tax saving strategies are also discussed. The publisher offers a telephone help line (not toll free) to answer any further questions, although, of course, they cannot give legal or tax advice (that's called practicing without a license, and it's illegal). Each book includes forms and elaborately decorated stock certificates.

Shaw, Karen A., Michael D. Jenkins, and Anthony J. Walters. *Starting and Operating a Business in Florida.* Grant's Pass, OR: Oasis Press, 1996. 1 vol.

The first chapter reviews basic considerations about going into business, including choosing the legal form and buying an existing business. General information for actually starting and staying in business is then offered, followed by a focus on the specific laws and practices of the state. The procedures and forms needed to start a business are provided and explained; checklists of regulatory requirements, tax-saving ideas, and names and addresses of organizations and government resources are also provided.

Warda, Mark. *How to Start a Business in Florida.* 4th ed. Clearwater, FL: Sphinx Publishing, 1995. 132p.

Information and ready-to-use forms to open your own business in Florida. Chapters cover choosing the form of your business, registering your business' name and trademarks, contracts, insurance, obtaining licenses, complying with laws and regulations, and paying state and Federal taxes. Includes a brief list of titles for further readings and tax timetable.

Georgia

Brown, W. Dean. *Incorporating in Georgia*. Knoxville, TN: Consumer Publishing Inc., 1991. 1 vol.

The *Incorporating in* . . . series explains the benefits of incorporation and the specific steps required to incorporate your business in the title state. Tax saving strategies are also discussed. The publisher offers a telephone help line (not toll free) to answer any further questions, although, of course, they cannot give legal or tax advice (that's called practicing without a license, and it's illegal). Each book includes forms and elaborately decorated stock certificates.

Dunleavy, Patricia Godwin and Mark Warda. *How to Start and Run a Georgia Business*. 2nd ed. Clearwater, FL: Sphinx Publishing, 1995. 136p.

Information and ready-to-use forms to open your own business in Georgia. Chapters cover: choosing the form of your business; registering your business' name and trademarks; contracts; insurance; obtaining licenses; complying with laws and regulations; and paying state and Federal taxes. Also includes a brief list of titles for further reading.

Shaw, Karen A., Michael D. Jenkins, and Anthony J. Walters. *Starting and Operating a Business in Georgia*. Grant's Pass, OR: Oasis Press, 1996. 1 vol.

The first chapter reviews basic considerations about going into business, including choosing the legal form and buying an existing business. General information for actually starting and staying in business is then offered, followed by a focus on the specific laws and practices of the state. The procedures and forms needed to start a business are provided and explained; checklists of regulatory requirements, tax-saving ideas, and names and addresses of organizations and government resources are also provided.

Hawaii

Shaw, Karen A., Michael D. Jenkins, and Anthony J. Walters. *Starting and Operating a Business in Hawaii.* Grant's Pass, OR: Oasis Press, 1996. 1 vol.

The first chapter reviews basic considerations about going into business, including choosing the legal form and buying an existing business. General information for actually starting and staying in business is then offered, followed by a focus on the specific laws and practices of the state. The procedures and forms needed to start a business are provided and explained; checklists of regulatory requirements, tax-saving ideas, and names and addresses of organizations and government resources are also provided.

Idaho

Shaw, Karen A., Michael D. Jenkins, and Anthony J. Walters. *Starting and Operating a Business in Idaho.* Grant's Pass, OR: Oasis Press, 1996. 1 vol.

The first chapter reviews basic considerations about going into business, including choosing the legal form and buying an existing business. General information for actually starting and staying in business is then offered, followed by a focus on the specific laws and practices of the state. The procedures and forms needed to start a business are provided and explained; checklists of regulatory requirements, tax-saving ideas, and names and addresses of organizations and government resources are also provided.

Illinois

Brown, W. Dean. *Incorporating in Illinois.* Knoxville, TN: Consumer Publishing Inc., 1991. 1 vol.

The *Incorporating in . . .* series explains the benefits of incorporation and the specific steps required to incorporate your business in the title state. Tax saving strategies are also discussed. The publisher offers a telephone help line (not toll free) to answer any further questions, although, of course, they cannot give legal or tax advice (that's called practicing without a license, and it's illegal). Each book includes forms and elaborately decorated stock certificates.

Shaw, Karen A., Michael D. Jenkins, and Anthony J. Walters. *Starting and Operating a Business in Illinois.* Grant's Pass, OR: Oasis Press, 1996. 1 vol.

The first chapter reviews basic considerations about going into business, including choosing the legal form and buying an existing business. General information for actually starting and staying in business is then offered, followed by a focus on the specific laws and practices of the state. The procedures and forms needed to start a business are provided and explained; checklists of regulatory requirements, tax-saving ideas, and names and addresses of organizations and government resources are also provided.

Indiana

Brown, W. Dean. *Incorporating in Indiana.* Knoxville, TN: Consumer Publishing Inc., 1991. 1 vol.

The *Incorporating in . . .* series explains the benefits of incorporation and the specific steps required to incorporate your business in the title state. Tax saving strategies are also discussed. The publisher offers a telephone help line (not toll free) to answer any further questions, although, of course, they cannot give legal or tax advice (that's called practicing without a license, and it's illegal). Each book includes forms and elaborately decorated stock certificates.

Shaw, Karen A., Michael D. Jenkins, and Anthony J. Walters. *Starting and Operating a Business in Indiana.* Grant's Pass, OR: Oasis Press, 1996. 1 vol.

The first chapter reviews basic considerations about going into business, including choosing the legal form and buying an existing business. General information for actually starting and staying in business is then offered, followed by a focus on the specific laws and practices of the state. The procedures and forms needed to start a business are provided and explained; checklists of regulatory requirements, tax-saving ideas, and names and addresses of organizations and government resources are also provided.

Iowa

Shaw, Karen A., Michael D. Jenkins, and Anthony J. Walters. Starting and Operating a Business in Iowa. Grant's Pass, OR: Oasis Press, 1996. 1 vol.

The first chapter reviews basic considerations about going into business, including choosing the legal form and buying an existing business. General information for actually starting and staying in business is then offered, followed by a focus on the specific laws and practices of the state. The procedures and forms needed to start a business are provided and explained; checklists of regulatory requirements, tax-saving ideas, and names and addresses of organizations and government resources are also provided.

Kansas

Brown, W. Dean. *Incorporating in Kansas.* Knoxville, TN: Consumer Publishing Inc., 1991. 1 vol.

The *Incorporating in* . . . series explains the benefits of incorporation and the specific steps required to incorporate your business in the title state. Tax saving strategies are also discussed. The publisher offers a telephone help line (not toll free) to answer any further questions, although, of course, they cannot give legal or tax advice (that's called practicing without a license, and it's illegal). Each book includes forms and elaborately decorated stock certificates.

Shaw, Karen A., Michael D. Jenkins, and Anthony J. Walters. *Starting and Operating a Business in Kansas.* Grant's Pass, OR: Oasis Press, 1996. 1 vol.

The first chapter reviews basic considerations about going into business, including choosing the legal form and buying an existing business. General information for actually starting and staying in business is then offered, followed by a focus on the specific laws and practices of the state. The procedures and forms needed to start a business are provided and explained; checklists of regulatory requirements, tax-saving ideas, and names and addresses of organizations and government resources are also provided.

Kentucky

Brown, W. Dean. *Incorporating in Kentucky*. Knoxville, TN: Consumer
    Publishing Inc., 1991. 1 vol.

The *Incorporating in . . .* series explains the benefits of incorporation and the
specific steps required to incorporate your business in the title state. Tax saving strategies are also discussed. The publisher offers a telephone help line
(not toll free) to answer any further questions, although, of course, they cannot give legal or tax advice (that's called practicing without a license, and it's
illegal). Each book includes forms and elaborately decorated stock certificates.

Shaw, Karen A., Michael D. Jenkins, and Anthony J. Walters. *Starting
    and Operating a Business in Kentucky*. Grant's Pass, OR: Oasis
    Press, 1996. 1 vol.

The first chapter reviews basic considerations about going into business,
including choosing the legal form and buying an existing business. General
information for actually starting and staying in business is then offered, followed by a focus on the specific laws and practices of the state. The procedures
and forms needed to start a business are provided and explained; checklists
of regulatory requirements, tax-saving ideas, and names and addresses of
organizations and government resources are also provided.

Louisiana

Shaw, Karen A., Michael D. Jenkins, and Anthony J. Walters. *Starting
    and Operating a Business in Louisiana*. Grant's Pass, OR: Oasis
    Press, 1996. 1 vol.

The first chapter reviews basic considerations about going into business,
including choosing the legal form and buying an existing business. General
information for actually starting and staying in business is then offered, followed by a focus on the specific laws and practices of the state. The procedures
and forms needed to start a business are provided and explained; checklists
of regulatory requirements, tax-saving ideas, and names and addresses of
organizations and government resources are also provided.

Maine

Shaw, Karen A., Michael D. Jenkins, and Anthony J. Walters. *Starting and Operating a Business in Maine*. Grant's Pass, OR: Oasis Press, 1996. 1 vol.

The first chapter reviews basic considerations about going into business, including choosing the legal form and buying an existing business. General information for actually starting and staying in business is then offered, followed by a focus on the specific laws and practices of the state. The procedures and forms needed to start a business are provided and explained; checklists of regulatory requirements, tax-saving ideas, and names and addresses of organizations and government resources are also provided.

Maryland

Brown, W. Dean. *Incorporating in Maryland*. Knoxville, TN: Consumer Publishing Inc., 1991. 1 vol.

The *Incorporating in . . .* series explains the benefits of incorporation and the specific steps required to incorporate your business in the title state. Tax saving strategies are also discussed. The publisher offers a telephone help line (not toll free) to answer any further questions, although, of course, they cannot give legal or tax advice (that's called practicing without a license, and it's illegal). Each book includes forms and elaborately decorated stock certificates.

Shaw, Karen A., Michael D. Jenkins, and Anthony J. Walters. *Starting and Operating a Business in Maryland*. Grant's Pass, OR: Oasis Press, 1996. 1 vol.

The first chapter reviews basic considerations about going into business, including choosing the legal form and buying an existing business. General information for actually starting and staying in business is then offered, followed by a focus on the specific laws and practices of the state. The procedures and forms needed to start a business are provided and explained; checklists of regulatory requirements, tax-saving ideas, and names and addresses of organizations and government resources are also provided.

Massachusetts

Brown, W. Dean. Incorporating in Massachusetts. Knoxville, TN: Consumer Publishing Inc., 1991. 1 vol.

The *Incorporating in . . .* series explains the benefits of incorporation and the specific steps required to incorporate your business in the title state. Tax saving strategies are also discussed. The publisher offers a telephone help line (not toll free) to answer any further questions, although, of course, they cannot give legal or tax advice (that's called practicing without a license, and it's illegal). Each book includes forms and elaborately decorated stock certificates.

Shaw, Karen A., Michael D. Jenkins, and Anthony J. Walters. *Starting and Operating a Business in Massachusetts.* Grant's Pass, OR: Oasis Press, 1996. 1 vol.

The first chapter reviews basic considerations about going into business, including choosing the legal form and buying an existing business. General information for actually starting and staying in business is then offered, followed by a focus on the specific laws and practices of the state. The procedures and forms needed to start a business are provided and explained; checklists of regulatory requirements, tax-saving ideas, and names and addresses of organizations and government resources are also provided.

Michigan

Brown, W. Dean. *Incorporating in Michigan.* Knoxville, TN: Consumer Publishing Inc., 1991. 1 vol.

The *Incorporating in . . .* series explains the benefits of incorporation and the specific steps required to incorporate your business in the title state. Tax saving strategies are also discussed. The publisher offers a telephone help line (not toll free) to answer any further questions, although, of course, they cannot give legal or tax advice (that's called practicing without a license, and it's illegal). Each book includes forms and elaborately decorated stock certificates.

Shaw, Karen A., Michael D. Jenkins, and Anthony J. Walters. *Starting and Operating a Business in Michigan.* Grant's Pass, OR: Oasis Press, 1996. 1 vol.

The first chapter reviews basic considerations about going into business, including choosing the legal form and buying an existing business. General information for actually starting and staying in business is then offered, followed by a focus on the specific laws and practices of the state. The procedures and forms needed to start a business are provided and explained; checklists of regulatory requirements, tax-saving ideas, and names and addresses of organizations and government resources are also provided.

Minnesota

Brown, W. Dean. *Incorporating in Minnesota.* Knoxville, TN: Consumer Publishing Inc., 1991. 1 vol.

The *Incorporating in* . . . series explains the benefits of incorporation and the specific steps required to incorporate your business in the title state. Tax saving strategies are also discussed. The publisher offers a telephone help line (not toll free) to answer any further questions, although, of course, they cannot give legal or tax advice (that's called practicing without a license, and it's illegal). Each book includes forms and elaborately decorated stock certificates.

Shaw, Karen A., Michael D. Jenkins, and Anthony J. Walters. *Starting and Operating a Business in Minnesota.* Grant's Pass, OR: Oasis Press, 1996. 1 vol.

The first chapter reviews basic considerations about going into business, including choosing the legal form and buying an existing business. General information for actually starting and staying in business is then offered, followed by a focus on the specific laws and practices of the state. The procedures and forms needed to start a business are provided and explained; checklists of regulatory requirements, tax-saving ideas, and names and addresses of organizations and government resources are also provided.

Mississippi

Brown, W. Dean. *Incorporating in Mississippi.* Knoxville, TN: Consumer Publishing Inc., 1991. 1 vol.

The *Incorporating in* . . . series explains the benefits of incorporation and the specific steps required to incorporate your business in the title state. Tax saving strategies are also discussed. The publisher offers a telephone help line (not toll free) to answer any further questions, although, of course, they cannot give legal or tax advice (that's called practicing without a license, and it's illegal). Each book includes forms and elaborately decorated stock certificates.

Shaw, Karen A., Michael D. Jenkins, and Anthony J. Walters. *Starting and Operating a Business in Mississippi*. Grant's Pass, OR: Oasis Press, 1996. 1 vol.

The first chapter reviews basic considerations about going into business, including choosing the legal form and buying an existing business. General information for actually starting and staying in business is then offered, followed by a focus on the specific laws and practices of the state. The procedures and forms needed to start a business are provided and explained; checklists of regulatory requirements, tax-saving ideas, and names and addresses of organizations and government resources are also provided.

Missouri

Brown, W. Dean. *Incorporating in Missouri*. Knoxville, TN: Consumer Publishing Inc., 1991. 1 vol.

The *Incorporating in . . .* series explains the benefits of incorporation and the specific steps required to incorporate your business in the title state. Tax saving strategies are also discussed. The publisher offers a telephone help line (not toll free) to answer any further questions, although, of course, they cannot give legal or tax advice (that's called practicing without a license, and it's illegal). Each book includes forms and elaborately decorated stock certificates.

Shaw, Karen A., Michael D. Jenkins, and Anthony J. Walters. *Starting and Operating a Business In Missouri*. Grant's Pass, OR: Oasis Press, 1996. 1 vol.

The first chapter reviews basic considerations about going into business, including choosing the legal form and buying an existing business. General information for actually starting and staying in business is then offered, followed by a focus on the specific laws and practices of the state. The procedures and forms needed to start a business are provided and explained; checklists of regulatory requirements, tax-saving ideas, and names and addresses of organizations and government resources are also provided.

Montana

Shaw, Karen A., Michael D. Jenkins, and Anthony J. Walters. *Starting and Operating a Business in Montana*. Grant's Pass, OR: Oasis Press, 1996. 1 vol.

The first chapter reviews basic considerations about going into business, including choosing the legal form and buying an existing business. General information for actually starting and staying in business is then offered, followed by a focus on the specific laws and practices of the state. The procedures and forms needed to start a business are provided and explained; checklists of regulatory requirements, tax-saving ideas, and names and addresses of organizations and government resources are also provided.

Nebraska

Shaw, Karen A., Michael D. Jenkins, and Anthony J. Walters. *Starting and Operating a Business in Nebraska*. Grant's Pass, OR: Oasis Press, 1996. 1 vol.

The first chapter reviews basic considerations about going into business, including choosing the legal form and buying an existing business. General information for actually starting and staying in business is then offered, followed by a focus on the specific laws and practices of the state. The procedures and forms needed to start a business are provided and explained; checklists of regulatory requirements, tax-saving ideas, and names and addresses of organizations and government resources are also provided.

Nevada

Brown, W. Dean. *Incorporating in Nevada*. Knoxville, TN: Consumer Publishing Inc., 1991. 1 vol.

The *Incorporating in . . .* series explains the benefits of incorporation and the specific steps required to incorporate your business in the title state. Tax saving strategies are also discussed. The publisher offers a telephone help line (not toll free) to answer any further questions, although, of course, they cannot give legal or tax advice (that's called practicing without a license, and it's illegal). Each book includes forms and elaborately decorated stock certificates.

Shaw, Karen A., Michael D. Jenkins, and Anthony J. Walters. *Starting and Operating a Business in Nevada.* Grant's Pass, OR: Oasis Press, 1996. 1 vol.

The first chapter reviews basic considerations about going into business, including choosing the legal form and buying an existing business. General information for actually starting and staying in business is then offered, followed by a focus on the specific laws and practices of the state. The procedures and forms needed to start a business are provided and explained; checklists of regulatory requirements, tax-saving ideas, and names and addresses of organizations and government resources are also provided.

New Hampshire

Shaw, Karen A., Michael D. Jenkins, and Anthony J. Walters. *Starting and Operating a Business in New Hampshire.* Grant's Pass, OR: Oasis Press, 1996. 1 vol.

The first chapter reviews basic considerations about going into business, including choosing the legal form and buying an existing business. General information for actually starting and staying in business is then offered, followed by a focus on the specific laws and practices of the state. The procedures and forms needed to start a business are provided and explained; checklists of regulatory requirements, tax-saving ideas, and names and addresses of organizations and government resources are also provided.

New Jersey

Brown, W. Dean. *Incorporating in New Jersey.* Knoxville, TN: Consumer Publishing Inc., 1991. 1 vol.

The *Incorporating in . . .* series explains the benefits of incorporation and the specific steps required to incorporate your business in the title state. Tax saving strategies are also discussed. The publisher offers a telephone help line (not toll free) to answer any further questions, although, of course, they cannot give legal or tax advice (that's called practicing without a license, and it's illegal). Each book includes forms and elaborately decorated stock certificates.

Shaw, Karen A., Michael D. Jenkins, and Anthony J. Walters. *Starting and Operating a Business in New Jersey.* Grant's Pass, OR: Oasis Press, 1996. 1 vol.

The first chapter reviews basic considerations about going into business, including choosing the legal form and buying an existing business. General information for actually starting and staying in business is then offered, followed by a focus on the specific laws and practices of the state. The procedures and forms needed to start a business are provided and explained; checklists of regulatory requirements, tax-saving ideas, and names and addresses of organizations and government resources are also provided.

New Mexico

Shaw, Karen A., Michael D. Jenkins, and Anthony J. Walters. *Starting and Operating a Business in New Mexico.* Grant's Pass, OR: Oasis Press, 1996. 1 vol.

The first chapter reviews basic considerations about going into business, including choosing the legal form and buying an existing business. General information for actually starting and staying in business is then offered, followed by a focus on the specific laws and practices of the state. The procedures and forms needed to start a business are provided and explained; checklists of regulatory requirements, tax-saving ideas, and names and addresses of organizations and government resources are also provided.

New York

Brown, W. Dean. *Incorporating in New York.* Knoxville, TN: Consumer Publishing Inc., 1991. 1 vol.

The *Incorporating in* . . . series explains the benefits of incorporation and the specific steps required to incorporate your business in the title state. Tax saving strategies are also discussed. The publisher offers a telephone help line (not toll free) to answer any further questions, although, of course, they cannot give legal or tax advice (that's called practicing without a license, and it's illegal). Each book includes forms and elaborately decorated stock certificates.

Shaw, Karen A., Michael D. Jenkins, and Anthony J. Walters. *Starting and Operating a Business in New York, New York*. Grant's Pass, OR: Oasis Press, 1996. 1 vol.

The first chapter reviews basic considerations about going into business, including choosing the legal form and buying an existing business. General information for actually starting and staying in business is then offered, followed by a focus on the specific laws and practices of the state. The procedures and forms needed to start a business are provided and explained; checklists of regulatory requirements, tax-saving ideas, and names and addresses of organizations and government resources are also provided.

North Carolina

Brown, W. Dean. *Incorporating in North Carolina*. Knoxville, TN: Consumer Publishing Inc., 1991. 1 vol.

The *Incorporating in . . .* series explains the benefits of incorporation and the specific steps required to incorporate your business in the title state. Tax saving strategies are also discussed. The publisher offers a telephone help line (not toll free) to answer any further questions, although, of course, they cannot give legal or tax advice (that's called practicing without a license, and it's illegal). Each book includes forms and elaborately decorated stock certificates.

Naylor, Wanda and Mark Warda. *How to Start a Business in North Carolina*. Clearwater, FL: Sphinx Publishing, 1994. 132p.

Information and ready-to-use forms to open your own business in North Carolina. Chapters cover choosing the form of your business, registering your business' name and trademarks, contracts, insurance, obtaining licenses, complying with laws and regulations, and paying state and Federal taxes. Includes a brief list of titles for further readings and contact information for regulatory offices.

Shaw, Karen A., Michael D. Jenkins, and Anthony J. Walters. *Starting and Operating a Business in North Carolina*. Grant's Pass, OR: Oasis Press, 1996. 1 vol.

The first chapter reviews basic considerations about going into business, including choosing the legal form and buying an existing business. General information for actually starting and staying in business is then offered, followed by a focus on the specific laws and practices of the state. The procedures and forms needed to start a business are provided and explained; checklists of regulatory requirements, tax-saving ideas, and names and addresses of organizations and government resources are also provided.

North Dakota

Shaw, Karen A., Michael D. Jenkins, and Anthony J. Walters. *Starting and Operating a Business in North Dakota*. Grant's Pass, OR: Oasis Press, 1996. 1 vol.

The first chapter reviews basic considerations about going into business, including choosing the legal form and buying an existing business. General information for actually starting and staying in business is then offered, followed by a focus on the specific laws and practices of the state. The procedures and forms needed to start a business are provided and explained; checklists of regulatory requirements, tax-saving ideas, and names and addresses of organizations and government resources are also provided.

Ohio

Brown, W. Dean. *Incorporating in Ohio*. Knoxville, TN: Consumer Publishing Inc., 1991. 1 vol.

The *Incorporating in . . .* series explains the benefits of incorporation and the specific steps required to incorporate your business in the title state. Tax saving strategies are also discussed. The publisher offers a telephone help line (not toll free) to answer any further questions, although, of course, they cannot give legal or tax advice (that's called practicing without a license, and it's illegal). Each book includes forms and elaborately decorated stock certificates.

Shaw, Karen A., Michael D. Jenkins, and Anthony J. Walters. *Starting and Operating a Business in Ohio*. Grant's Pass, OR: Oasis Press, 1996. 1 vol.

The first chapter reviews basic considerations about going into business, including choosing the legal form and buying an existing business. General information for actually starting and staying in business is then offered, followed by a focus on the specific laws and practices of the state. The procedures and forms needed to start a business are provided and explained; checklists of regulatory requirements, tax-saving ideas, and names and addresses of organizations and government resources are also provided.

Oklahoma

Brown, W. Dean. *Incorporating in Oklahoma*. Knoxville, TN: Consumer Publishing Inc., 1991. 1 vol.

The *Incorporating in . . .* series explains the benefits of incorporation and the specific steps required to incorporate your business in the title state. Tax saving strategies are also discussed. The publisher offers a telephone help line (not toll free) to answer any further questions, although, of course, they cannot give legal or tax advice (that's called practicing without a license, and it's illegal). Each book includes forms and elaborately decorated stock certificates.

Shaw, Karen A., Michael D. Jenkins, and Anthony J. Walters. *Starting and Operating a Business in Oklahoma*. Grant's Pass, OR: Oasis Press, 1996. 1 vol.

The first chapter reviews basic considerations about going into business, including choosing the legal form and buying an existing business. General information for actually starting and staying in business is then offered, followed by a focus on the specific laws and practices of the state. The procedures and forms needed to start a business are provided and explained; checklists of regulatory requirements, tax-saving ideas, and names and addresses of organizations and government resources are also provided.

Oregon

Brown, W. Dean. *Incorporating in Oregon*. Knoxville, TN: Consumer Publishing Inc., 1991. 1 vol.

The *Incorporating in . . .* series explains the benefits of incorporation and the specific steps required to incorporate your business in the title state. Tax saving strategies are also discussed. The publisher offers a telephone help line (not toll free) to answer any further questions, although, of course, they cannot give legal or tax advice (that's called practicing without a license, and it's illegal). Each book includes forms and elaborately decorated stock certificates.

Shaw, Karen A., Michael D. Jenkins, and Anthony J. Walters. *Starting and Operating a Business in Oregon*. Grant's Pass, OR: Oasis Press, 1996. 1 vol.

The first chapter reviews basic considerations about going into business, including choosing the legal form and buying an existing business. General information for actually starting and staying in business is then offered, followed by a focus on the specific laws and practices of the state. The procedures and forms needed to start a business are provided and explained; checklists of regulatory requirements, tax-saving ideas, and names and addresses of organizations and government resources are also provided.

Pennsylvania

Brown, W. Dean. *Incorporating in Pennsylvania*. Knoxville, TN: Consumer Publishing Inc., 1991. 1 vol.

The *Incorporating in . . .* series explains the benefits of incorporation and the specific steps required to incorporate your business in the title state. Tax saving strategies are also discussed. The publisher offers a telephone help line (not toll free) to answer any further questions, although, of course, they cannot give legal or tax advice (that's called practicing without a license, and it's illegal). Each book includes forms and elaborately decorated stock certificates.

Shaw, Karen A., Michael D. Jenkins, and Anthony J. Walters. *Starting and Operating a Business in Pennsylvania*. Grant's Pass, OR: Oasis Press, 1996. 1 vol.

The first chapter reviews basic considerations about going into business, including choosing the legal form and buying an existing business. General information for actually starting and staying in business is then offered, followed by a focus on the specific laws and practices of the state. The procedures and forms needed to start a business are provided and explained; checklists of regulatory requirements, tax-saving ideas, and names and addresses of organizations and government resources are also provided.

Rhode Island

Shaw, Karen A., Michael D. Jenkins, and Anthony J. Walters. *Starting and Operating a Business in Rhode Island*. Grant's Pass, OR: Oasis Press, 1996. 1 vol.

The first chapter reviews basic considerations about going into business, including choosing the legal form and buying an existing business. General information for actually starting and staying in business is then offered, followed by a focus on the specific laws and practices of the state. The procedures and forms needed to start a business are provided and explained; checklists of regulatory requirements, tax-saving ideas, and names and addresses of organizations and government resources are also provided.

South Carolina

Shaw, Karen A., Michael D. Jenkins, and Anthony J. Walters. *Starting and Operating a Business in South Carolina.* Grant's Pass, OR: Oasis Press, 1996. 1 vol.

The first chapter reviews basic considerations about going into business, including choosing the legal form and buying an existing business. General information for actually starting and staying in business is then offered, followed by a focus on the specific laws and practices of the state. The procedures and forms needed to start a business are provided and explained; checklists of regulatory requirements, tax-saving ideas, and names and addresses of organizations and government resources are also provided.

South Dakota

Shaw, Karen A., Michael D. Jenkins, and Anthony J. Walters. *Starting and Operating a Business In South Dakota.* Grant's Pass, OR: Oasis Press, 1996. 1 vol.

The first chapter reviews basic considerations about going into business, including choosing the legal form and buying an existing business. General information for actually starting and staying in business is then offered, followed by a focus on the specific laws and practices of the state. The procedures and forms needed to start a business are provided and explained; checklists of regulatory requirements, tax-saving ideas, and names and addresses of organizations and government resources are also provided.

Tennessee

Brown, W. Dean. *Incorporating in Tennessee.* Knoxville, TN: Consumer Publishing Inc., 1991. 1 vol.

The *Incorporating in . . .* series explains the benefits of incorporation and the specific steps required to incorporate your business in the title state. Tax saving strategies are also discussed. The publisher offers a telephone help line (not toll free) to answer any further questions, although, of course, they cannot give legal or tax advice (that's called practicing without a license, and it's illegal). Each book includes forms and elaborately decorated stock certificates.

Shaw, Karen A., Michael D. Jenkins, and Anthony J. Walters. *Starting and Operating a Business in Tennessee*. Grant's Pass, OR: Oasis Press, 1996. 1 vol.

The first chapter reviews basic considerations about going into business, including choosing the legal form and buying an existing business. General information for actually starting and staying in business is then offered, followed by a focus on the specific laws and practices of the state. The procedures and forms needed to start a business are provided and explained; checklists of regulatory requirements, tax-saving ideas, and names and addresses of organizations and government resources are also provided.

Texas

Brown, W. Dean. *Incorporating in Texas*. Knoxville, TN: Consumer Publishing Inc., 1991. 1 vol.

The *Incorporating in . . .* series explains the benefits of incorporation and the specific steps required to incorporate your business in the title state. Tax saving strategies are also discussed. The publisher offers a telephone help line (not toll free) to answer any further questions, although, of course, they cannot give legal or tax advice (that's called practicing without a license, and it's illegal). Each book includes forms and elaborately decorated stock certificates.

Brown, William R. and Mark Warda. *How to Start a Business in Texas*. Clearwater, FL: Sphinx Publishing, 1994. 124p.

Information and ready-to-use forms to open your own business in Texas. Chapters cover choosing the form of your business, registering your business' name and trademarks, contracts, insurance, obtaining licenses, complying with laws and regulations, and paying state and Federal taxes. Includes a brief list of titles for further readings and a few pages of anti-government, anti-regulation sentiment.

Shaw, Karen A., Michael D. Jenkins, and Anthony J. Walters. *Starting and Operating a Business in Texas*. Grant's Pass, OR: Oasis Press, 1996. 1 vol.

The first chapter reviews basic considerations about going into business, including choosing the legal form and buying an existing business. General information for actually starting and staying in business is then offered, followed by a focus on the specific laws and practices of the state. The procedures and forms needed to start a business are provided and explained; checklists of regulatory requirements, tax-saving ideas, and names and addresses of organizations and government resources are also provided.

Utah

Brown, W. Dean. *Incorporating in Utah.* Knoxville, TN: Consumer Publishing Inc., 1991. 1 vol.

The *Incorporating in . . .* series explains the benefits of incorporation and the specific steps required to incorporate your business in the title state. Tax saving strategies are also discussed. The publisher offers a telephone help line (not toll free) to answer any further questions, although, of course, they cannot give legal or tax advice (that's called practicing without a license, and it's illegal). Each book includes forms and elaborately decorated stock certificates.

Shaw, Karen A., Michael D. Jenkins, and Anthony J. Walters. *Starting and Operating a Business in Utah.* Grant's Pass, OR: Oasis Press, 1996. 1 vol.

The first chapter reviews basic considerations about going into business, including choosing the legal form and buying an existing business. General information for actually starting and staying in business is then offered, followed by a focus on the specific laws and practices of the state. The procedures and forms needed to start a business are provided and explained; checklists of regulatory requirements, tax-saving ideas, and names and addresses of organizations and government resources are also provided.

Vermont

Shaw, Karen A., Michael D. Jenkins, and Anthony J. Walters. *Starting and Operating a Business in Vermont.* Grant's Pass, OR: Oasis Press, 1996. 1 vol.

The first chapter reviews basic considerations about going into business, including choosing the legal form and buying an existing business. General information for actually starting and staying in business is then offered, followed by a focus on the specific laws and practices of the state. The procedures and forms needed to start a business are provided and explained; checklists of regulatory requirements, tax-saving ideas, and names and addresses of organizations and government resources are also provided.

Virginia

Brown, W. Dean. *Incorporating in Virginia*. Knoxville, TN: Consumer
    Publishing Inc., 1991. 1 vol.

The *Incorporating in* . . . series explains the benefits of incorporation and the
specific steps required to incorporate your business in the title state. Tax saving strategies are also discussed. The publisher offers a telephone help line
(not toll free) to answer any further questions, although, of course, they cannot give legal or tax advice (that's called practicing without a license, and it's
illegal). Each book includes forms and elaborately decorated stock certificates.

Shaw, Karen A., Michael D. Jenkins, and Anthony J. Walters. *Starting
    and Operating a Business in Virginia*. Grant's Pass, OR: Oasis
    Press, 1996. 1 vol.

The first chapter reviews basic considerations about going into business,
including choosing the legal form and buying an existing business. General
information for actually starting and staying in business is then offered, followed by a focus on the specific laws and practices of the state. The procedures
and forms needed to start a business are provided and explained; checklists
of regulatory requirements, tax-saving ideas, and names and addresses of
organizations and government resources are also provided.

Washington

Brown, W. Dean. *Incorporating in Washington*. Knoxville, TN:
    Consumer Publishing Inc., 1991. 1 vol.

The *Incorporating in* . . . series explains the benefits of incorporation and the
specific steps required to incorporate your business in the title state. Tax saving strategies are also discussed. The publisher offers a telephone help line
(not toll free) to answer any further questions, although, of course, they cannot give legal or tax advice (that's called practicing without a license, and it's
illegal). Each book includes forms and elaborately decorated stock certificates.

Washington, D.C.

Shaw, Karen A., Michael D. Jenkins, and Anthony J. Walters. *Starting and Operating a Business in Washington, D.C.* Grant's Pass, OR: Oasis Press, 1996. 1 vol.

The first chapter reviews basic considerations about going into business, including choosing the legal form and buying an existing business. General information for actually starting and staying in business is then offered, followed by a focus on the specific laws and practices of the state. The procedures and forms needed to start a business are provided and explained; checklists of regulatory requirements, tax-saving ideas, and names and addresses of organizations and government resources are also provided.

West Virginia

Shaw, Karen A., Michael D. Jenkins, and Anthony J. Walters. *Starting and Operating a Business in West Virginia.* Grant's Pass, OR: Oasis Press, 1996. 1 vol.

The first chapter reviews basic considerations about going into business, including choosing the legal form and buying an existing business. General information for actually starting and staying in business is then offered, followed by a focus on the specific laws and practices of the state. The procedures and forms needed to start a business are provided and explained; checklists of regulatory requirements, tax-saving ideas, and names and addresses of organizations and government resources are also provided.

Wisconsin

Brown, W. Dean. *Incorporating in Wisconsin.* Knoxville, TN: Consumer Publishing Inc., 1991. 1 vol.

The *Incorporating in . . .* series explains the benefits of incorporation and the specific steps required to incorporate your business in the title state. Tax saving strategies are also discussed. The publisher offers a telephone help line (not toll free) to answer any further questions, although, of course, they cannot give legal or tax advice (that's called practicing without a license, and it's illegal). Each book includes forms and elaborately decorated stock certificates.

Shaw, Karen A., Michael D. Jenkins, and Anthony J. Walters. *Starting and Operating a Business in Wisconsin.* Grant's Pass, OR: Oasis Press, 1996. 1 vol.

The first chapter reviews basic considerations about going into business, including choosing the legal form and buying an existing business. General information for actually starting and staying in business is then offered, followed by a focus on the specific laws and practices of the state. The procedures and forms needed to start a business are provided and explained; checklists of regulatory requirements, tax-saving ideas, and names and addresses of organizations and government resources are also provided.

Wyoming

Shaw, Karen A., Michael D. Jenkins, and Anthony J. Walters. *Starting and Operating a Business in Wyoming.* Grant's Pass, OR: Oasis Press, 1996. 1 vol.

The first chapter reviews basic considerations about going into business, including choosing the legal form and buying an existing business. General information for actually starting and staying in business is then offered, followed by a focus on the specific laws and practices of the state. The procedures and forms needed to start a business are provided and explained; checklists of regulatory requirements, tax-saving ideas, and names and addresses of organizations and government resources are also provided.

CHARITIES

Mackey, Philip English. *The Giver's Guide: Making Your Charity Dollars Count.* Highland Park, NJ: Catbird Press, 1990. 275p.

Information about more than 300 national charities, taken from the records of the National Charities Information Bureau, an independent watchdog agency that evaluates charitable organizations. The guide offers to help the reader evaluate how efficiently a gift of money, goods, or time is likely to be used by these agencies, and how to budget your charitable giving to produce the greatest tax break. Also included are ways to introduce your children to charitable giving, to recognize and report fraud, deal with solicitations, persuade your employer to match charitable gifts, and find the most satisfying volunteer position for you.

CHILDREN

Waters, Robert C. *Kids, the Law, and You.* Bellingham, WA: Self-Counsel Press, 1994. 200p.

A book for adults about legal protections for children. Deals with suspected child abuse, the legal status of children, parent's rights, medical issues involving children and the law, and children in trouble with the law. A large section discusses "preventative law": things you can do to plan ahead for your children's welfare in the event of divorce, disability, or death. Sample nomination of guardian documents, living will, and health care proxy are included. Appendices list child welfare, labor, service, support enforcement, and missing children organizations.

COMPUTERS AND COMPUTER SOFTWARE

Benzel, Rick. *Legal Services on Your Home-Based PC.* Blue Ridge Summit, PA: Windcrest/McGraw-Hill, 1994. 1 vol.

Fishman, Stephen. *Software Development: A Legal Guide.* 1st ed. Berkeley, CA: Nolo Press, 1994. 576p.

Explains the various legal protections available for software developers, including the new multimedia patent, and how to avoid infringement. Offers step-by- step instructions for drafting publishing, employment, contractor or consultant agreements, and agreements for the development of custom software. Also discusses when and how to obtain permission to use existing materials in your multimedia projects. Includes contracts and agreements on disk for us on a DOS-based PC and any word processing program.

Fishman, Stephen. *Copyright Your Software.* 1st ed. Berkeley, CA: Nolo Press, 1994. 304p.

CONSTRUCTION AND CONSTRUCTION LIENS

Bianchina, Paul. *How to Hire the Right Contractor: Getting the Right Prices, Workmanship and Scheduling for Home Remodeling.* Mt. Vernon, NY: Consumer Reports Books, 1991. 164p.

This book discusses how to: choose the best contractor for your job; save money by doing some of the work yourself; avoid being overcharged or having work left undone or done late; arrange loans, permits, and insurance; and evaluate contracts and contractor credentials. Includes contact information for state licensing authorities, organizations to contact for additional information, sample forms for bids, construction contract, liens, and 17 pages of home repair product ratings.

Florida

Kalmanson, Barry. *How to File a Florida Construction Lien (and Collect!).* 2nd ed. Clearwater, FL: Sphinx Publishing, 1995. 134p.

If you provide goods or services to real property in Florida, then you can file a construction lien (formerly known as a mechanics lien) to assure that you will be paid. This book explains: what services and materials are lienable; who can file a lien; how to handle bonded projects; when you must file a lawsuit; recovery of attorney fees and costs; and how to obtain a release or waiver of a lien. Notes criminal and disciplinary penalties available against erring contractors and offers text of selected portions of relevant statutes. Includes ready-to-use forms and completed sample forms including notices to owners, affidavits, releases, sworn statement of account, and a project tracking sheet.

CONSUMER LAW

The Consumer Handbook. Irvine, CA: LawPrep Press, 1991. 1 vol.

Smith, Wesley. *The Smart Consumer: Legal Guide to Your Rights in the Marketplace.* Washington, DC: HALT, 1994. 235p.

Discusses legal protections available to consumers and how to take advantage of them, and offers advice on exerting your rights in and out of court. Appendices include contact information for state insurance regulators, medical boards, consumer hotlines, and state bar programs for resolving disputes against lawyers. Also includes a six-page glossary of legal terms and a three-page annotated bibliography of recommended reading.

California

Kaufman, Barbara. *Nolo's Pocket Guide to Consumer's Rights: A Resource for All Californians.* 2nd Cal. ed. Berkeley, CA: Nolo Press, 1994. 250p.

Details California consumer protection laws and contact information for federal, state, local, and private agencies that can help with consumer complaints. Brief information on approximately 200 specific products and consumer protection topics are listed from A to Z. Each topic includes a very brief explanation of applicable rights and relevant agencies that may be helpful; many also include advice on how to proceed with possible remedies, and where to get additional information.

CONTRACTS

Barret, E.T. *Write Your Own Business Contracts: What Your Attorney Won't Tell You.* Grant's Pass, OR: Oasis Press, 1994. 337p.

The author, a lawyer, provides a clause-by-clause analysis of various business contracts, and examples of good and bad legal writing. He critically examines sample documents and shows how to evaluate them for loopholes and/or ambiguous language. A separate chapter covers "Forming and Maintaining a Corporation," offering a straightforward discussion of the corporate entity. The author suggests that all contracts be reviewed by an attorney.

Elias, Stephen and Lisa Goldoftas. *Nolo's Law Form Kit: Buy & Sell Contracts: Bills of Sale for Cars, Boats, Electronic Equipment and Other Personal Property.* Berkeley, CA: Nolo Press, 1993. 50p.

Elias, Stephen and Marcia Stewart. *Simple Contracts for Personal Use.* 2nd ed. Berkeley, CA: Nolo Press, 1994. 1 vol.

Provides "ready-to-use" contracts for various private transactions, as opposed to business or commercial enterprises. Each form uses simple terms and is basically self-explanatory, although notes and examples are provided to help the reader understand various clauses. Each chapter deals with a specific type of contract: promissory notes; bills of sale; storage contracts; releases; home-repair agreements; and contracts for in-home child care and other household help. Sample forms are provided throughout, many filled in, or with instructions on the specific information that should be provided.

Milko, George, Kay Ostberg, and Theresa Rudy. *Everyday Contracts: Protecting Your Rights, A Step-by-Step Guide.* Rev. ed. New York, NY/Washington, DC: HALT, 1991. 1 vol.

Sigman, Robert. *Contracts.* Altamonte Springs, FL: Legovac, 1990. Audio

COPYRIGHTS, PATENTS, AND TRADEMARKS

Amernick, Burton A. *Patent Law for the Nonlawyer: A Guide for the Engineer, Technologist, and Manager.* 2nd ed. New York, NY: Van Nostrand Reinhold, 1991. 240p.

This book is intended "to provide inventors and those who manage technology with sufficient understanding of the patent system to permit them to use it with the greatest possible accuracy and comfort." The author hopes to facilitate communication between technical people and their legal representatives by providing "an overall understanding of the basic principles . . . of patent law." Introductory chapters distinguish between patent law and other forms of protection such as copyright, trade secrets, and trademarks; review jurisdiction for administering laws pertaining to intellectual property; and consider the relationship between patentability and inventorship. Subsequent chapters provide practical information on the patent application and the procedures involved in obtaining a patent. Appendices include a glossary, a list of important addresses, standard forms, and applicable laws and regulations.

Barber, Hoyt L. *Copyrights, Patents and Trademarks: Protect Your Rights Worldwide.* Blue Ridge Summit, PA: Tab Books, 1990. 258p.

Provides extensive information on the various forms of intellectual property protection, explaining in detailed, step-by-step procedures how to obtain exclusive protection for ideas, inventions, names, identifying marks, or artistic, literary, musical, photographic or cinematographic works. The purpose is to simplify the process of securing a copyright, patent, or trademark in most countries where protection would be beneficial. Parts 1 through 3 cover federal and state protection in the United States; Part 4 provides international information, including country-by-country profiles; Part 5 offers contacts/sources of further information.

Burshtein, Sheldon. *Patent Your Own Invention in Canada: A Complete Step-by-Step Guide.* 2nd ed. Bellingham, WA: Self-Counsel Press, 1991. 228p.

Elias, Stephen. *Patent, Copyright and Trademark: A Desk Reference to Intellectual Property Law.* Berkeley, CA: Nolo Press, 1996. 430p.

A comprehensive dictionary of words and phrases used in each of the substantive areas of intellectual property law (trade secret, copyright, trademark, patent, and contract & warranty), this book is designed to bridge the gap between the scientist, educator, and author and the lawyer. Each part focuses on a particular area and begins with an overview of the legal issues, followed by an alphabetical listing of the terms. The definitions present the context in which the words are used. Entries provide cross references to related terms, as well as notations where terms used in the definition are defined elsewhere. An index is included.

Fishman, Stephen. *The Copyright Handbook: How to Protect and Use Written Works.* 2nd National ed. Berkeley, CA: Nolo Press, 1992. 1 vol.

A book about "copyright for written works," this *Handbook* is directed to "the entire universe of people who deal with the written word," including novelists, poets, playwrights, screenwriters, how-to authors, journalists, editors, librarians, and literary agents. The first part of the book consists of an overview of copyright law and a "how-to" guide on copyright notice and registration. The second half is a copyright resource, discussing the most important aspects of copyright law in detail. For instance, Chapter 9 addresses the transfer of copyright rights; Chapter 11, the fair use privilege; and Chapter 12, copyright infringement. Short examples and case studies appear throughout the book to clarify the text, as do highlighted "copyright tips." The appendix contains both sample filled-in forms and blank forms which can be removed and used.

Goldstein, Paul. *Copyright's Highway: From Gutenberg to the Celestial Jukebox.* 2nd ed. New York, NY: Hill and Wang, 1994. 1 vol.

A detailed examination of the nature and implications of copyright law, with emphasis on changes on the horizon for copyright law and the transmission of information in general and how various possible approaches could affect society and creative productivity. Although this book offers no forms or instructions on the practicalities of copyright laws, and thus is arguably not a self-help book per se, it does offer a clear, plain-language explanation of a very complicated area of law which may be helpful to laypeople trying to stay on the right side of the often-murky copyright line.

Klavens, Kent J. *Protecting Your Songs & Yourself.* Cincinnati, OH: Writer's Digest Books, 1989. 112p.

Provides a basic legal background for songwriters, covering the fundamental laws and business principles that affect the craft of songwriting. Begins with an analysis of copyright law since this provides the basis for all rights, agreements, and other legal issues that relate to protecting one's songs. Other chapters examine limits on song creation (e.g., parody, libel, right of publicity), co-writers, song contests, and transfers of publishing rights.

Lee, Robert E. *A Copyright Guide for Authors.* Stanford CT: Kent Press, 1996. 200p.

Levy, Richard C. *Inventing and Patenting Sourcebook: How to Sell and Protect Your Ideas.* Detroit, MI: Gale Research Inc., 1990. 922p.

Designed to provide inventors, innovators, and marketers of new products and inventions with a comprehensive and practical "how-to" guide to developing, patenting, licensing, and marketing their ideas and concepts. Contains a step-by-step discussion of the inventing and patenting process, including such topics as patent searches, selecting companies to market inventions, licensing agreements, and procuring federal R & D funds. The *Sourcebook* also includes an extensive directory of inventing and patenting information (e.g., invention consultants; publications for the inventor; patent depository libraries; registered patent attorneys).

McGrath, Kate, Stephen Elias, and Sarah Shena. *Trademark: How to Name Your Business & Product.* 2nd ed. Berkeley, CA: Nolo Press, 1996. 352p.

Extensive explanation of the importance of trademarks and how to find the best trademark for your business and register it yourself. Covers how to choose a trademark that competitors can't copy and how to assert your rights in a trademark dispute. Includes all the information and official forms with instructions you need to register a trademark, with clear, detailed step-by-(tiny) step instructions. An excellent guide.

Pressman, David. *Patent It Yourself.* 3rd ed. Berkeley, CA: Nolo Press, 1991. 1 vol.

Presented in a chronological format, starting with an overview of the patent process and then covering the steps most often taken to protect and profit from an invention, this book is designed to show the inventor how to patent and commercially exploit an invention. It provides step-by-step guidance for obtaining a patent (including tear-out forms), an overview of procedures for getting patent protection abroad, and introduction to alternative and supplementary forms of protection (e.g., copyright, trademarks, trade secrets), and detailed information on how to commercially evaluate and market an invention.

Warda, Mark. *How to Register Your Own Trademark.* Clearwater, FL: Sphinx Publishing. 1994. 146p.

Warda, Mark. *How to Register Your Own Copyright.* Clearwater, FL: Sphinx Publishing, 1995. 146p.

Everything you need to copyright your written, artistic, dramatic, audio-visual, three-dimensional or musical works, computer chip designs, or computer programs. Ready-to-use forms and simple explanations of the law of copyright, covering what copyright is and why you want to take advantage of it, what it covers, how to file and protect your copyright, and what you can and cannot copy from others without violating copyright laws.

CORPORATIONS AND PARTNERSHIPS

Clifford, Denis. *The Partnership Book: How to Write a Partnership Agreement: Sample Clauses for All Key Issues.* 4th ed. Berkeley, CA: Nolo Press, 1991. 350p.

Designed as a workbook which provides the tools you can use to create a viable partnership based on a solid legal foundation that should meet both present and future needs of the small business. The initial chapters provide background information on partnerships and getting a business started. Subsequent chapters focus on the partnership agreement itself, covering basic issues (e.g., financial matters, handling disputes, changes in the partnership, tax matters) to be resolved and providing numerous sample clauses. Limited partnerships are separately reviewed. Finally, a step-by-step illustration of how to construct the agreement is offered.

Cooke, Robert A. *How to Start Your Own Subchapter S Corporation.* New York, NY: John Wiley and Sons, 1995. 240p.

A book about how to start your own Subchapter S corporation which focuses on tax consequences and alternatives, including the limited liability company. Explains advantages and disadvantages of various legal forms of business and tells you how to set up the one you want with "affordable professional assistance." The author stresses that if you will do most of the background work to educate yourself about the issues involved you can get good legal help take care of the formalities correctly at lower cost. Contains some forms but, curiously, "most of the 'boilerplate' forms that require little or no change from corporation to corporation have been omitted." The author notes that "Your attorney will have an ample supply of those."

Essential Limited Liability Company Handbook. Grant's Pass, OR: Oasis Press/PSI Research, 1995. 259p.

Explains the legal and financial ramifications of limited liability companies, including protecting personal assets and avoiding corporate taxes. Describes basically how to form a limited liability company, as a new venture or a conersion of an existing business. Includes additional specifics for various states (note that Hawaii, Massachusetts, and Vermont don't encourage LLCs, so you might not want to buy this book if your business is there) and sources of additional state information. The book intends to give information to allow you to speak intelligently with legal and accounting professionals, but does not act as a complete do-it-yourself guide.

Friedman, Scott E. *Forming Your Own Limited Liability Company.* Chicago, IL: Dearborn, 1995. 176p.

Goldstein, Arnold S. and Robert L. Davidson. *Starting Your Subchapter "S" Corporation: How to Build a Business the Right Way.* 2nd ed. New York, NY: John Wiley & Sons, Inc., 1992. 242p.

The authors explain how the Subchapter S form of incorporation can enable you to: avoid paying any corporate or accumulated earnings tax; claim unlimited passive income; give your spouse a tax-deferred check for $144,000; sell personal property tax free; and utilize your business as a personal tax shelter. It also gives you the checklists and ready-to-use forms you need to incorporate without a lawyer.

Howell, John C. *Forming Corporations and Partnerships: An Easy, Do-It-Yourself Guide.* 2nd ed. Blue Ridge Summit, PA: TAB Books, 1991. 220p.

Explains the three types of organization commonly used for small businesses (including the advantages and disadvantages of each): a corporation, a partnership (general or limited), or a sole proprietorship. Descriptions of the necessary forms and step-by-step instructions as to formation of each entity are provided. Appendices include the names and addresses of state offices where corporation papers are filed and a glossary of legal terms.

Kirk, John. *Incorporating Your Business.* Chicago, IL: Contemporary Books, 1994. 1 vol.

Legal Expense Defense: How to Control Your Business' Legal Costs and Problems. Grant's Pass, Oregon: Oasis Press, 1995. 326p.

Offers strategies and checklists for minimizing your legal expenses, from alternatives to courts and lawyers to negotiating low-cost, value-based billing fee structures with your attorney. Emphasizes preventative legal strategies, doing more of your own legal work using in-house staff, and being involved in what your attorney is doing for you so that you make the decisions. Includes worksheets for monitoring your costs, model letters, contracts, and notices, and some reproducible forms.

Mancuso, Anthony. *Form Your Own Limited Liability Company.* 1st ed. Berkeley, CA: Nolo Press, 1996. 300p.

Mancuso, Anthony. *How to Form a Nonprofit Corporation*. 3rd ed. Berkeley, CA: Nolo Press, 1996. 1 vol.

Everything you need to set up a nonprofit corporation, right up to forms for taking down the minutes of your first meeting. Also covers legal and tax regulations for each state and applying and qualifying for a nonprofit tax exemption. Well-organized, clear, step-by-step instructions with ready-to-use, tear-out forms. Another exemplary Nolo Press publication.

Mancuso, Anthony. *Taking Care of Your Corporation, Vol. 1: Director and Shareholder Meetings Made Easy*. 1st ed. Berkeley, CA: Nolo Press, 1994. 304p.

Mancuso, Anthony. *Taking Care of Your Corporation, Vol 2: Key Corporate Decisions Made Easy*. 1st ed. Berkeley, CA: Nolo Press, 1995. 320p.

Advice and forms for major corporate business and tax actions, including: setting up your business; buying or leasing commercial property and company cars; authorizing corporate contracts and loans; hiring and compensating employees; authorizing loans and expense payments; authorizing the issuance of stock and dividends; and making various strategic tax decisions. Includes forms on disk that are "good in all 50 states," and brief instructions on how to install and use the disk and find the form you are looking for on it. Also includes tear-out forms for written consent to action without meeting, minutes of a meeting, waiver of notice of meeting, and S corporation tax election (IRS Form 2553).

Nicholas, Ted. *How to Form Your Own "S" Corporation and Avoid Double Taxation*. Chicago, IL: Dearborn, 1995. 208p.

Nicholas, Ted. *How to Form Your Own Corporation Without a Lawyer for Under $75.00*. 20th ed. Chicago, IL: Dearborn Trade, 1992. 1 vol.

Nolo Press. *Nolo's Partnership Maker*. Berkeley, CA: Nolo Press, 1994. 256p.

Ray, James C. *The Most Valuable Corporate Forms You'll Ever Need*. Clearwater, FL: Sphinx Publishing, 1995. 220p.

Forms and instructions dealing with: meetings and adoption of resolutions; minutes; minute books; board of directors actions and meetings; shares and shareholders; officers; employees; agents; amending bylaws and articles of incorporation; protecting the officers and directors from liability; changing the corporate name; mergers; stock and asset transactions; and various financial transactions. Includes blank and sample completed forms, but blank forms have headers and page numbers and are not perforated, so you might have to do some creative copying if you are particular. Includes a list of citations to the corporations statutes of each state.

Sitarz, Dan. *Incorporate Your Business: The National Corporation Kit.* 1st ed. Carbondale, IL: Nova Publishing Co., 1995. 256p.

Explains the benefits of incorporating a small business, and how to incorporate your own without hiring a lawyer, with all the forms and information that you need to form a C or S corporation in any state. Forms will need to be retyped or creatively Xeroxed to avoid including the chapter headers. Also offers brief advice on filing corporate tax returns. Includes an appendix of state-specific incorporation information and a glossary of corporate legal terms.

Sniffen, Carl J. *The Essential Corporation Handbook.* 2nd ed. Grant's Pass, OR: Oasis Press, 1995. 236p.

Explains how to form a corporation and why you would want to. Includes checklists, sample forms, and sample documents, but no ready-to-use forms. With glossary and appendix of secretaries of state and corporation divisions. Includes brief chapters on professional, not-for-profit, close, and limited liability corporations, and one chapter aptly named "Horror Stories," about what can happen if you aren't scrupulously careful to follow all the formalities in the incorporation process.

Tuller, Lawrence W. *Tap the Hidden Wealth in Your Business.* Blue Ridge Summit, PA: TAB Books/McGraw-Hill 1991. 1 vol.

Van Hof, Victoria. *Incorporation and Business Guide for Washington: How to Form Your Own Corporation.* 6th ed. Bellingham, WA: Self-Counsel Press, 1993. 128p.

After considering the methods of carrying on a business and the advantages of doing so as a corporation, this book offers a simplified examination of the basic procedure for incorporating a business in Washington. Also presented are step-by-step instructions on how to start a business, including an explanation of tax and license requirements, and a chapter devoted to a "Pre-Incorporation Checklist." A multitude of filled-in forms to be used as samples are provided throughout the book. Also available from the publisher is a separately sold "Incorporation Forms for Washington" kit, with complete blank forms necessary to form a corporation (e.g., applications to reserve name; articles of incorporation; consents to board action; and bylaws.

Wilber, W. Kelsea and Arthur G. Sartorius III. *How to Form Your Own Corporation.* Clearwater, FL: Sphinx Publishing, 1993. 148p.

Forms, instructions and selected statutes on forming a corporation in all 50 states and the District of Columbia. Discusses advantages and disadvantages of C and S corporations, a checklist for forming a simple corporation, and information on selling corporate stock and running a corporation using appropriate procedures and paperwork.

Alabama

Haman, Edward A. *How to Form Your Own Partnership.* Southeast ed. Clearwater, FL: Sphinx Publishing, 1995. 144p.

Instructions and forms for evaluating, creating, changing, or dissolving a partnership in Alabama, Florida, Georgia, Louisiana, Mississippi, North Carolina, South Carolina, or Texas. Addresses the implications of the Uniform Partnership Act and the partnership laws of the states in question. In addition to basic forms covering forming, buying-out, terminating or amending a partnership, (and registering a partnership in Louisiana) a 26-page appendix of optional partnership clauses is included.

California

Mancuso, Anthony. *The California Nonprofit Corporation Handbook.* 6th ed. Berkeley, CA: Nolo Press, 1992. 352p.

Although primarily a guide to forming a nonprofit corporation eligible for tax exempt status under IRC Section 501(c)(3), this book also presents much information on the federal, state, and local tax advantages and requirements and a discussion of California corporate law provisions. Separate chapters explain how to prepare and submit federal and California tax exemption applications. Step-by-step instructions are given for the initial and final steps in organizing a nonprofit corporation under California law, including: choosing a name; preparing articles of incorporation and bylaws; filing incorporation papers; preparing minutes of the first board meeting; registering with the attorney general; and filing articles with county recorders. Sample forms are included in the text, and the appendix provides tear-out, ready-to-use forms.

Mancuso, Anthony. *California Professional Corporation Handbook.*
6th ed. Berkeley, CA: Nolo Press, 1996. 224p.

The information and forms you need to form a professional corporation in California, elect corporation tax status, and save on your taxes, while protecting yourself from personal liability for the malpractice of the other professionals in your practice. Only the following categories of professionals are required to form a professional corporation (other can form a regular corporation): accountants; acupuncturists; attorneys; clinical social workers; chiropractors; dentists; doctors; marriage, family, and child counselors; nurses; optometrists; osteopaths; pharmacists; physical therapists; physicians assistants; podiatrists; psychologists; shorthand reporters; speech pathologists; and audiologists. Architects and veterinarians have the option to form a professional corporation of a regular business corporation. It is a little hard to guess the reasoning on this breakdown, but there it is.

Mancuso, Anthony. *How to Form Your Own California Corporation.*
8th ed. Berkeley, CA: Nolo Press, 1994. 1 vol.

This book gives the instructions and forms necessary to organize a small, privately held profit corporation, eligible to issue initial shares under California's limited offering exemption (the state securities law exemption explained in Chapter 3). More than just a corporate kit, the first chapters give background information about the practical, legal, and tax issues related to forming and operating a corporation (e.g., Chapter 1 covers the "Advantages and Disadvantages of Forming a California Corporation"). Chapter 5 has "how-to-do-it" material on forming a corporation in a systematic, step-by-step presentation, including many sample forms and detailed instructions as to how to fill them out. A final chapter specifies what to do after the corporation is organized, emphasizing the tax-related forms to be completed and also explaining the final formalities which must be taken. The appendix contains a complete set of tear-out forms ready for use, including multiple copies of stock certificates. This book is also available in a ring-binder format with: index dividers to organize corporate documents and records; 10 stock certificates; and all incorporation forms on Macintosh and PC diskettes.

Florida

Haman, Edward A. *How to Form Your Own Partnership*. Southeast ed. Clearwater, FL: Sphinx Publishing, 1995. 144p.

Instructions and forms for evaluating, creating, changing, or dissolving a partnership in Alabama, Florida, Georgia, Louisiana, Mississippi, North Carolina, South Carolina, or Texas. Addresses the implications of the Uniform Partnership Act and the partnership laws of the states in question. In addition to basic forms covering forming, buying-out, terminating or amending a partnership, (and registering a partnership in Louisiana) a 26-page appendix of optional partnership clauses is included.

Mackie, Sam. *How to Form a Nonprofit Corporation in Florida*. 3rd ed. Clearwater, FL: Sphinx Publishing, 1994. 138p.

Mancuso, Anthony. *How to Form Your Own Florida Corporation*. 3rd ed. Berkeley, CA: Nolo Press, 1991. 272p.

Step-by-step instructions and all the forms you need (includes both ready-to-use, tear-out paper forms and a computer disk of forms) to incorporate your business in Florida under the Florida Business Corporation Act, and an explanation of the advantages and disadvantages of incorporation in Florida (in comparison to adopting other forms of business organization or incorporating in another state). Describes relevant tax, corporation, workers' compensation, and securities law information, and how to secure federal S corporation tax status, advice about personal insurance coverage, and when you do and don't need a lawyer or accountant.

Warda, Mark. *How to Form a Simple Corporation in Florida*. Clearwater, FL: Sphinx Publishing, 1994. 147p.

Explains the advantages and disadvantages of various types of corporations, and how to deal with taxes, licenses, securities, and required corporate formalities. Includes the forms and instructions you need to start up a corporation (even an S or professional corporation), including ready-to-use stock certificates. Sample filled-in forms are also included for guidance, and the text of selected portions of relevant Florida statutes and rules of the Department of State regarding corporate names are included in an appendix.

Waters, Robert C. *Incorporation and Business Guide for Florida: How to Form Your Own Corporation.* Bellingham, WA: Self-Counsel Press, 1992. 192p.

Step-by-step guidance on forming your own corporation or professional association in Florida and why you may or may not want to do so. Includes many sample, filled-in forms, and two tear-out copies of each of the forms you will be most likely to need. Also discusses the advantages and disadvantages (tax and otherwise) of various forms of business organization, what you should know before you incorporate, and the basics of running meetings, dealing with shareholders, daily operation as a corporation, and making changes after you incorporate.

Georgia

Haman, Edward A. *How to Form Your Own Partnership.* Southeast ed. Clearwater, FL: Sphinx Publishing, 1995. 144p.

Instructions and forms for evaluating, creating, changing, or dissolving a partnership in Alabama, Florida, Georgia, Louisiana, Mississippi, North Carolina, South Carolina, or Texas. Addresses the implications of the Uniform Partnership Act and the partnership laws of the states in question. In addition to basic forms covering forming, buying-out, terminating or amending a partnership, (and registering a partnership in Louisiana) a 26-page appendix of optional partnership clauses is included.

Indiana

Williams, Phillip G. *How to Form Your Own Indiana Corporation Before the Inc. Dries!* Oak Park, IL: P. Gaines Co., 1992. 155p.

Standard entry in the author's *Small Business Administration* series covering the basic steps for incorporating a small business in the state of Indiana. Complete with sample forms and instructions as well as brief background information on the various forms of business ownership, taxation and corporations, and special types of corporations in Indiana (e.g., professional and not for profit). Includes an incorporation checklist keyed to pages where the matters are discussed in the book, important Indiana addresses and phone numbers, and an index.

Louisiana

Haman, Edward A. *How to Form Your Own Partnership.* Southeast ed. Clearwater, FL: Sphinx Publishing, 1995. 144p.

Instructions and forms for evaluating, creating, changing, or dissolving a partnership in Alabama, Florida, Georgia, Louisiana, Mississippi, North Carolina, South Carolina, or Texas. Addresses the implications of the Uniform Partnership Act and the partnership laws of the states in question. In addition to basic forms covering forming, buying-out, terminating or amending a partnership, (and registering a partnership in Louisiana) a 26-page appendix of optional partnership clauses is included.

Mississippi

Haman, Edward A. *How to Form Your Own Partnership.* Southeast ed. Clearwater, FL: Sphinx Publishing, 1995. 144p.

Instructions and forms for evaluating, creating, changing, or dissolving a partnership in Alabama, Florida, Georgia, Louisiana, Mississippi, North Carolina, South Carolina, or Texas. Addresses the implications of the Uniform Partnership Act and the partnership laws of the states in question. In addition to basic forms covering forming, buying-out, terminating or amending a partnership, (and registering a partnership in Louisiana) a 26-page appendix of optional partnership clauses is included.

Missouri

Williams, Phillip G. *How to Form Your Own Missouri Corporation Before the Inc. Dries!* Oak Park, IL: P. Gaines Co., 1992. 155p.

Volume Five in the author's *Small Business Incorporation* series (volumes one through four cover Illinois, Ohio, Michigan, and Indiana), this work follows the standard format. General discussions on the forms of business ownership, Delaware corporations, and using the corporation as a tax shelter and other tax ramifications of corporate status are followed by detailed chapters on specific aspects of Missouri corporations (e.g., how to form a corporation; professional corporations; not-for-profit corporations). Among the sample forms included in the appendices are articles of incorporation, bylaws, minutes of first meetings for shareholders and boards of directors, name reservation application, and preorganization subscription agreement. An incorporation checklist is also provided.

New York

Mancuso, Anthony. *How to Form Your Own New York Corporation.* 3rd ed. Berkeley, CA: Nolo Press, 1994. 304p.

This book gives the instructions and forms necessary to organize a business corporation which has less than ten New York shareholders; it can also be used if a corporation will offer its initial shares to a limited number of New York residents for a relatively small amount of money. The first four chapters give background information about how corporations work and potential danger areas (e.g., Chapter 1 covers the "Advantages and Disadvantages of Forming a New York Corporation"). Chapter 5 has "how-to-do-it" material on forming a corporation in a systematic, step-by-step presentation, including many sample forms and detailed instructions as to how to fill them out. A final chapter specifies what to do after the corporation is organized, emphasizing the tax forms which must be submitted. The appendix contains a complete set of tear-out forms (also included on computer diskette) ready to use in forming a New York corporation, including extra copies of share certificates.

North Carolina

Haman, Edward A. *How to Form Your Own Partnership.* Southeast ed. Clearwater, FL: Sphinx Publishing, 1995. 144p.

Instructions and forms for evaluating, creating, changing, or dissolving a partnership in Alabama, Florida, Georgia, Louisiana, Mississippi, North Carolina, South Carolina, or Texas. Addresses the implications of the Uniform Partnership Act and the partnership laws of the states in question. In addition to basic forms covering forming, buying-out, terminating or amending a partnership, (and registering a partnership in Louisiana) a 26-page appendix of optional partnership clauses is included.

Oregon

Davis, Thomas C. *Incorporation and Business Guide for Oregon: How to Form Your Own Corporation.* 4th ed. Bellingham, WA: Self-Counsel Press, 1992. 120p.

After considering the methods of carrying on a business and the advantages of doing so as a corporation, this book offers a simplified examination of the basic procedure for incorporating a business in Oregon. Also presented are step-by-step instructions on how to start a business, including an explanation of tax and license requirements. A multitude of filled-in forms to be used as samples are provided throughout the book and a checklist of steps to be followed in incorporation is included in the Appendix. Also available from the publisher is a separately sold "Incorporation Forms for Oregon" kit, with complete blank forms necessary to form a corporation (e.g., articles of incorporation; bylaws; share certificates).

South Carolina

Haman, Edward A. *How to Form Your Own Partnership*. Southeast ed. Clearwater, FL: Sphinx Publishing, 1995. 144p.

Instructions and forms for evaluating, creating, changing, or dissolving a partnership in Alabama, Florida, Georgia, Louisiana, Mississippi, North Carolina, South Carolina, or Texas. Addresses the implications of the Uniform Partnership Act and the partnership laws of the states in question. In addition to basic forms covering forming, buying-out, terminating or amending a partnership, (and registering a partnership in Louisiana) a 26-page appendix of optional partnership clauses is included.

Texas

Haman, Edward A. *How to Form Your Own Partnership*. Southeast ed. Clearwater, FL: Sphinx Publishing, 1995. 144p.

Instructions and forms for evaluating, creating, changing, or dissolving a partnership in Alabama, Florida, Georgia, Louisiana, Mississippi, North Carolina, South Carolina, or Texas. Addresses the implications of the Uniform Partnership Act and the partnership laws of the states in question. In addition to basic forms covering forming, buying-out, terminating or amending a partnership, (and registering a partnership in Louisiana) a 26-page appendix of optional partnership clauses is included.

Mancuso, Anthony. *How to Form Your Own Texas Corporation*. 4th ed. Berkeley, CA: Nolo Press, 1989. 272p.

Step-by-step instructions and all the forms you need (includes both ready-to-use, tear-out paper forms and a computer diskette of forms) to incorporate your business in Texas, and an explanation of the advantages and disadvantages of incorporation in Florida (in comparison to adopting other forms of business organization or incorporating in another state like Delaware). Describes relevant tax, corporation, workers' compensation and securities law information, how to secure federal S corporation tax status, advice about personal insurance coverage, and when you do and don't need a lawyer or accountant.

Rolcik, Karen Ann and Mark Warda. *How to Form a Simple Corporation in Texas.* Clearwater, FL: Sphinx Publishing, 1995. 148p.

Explains the advantages and disadvantages of various types of corporations, and how to deal with taxes, licenses, securities, and required corporate formalities. Includes the forms and instructions you need to start up a corporation (even an S or professional corporation), including ready-to-use stock certificates with eagles and colored borders—cut them out carefully and nobody would guess you got them out of a paperback incorporation book. Sample filled-in forms are also included for guidance, and the text of selected portions of relevant Texas statutes is included in an appendix.

COURTS

Bergman, Paul and Sara J. Berman-Barrett. *Represent Yourself in Court: How to Prepare and Try a Winning Case.* 1st ed. Berkeley, CA: Nolo Press, 1993. 384p.

LeValliant, Ted and Marcel Theroux. *What's the Verdict?: Real Life Court Cases to Test Your Legal IQ.* New York, NY: Sterling Pub. Co., 1991. 1 vol.

A book of "legal puzzles": brief statements of real cases for the reader to judge and try to guess what the real trial and appeals courts held. Really more of a game than a self-help book (the authors include instructions for using the book as a game), but readers will doubtless pick up some legal principles which are summarized where they result in a given decision. The court decisions are in the back of the book, separate from the facts of the cases, and are "scrambled so that your crafty legal eye won't pick up the answer to the next case by mistake." Legal principles which led to the decisions are also summarized.

California

Duncan, Roderic. *Everybody's Guide to Municipal Court.* Berkeley, CA: Nolo Press, 1991. 1 vol.

Written by a municipal court judge, this guide covers the basics of handling cases for up to $2,500 in California's municipal courts. Tear-out legal forms are included for plaintiffs and defendants, along with advice on completing and filing them, arbitration, preparing witnesses and evidence, whether to request a jury trial, and how to conduct yourself in front of a jury. It also suggests ways to enlist the aid of an attorney without turning your case and your wallet over to him or her completely.

Duncan, Roderic. *Everybody's Guide to Municipal Court: Sue and Defend Cases for Up to $25,000.* 1st ed. Berkeley, CA: Nolo Press, 1992. 368p.

Scott, Gini Graham. *Collect Your Court Judgment.* 2nd ed. Berkeley, CA: Nolo Press, 1992. 1 vol.

This book explains how to collect a court judgment for money in California, whether from a small claims, municipal, or superior court in-state, or from a court in another state. It examines a variety of procedures for collecting a judgment, including getting the debtor to pay voluntarily, placing a lien on the debtor's property, and obtaining a writ of execution. The authors review the various types of assets which may be levied against: bank accounts; wages; obligations owed to the debtor; business records or assets; motor vehicles; personal property; and real estate. In each instance, step-by-step procedures are outlined, often in a checklist, and sample filled-in forms are generally included. Steps to follow in special situations (e.g., debtor dies, files for bankruptcy, or is "judgement-proof") are outlined in separate chapters. Procedures to follow for out-of-state judgments, where assets or the debtor is located in California are also developed in a separate chapter.

CRIME AND CRIME VICTIMS

Ginsburg, William L. *Victims' Rights: The Complete Guide to Crime Victim Compensation.* Clearwater, FL: Sphinx Publishing, 1994. 163p.

A detailed guide to collecting compensation from crime victim compensation funds if you are the victim of a violent crime, or are a dependent of someone who is. Explains who qualifies, and what you need to do to document your qualifications, how to apply, and how much you may be eligible for. Includes a summary of relevant laws contact information for funds in each state, a checklist of things to be sure to include on you application for compensation, and a sample filled-in application form for California (the scope of the book is national; it is not limited to California in any other respect).

Mann, Stephanie and M.C. Blakeman. *Safe Homes, Safe Neighborhoods: Stopping Crime Where You Live.* 1st ed. Berkeley, CA: Nolo Press, 1993. 320p.

CRIMINAL LAW

Rudovsky, David, Alvin J. Bronstein, Edward I. Koren, and Julia D. Cade. *The Rights of Prisoners: The Basic ACLU Guide to Prisoners' Rights.* 4th ed. Carbondale, IL: Southern Illinois University Press, 1988. 127p.

Written in the question-and-answer format typically used in the ACLU *Guides,* this book uses court decisions interpreting the U.S. Constitution and federal and state statutory law to enunciate the rights of individuals incarcerated in correctional institutions in a variety of contexts. General topics covered include: problems of prison censorship; political and religious rights; racial discrimination; privacy and personal appearance; medical care and rehabilitation; and jail conditions and practices in pretrial confinement. A separate chapter focuses on the special concerns of women prisoners. A final chapter reviews the remedies and procedures for challenging conditions of confinement. Names and addresses of prisoners' rights organizations are provided in an appendix.

Siegel, Warren. *The Criminal Records Book.* 4th ed. Berkeley, CA: Nolo
     Press, 1995. 176p.

A step-by-step guide through the procedures used to seal, destroy, or
change records established in juvenile or criminal courts of the California
criminal justice system. The author explains what a criminal record is, how
it can harm the subject, how to get a copy of it, and how to correct inac-
curacies. The book considers the following types of records: juvenile delin-
quency and status offenses; marijuana possession; criminal convictions with
probation and misdemeanor convictions without probation; adult arrest and
detentions; juvenile misdemeanor convictions; and youth parole board discharges. Sample forms, charts, and graphic illustrations simplify usage of the
book and make it easier to understand. The appendix contains a variety of
reproducible forms.

DEBTOR AND CREDITOR

American Bar Association. *Your Legal Guide to Consumer Credit.* You
     and the Law Series. Chicago, IL: American Bar Association
     Public Education Division, 1994. 1 vol.

Focusing on transactions such as credit card purchases and cars or appli-
ances bought on installment, this booklet tells how to determine if the credit-
debt limit has been reached and, if so, what to do when the limit is
exceeded. It seeks to provide an understanding of the federal regulations
and laws pertaining to consumer installment credit that are designed to protect the consumer. A variety of practical topics are reviewed: how to apply
for credit; how to establish a credit record; how to correct credit mistakes;
key questions about debt collection; the use of bankruptcy and other alternatives; and where to get help.

Elias, Stephen, Marcia Stewart, and Lisa Goldoftas. *Nolo's Law Form
     Kit: Loan Agreements: Borrow and Lend Money.* 1st ed.
     Berkeley, CA: Nolo Press, 1993. 120p.

Faron, Fay. *A Private Eye's Guide to Collecting a Bad Debt.*
     Emeryville, CA: Creighton-Morgan Publishing, 1991. 209p.

Leonard, Robin. *Nolo's Law Form Kit: Rebuild Your Credit: Solve Your
     Debt Problems.* 1st ed. Berkeley, CA: Nolo Press, 1993. 120p.

Leonard, Robin. *Money Troubles: Legal Strategies to Cope with Your Debts.* 1st ed. Berkeley, CA: Nolo Press, 1991. 360p.

Directed to the individual in debt, this book covers much ground in its attempt to educate the reader about the legal rights of a debtor. Topics discussed include: credit ratings; different types of debts (e.g., secured vs. unsecured); the consequences of ignoring debts; credit cards; student loans; bankruptcy; and rebuilding one's credit. Practical suggestions are offered in explaining how to negotiate with creditors, how to respond to being sued, what to do when a bill collector calls, and how to avoid bankruptcy when appropriate. Included along the way are many sample letters and statements for use in various interactions with creditors (e.g., requesting additional time to pay or to lower the amount of a bill). Worksheets are also provided to help debtors evaluate their financial situations by determining how much they earn, how much they owe, how much they spend, and what they own.

Nickel, Gudrun M. *Debtors' Rights: A Legal Self Help Guide with Forms.* Clearwater, FL: Sphinx International, 1996. 158p.

This book is designed to help people in financial difficulty by giving them a better understanding of the different types of debt they have incurred and what their legal rights are in reference to these debts. The author explains what types of actions can be taken by creditors to collect for non-payment of debts and what defenses a debtor may have to such actions. Readers are warned that the complexity and potential cost of handling their problem without the assistance of an attorney should be carefully considered. In the event they do choose to pursue the matter on their own, many chapters include sections on how to exercise your rights (and includes sample letters and forms). Major areas covered include: duties and responsibilities of collection and consumer reporting agencies; disclosures required by truth-in-lending laws; laws pertaining to judgments and foreclosures; and the use of bankruptcy as an option to dealing with debt.

California

Scott, Gini Graham. *Collect Your Court Judgment.* 2d ed. Berkeley, CA: Nolo Press, 1992. 1 vol.

This book explains how to collect a court judgment for money in California, whether from a small claims, municipal, or superior court in-state, or from a court in another state. It examines a variety of procedures for collecting a judgment, including getting the debtor to pay voluntarily, placing a lien on the debtor's property, and obtaining a writ of execution. The authors review the various types of assets which may be levied against: bank accounts; wages; obligations owed to the debtor; business records or assets; motor vehicles; personal property; and real estate. In each instance, step-by-step procedures are outlined, often in a checklist, and sample filled-in forms are generally included. Steps to follow in special situations (e.g., debtor dies, files for bankruptcy, or is "judgment-proof") are outlined in separate chapters. Procedures to follow for out-of-state judgments, where assets or the debtor is located in California are also developed in a separate chapter.

DICTIONARIES

Gifis, Steven. *Dictionary of Legal Terms.* Hauppage, NY: Barron's Educational Series, Inc., 1993. 517p.

A legal dictionary designed specifically for the layperson. Includes examples to clarify some particularly difficult terms.

DIRECTORIES

Brownson, Ann L. *Judicial Staff Directory.* Mount Vernon, VA: Staff Directories, 1996. 906p.

Contact information for judges and staff of all courts in the United States. Also includes: biographies of judges; maps of court jurisdictions; department of justice information; and an index of individuals.

DOMESTIC VIOLENCE

Sigman, Robert. *Family Violence and the Law.* Altamonte Springs, FL: Legovac, 1990. Audio

EDUCATION

Kaplin, William A. and Barbara A. Lee. *The Law of Higher Education.* 3rd ed. San Francisco, CA: Jossey-Bass Publications, 1995. 1,075p.

Texas

Kemerer, Frank R. and Jim Walsh. *The Educator's Guide to Texas School Law.* 3rd ed. Austin, TX: University of Texas, 1994. 368p.

ENVIRONMENTAL LAW

Stoloff, Neil. *Regulating the Environment: An Overview of Federal Environmental Laws.* Dobbs Ferry, NY: Oceana Publications, 1991. 176p.

This book offers descriptions of the major laws pertaining to environmental protection which are administered by agencies of the federal government. The descriptions are written to be understood by lay readers and, for the most part, avoid "legalese" and excessive legal citations. The laws are divided by subject: air; water; hazardous substances and solid waste; mining; public lands; and wildlife and wilderness. The author recognizes the failure to include state laws as a major limitation, but does provide a long list of other governmental entities (including those in individual states) in an appendix covering "Environmental Information Sources." A second lengthy appendix is a "Glossary of Environmental Acronyms," covering statutory and regulatory abbreviations, government agencies, and other terms of art. A final chapter ("Unfinished Business") examines a variety of "problem areas" inadequately addressed by laws currently in effect.

ESTATE PLANNING

Clifford, Denis and Cora Jordan. *Plan Your Estate*. 3rd ed. Berkeley,
    CA: Nolo Press, 1994. 416p.

Designed to help the reader understand and prepare for the practical consequences following a death, primarily to transfer property and to provide
for loved ones. It is written for people with small or moderate estates (i.e.,
net worth less than $600,000). Seeks to help the reader understand the
choices available, how they work, and their advantages and disadvantages.
Separate parts offer an introduction to estate planning, help in gathering
relevant information, advice on avoiding probate (e.g., living trusts, joint
tenancy), discussion of taxes, and information on wills. A variety of sample
estate plans are provided.

Dowd, Merle E. *Estate Planning Made Simple*. 1st ed. New York, NY:
    Doubleday, 1991. 176p.

How and why you should plan your estate, focusing on minimizing taxes
and costs. Discusses wills, probate, living trusts, trusts, joint ownership, and
gifts in clear, simple terms. Includes some worksheets and sample documents, but overall more of an clarifying informational book than a do-it-
yourself guide.

Nigito, Daniel G. *Avoiding the Estate Tax Trap*. Chicago, IL: Con-
    temporary Books, 1991. 1 vol.

Platt, Harvey J. *Your Living Trust and Estate Plan: How to Maximize
    Your Family's Assets and Protect Your Loved Ones*. New York,
    NY: Allworth Press, 1995. 224p.

Strategies for saving your estate money and assets, and saving those close
to you from necessary stress and difficulties. Discusses retirement benefits,
subsequent marriages, powers of surviving spouses, Medicaid, minimizing
taxes, and asset protection. Covers special situations such as estate planning
for the HIV positive and planning for children with special needs. The
author emphasizes that this book is not a do-it-yourself kit, but will help you
understand your options and work intelligently with professional advisors to
create a plan to suit your specific needs. Includes a worksheet for figuring
your net worth and a glossary of terms.

Florida

Berteau, John. *Estate Planning in Florida.* Sarasota, FL: Pineapple
        Press, 1993. 240p.

The basics of good estate planning in Florida, including living wills and
trusts, gifts, charitable donations, pension plans and IRAs, life insurance,
and tax considerations, and special considerations for married or single
readers. A chapter on qualifying as a Floridian whose estate is subject to
Florida law. The concepts and implications of durable powers of attorney,
homesteads, and joint property are explained. The author points out that
differences in death and inheritance taxes assessed by various states can be
significant, with Florida being one of the choicer states for decreased tax
burdens. Some forms are included, but basic forms, such as those for a
simple will or a living trust, are notably absent.

FAMILY LAW

Agran, Libbie. *The Economics of Divorce: A Financial Survival Guide
        for Women.* Pasadena, CA: Trilogy Books, 1990. 1 vol.

Anderson, Keith and Roy MacSkimming. *On Your Own Again: The
        Down-to-Earth Guide to Getting Through a Divorce or Separa-
        tion & Getting On with Your Life.* New York, NY: St. Martin's
        Press, 1992. 1 vol.

Biracree, Tom. *How to Protect Your Spousal Rights: The Complete
        Guide to Your Legal and Financial Rights.* Chicago, IL: Con-
        temporary Books, 1991. 1 vol.

Chambers, Carole A. *Child Support: How to Get What Your Child
        Needs and Deserves.* New York, NY: Summit Books, 1991. 283p.

Written for the custodial parent, this book provides a thorough explanation
of all aspects of child support and is intended to prepare the reader to
handle the economic and emotional trauma of child support negotiations.
The book follows a chronological format corresponding to the typical stages
of the process: Part 1 covers "Preparation" (e.g., taking inventory, determining a child's expenses, figuring insurance, evaluating the spouse); Part
2, "The Proceeding and the Aftermath" (e.g., selecting an attorney and the

attorney-client relationship, what happens in court, post-hearing evaluations); Part 3, "Your Remedies" (e.g., contempt; uniform laws on support enforcement; wage deduction); and Part 4, "In the Future" (e.g., modification of awards). Sample forms are provided in the text and appendices. State-by-state lists of child support advocacy groups and child support enforcement offices are also found in separate appendices.

Folberg, Jay. *Joint Custody and Shared Parenting*. 2nd ed. New York, NY: Guilford Press, 1991. 380p.

An extensive discussion of all aspects of joint custody and shared parenting which focuses on psychological and public policy issues for parents and children. Divided into four parts: (1) an overview of the history and current state of joint custody arrangements and its impact on children, (2) factors influencing the choice of joint custody, (3) what research tells us about joint custody, and (4) the law of joint custody. Appendices contain joint custody statutes and judicial interpretations and sample joint custody agreements and provisions.

Freidman, Gary. *Taking Charge of Your Own Divorce: A Guide to Mediation*. New York, NY: Workman Publishers, 1993. 1 vol.

Guggenheim, Martin. *The Rights of Families*. Carbondale, IL: Southern Illinois University Press, 1996. 1 vol.

Haman, Edward A. *How to File Your Own Divorce*. Clearwater, FL: Sphinx Publishing, 1993. 146p.

Haman, Edward A. *How to Write Your Own Premarital Agreement*. Clearwater, FL: Sphinx Publishing, 1993. 150p.

Includes the text of the Uniform Premarital Agreement Act and selected relevant laws from each state. These take up most of the book. The author contends that a premarital agreement "can help direct your marriage toward greater understanding and financial success. . . ."

Ihara, Toni and Ralph Warner. *The Living Together Kit*. 7th ed. Berkeley, CA: Nolo Press, 1994. 256p.

This book is designed to help unmarried couples who live together understand the rules which apply to them on a whole variety of subjects, including: renting a home or buying a house; starting a family; division of property and custody of children if the relationship dissolves; and estate planning. Practical matters such as bank accounts; credit; income taxes; public benefits; and insurance are also covered. The use of Living Together contracts is reviewed and a number of samples are provided. The appendix contains several different tear-out documents covering various situations, depending on what course the parties choose to follow (i.e., keeping things separate or sharing).

Leonard, Robin and Stephen Elias. *Nolo's Pocket Guide to Family Law.* 4th ed. Berkeley, CA: Nolo Press, 1996. 1 vol.

104 Legal Secrets Before You Say I Do. Irvine, CA: LawPrep Press, 1991. 1 vol.

Phillips, Patricia. *Divorce: A Guide for Women: What Every Woman Needs to Know About Getting a Fair Divorce Even When She Thinks She Doesn't Need to Know It.* New York, NY: Macmillan, 1995. 1 vol.

Sigman, Robert. *Collecting Child Support and Alimony.* Altamonte Springs, FL: Legovac, 1990. Audio

Sigman, Robert. *Waging Custody Battles.* Altamonte Springs, FL: Legovac, 1990. Audio

Sitarz, Daniel. *Divorce Yourself: The National No-Fault Divorce Kit.* 3rd ed. Carbondale, IL: Nova Publishing Co., 1994. 334p.

Designed to avoid turning a divorce into a "war waged by competing lawyers," this book tells how to utilize a Marital Settlement Agreement as the basis for a no-fault divorce. A general overview of the law and procedure relating to divorce is provided, followed by chapters on the actual preparation of an agreement (e.g., property division, alimony, child custody and visitation, child support). Guidelines, questionnaires, worksheets, and sample clauses are included for each area. Using the agreement to obtain a divorce is described (i.e., appearing in court) and the divorce laws of all 50 states are detailed. A glossary of legal terms from "action" to "waiver" is included. Selected as one of the "Best Law Books of the Year" by *Library Journal.*

Truly, Traci. *Grandparents' Rights: With Forms.* Clearwater, FL: Sphinx Publishing, 1995. 146p.

Intended to help grandparents secure visitation or custody rights to their grandchildren without hiring a lawyer. Discusses pros of cons of suing for these rights, and legal issues involved in most states. An appendix summarizes particularly relevant laws of specific states. Sample forms are included, some of which are for specific states. Others are general in nature, and the author recommends modifying them for use in particular states. No specific instructions for such modifications are included. The author strongly recommends that the reader do additional legal research before pursuing a claim, and offers brief instructions, including state-specific titles, on how to approach such research.

Woodhouse, Violet, Victoria F. Collins, and M.C. Blakeman. *Divorce and Money: How to Make the Best Financial Decisions During Divorce.* 2nd ed. Berkeley, CA: Nolo Press, 1992. 304p.

Intended to show the reader "how to avoid the financial disasters of divorce," focusing on the differences between legal and financial reality. A practical, step-by-step plan is offered, beginning with what to do in the "First 30 Days" (i.e., handling joint accounts, gathering financial facts), followed by chapters on: analyzing assets; income vs. debts; expenses and the division of specific types of assets (e.g., property, retirement debts, investments). Separate chapters on the division of debts, alimony and child support, and negotiating the settlement complete the coverage provided by authors, each a "Certified Financial Planner." Worksheets, numerous examples, and excellent graphics facilitate the utility of this book for the lay reader.

Alabama

DeRamus, Sterling and Edward A. Haman. *How to File for Divorce in Alabama.* Clearwater, FL: Sphinx Publishing, 1995. 148p.

A guide to divorce, with a good deal of space devoted to the realities of divorce beyond the textbook legal procedures. For example, one chapter is entitled "Do you really want a divorce?" and another section is "The legal system: theory vs. reality." Introduces relevant legal terms and concepts, invites you to evaluate your situation in specific ways, and offers advice on where to go from there, including the specific steps you must take to file your own divorce. Includes suggestions for dealing with special problems, such as not knowing where your spouse is or not being able to afford court costs. Includes ready-to-use forms and the text of especially relevant portions of Alabama laws.

California

Warner, Ralph E. *California Marriage & Divorce Law*. 11th ed. Berkeley, CA: Nolo Press, 1992. 1 vol.

The authors offer practical information about the laws affecting marriage and divorce in California, written in a style that is understandable to the non-attorney reader. Separate chapters cover marriage requirements and how to get married, non-traditional lifestyles (e.g., living together, group, and gay marriages), names, marital property issues, buying a house, children, spousal support, the mechanics of getting a divorce, and domestic emergencies (e.g., spousal rape, battered women, expedited child support orders). Several sample forms accompany the discussion of the legal issues (e.g., enforceable and unenforceable provisions) surrounding marriage contracts.

Duncan, Roderic and Warren Siegel. *How to Raise or Lower Child Support in California*. 3rd ed. Berkeley, CA: Nolo Press, 1995. 192p.

Sherman, Charles Edward. *Practical Divorce Solutions*. Berkeley, CA: Nolo Press, 1994. 151p.

Beginning from the premise that a better divorce can be achieved if the parties are informed about the law and prepared for the process, this book is intended to help the reader avoid an "uncontrolled battle" and achieve a good outcome (e.g., better compliance with agreements, less chance of litigation, increased goodwill, better co-parenting). It offers an overview of the divorce process, suggestions for structured problem solving and how to deal with the "business end" of divorce, and a chapter explaining "how to get organized" (including tear-out worksheets for gathering information). Other chapters deal with the practical aspects of cases with no legal opposition and cases where there is opposition and conflict (with advice on how to reduce conflict to reach an agreement). A final chapter explains how to choose and use a lawyer.

Canada

Meyric, Sandra J., LL.B. *Divorce Guide for Ontario: Step-by-Step Guide for Obtaining Your Own Divorce*. 12th ed. Bellingham, WA: Self-Counsel Press, 1995. 141p.

The author claims that you can follow the instructions in this book to obtain your own divorce without a lawyer for under $400. Step-by-step instructions are given for obtaining a divorce, along with related information on financial relief and tax and credit aspects of divorce. Includes sample documents (not ready to use), a step-by-step checklist for a typical divorce, addresses of courts and for record offices, and the text of the Divorce Act and its amendments. The publisher offers sets of pre-printed forms in two versions: one for sole petitioners and one for spouses filing as joint petitioners. These forms are to be completed in accordance with the instructions in this book.

Connecticut

Avery, Michael. *Do Your Own Divorce in Connecticut.* Pro Se Divorce Group/Cobblesmith, 1991. 1 vol.

Avery, Michael, Diane Polan, and Sarah D. Eldrich. *Do Your Own Divorce in Connecticut.* Freeport, ME: Cobblesmith, 1991. 142p.

A step-by-step guide to getting a no fault divorce without a lawyer. Includes sample court documents but no ready-to-use forms. Appendices include a glossary of definitions, contact information for judicial districts, and a judicial district locator to help you find the district where you need to file. Special attention is given to procedures to be attended to if you have children and/or are on welfare.

Florida

Haman, Edward A. *How to File for Divorce in Florida.* 3rd ed. Clear-water, FL: Sphinx Publishing, 1994. 138p.

A guide to divorce, with a good deal of space devoted to the realities of divorce beyond the textbook legal procedures. For example, one chapter is entitled "Do you really want a divorce?" and another section is "The legal system: theory vs. reality." Introduces relevant legal terms and concepts, invites you to evaluate your situation in specific ways, and offers advice on where to go from there, including the specific steps you must take to file your own divorce, Includes suggestions for dealing with special problems, such as not knowing where your spouse is or not being able to afford court costs. Includes ready-to-use forms and the text of especially relevant portions of Florida law.

Haman, Edward A. *How to Modify Your Florida Divorce Judgment.* 2nd ed. Clearwater, FL: Sphinx Publishing, 1995. 138p.

Leads you through the process of petitioning a court to modify your divorce judgment. Explains how alimony, child support, child visitation, and custody are determined, and when changed circumstances may merit a changed judgment. Includes Florida Supreme Court-approved forms addressing most possible changes, sample completed forms, and text of selected statutes.

Waters, Robert C. *Divorce Guide for Florida.* Bellingham, WA: Self-Counsel Press, 1992. 240p.

An excellent and detailed guide to getting an uncontested divorce in Florida without an attorney. Offers advice and instructions on every step of the divorce process, and draws your attention to issues which may warrant hiring an attorney. Also covers child support and alimony payments. Includes tear-out forms and instructions for completing them.

Georgia

Robertson, Charles T. and Edward A. Haman. *How to File for Divorce in Georgia.* Clearwater, FL: Sphinx Publishing, 1995. 140p.

A guide to divorce, with a good deal of space devoted to the realities of divorce beyond the textbook legal procedures. For example, one chapter is entitled "Do you really want a divorce?" and another section is "The legal system: theory vs. reality." Introduces relevant legal terms and concepts, invites you to evaluate your situation in specific ways, and offers advice on where to go from there, including the specific steps you must take to file your own divorce, Includes suggestions for dealing with special problems, such as not knowing where your spouse is or not being able to afford court costs. Includes ready-to-use forms and the text of especially relevant portions of Georgia laws.

Hawaii

Herman, Peter J. *A Practical Guide to Divorce in Hawaii.* 2nd ed. Honolulu, HI: University of Hawaii Press, 1991. 132p.

The author notes that this book is not intended as a substitute for an attorney, but only to offer "a broad understanding of the divorce process in Hawaii and the knowledge of how to fully protect your rights." Begins with a chapter on questions to ask before you file for divorce, and moves on to discussions of filing, negotiations, child custody and visitation, child support and alimony, property division, going to court, and modifications and enforcement of court orders. Also includes some information on pre- and post-marital agreements, and palimony and the effect of divorce on estate planning. One chapter deals with special problems of divorce for military personnel involving process and benefits problems, and where to file.

Illinois

Whittingham, Nikki. *Do-It-Yourself Divorce. Cook County, Illinois.* Chicago, IL: ENAAQ Publications, 1990. 1 vol.

Maine

Pine Tree Legal Assistance Inc. Staff. *Do Your Own Divorce in Maine.* Book by Village, 1991. 1 vol.

Maryland

Kalenik, Sandra. *How to Get a Divorce: A Practical Guide for the Residents of the District of Columbia, Maryland & Virginia Who Are Contemplating Divorce.* Washington Book Trading Co. 1991. 1 vol.

Massachusetts

Jancourtz, Isabella. *The Massachusetts Women's Divorce Handbook.* Isabella Jancourtz, 1990. 1 vol.

Michigan

Haman, Edward A. *How to File for Divorce in Michigan.* Clearwater, FL: Sphinx Publishing, 1995. 148p.

A guide to divorce, with a good deal of space devoted to the realities of divorce beyond the textbook legal procedures. For example, one chapter is entitled "Do you really want a divorce?" and another section is "The legal system: theory vs. reality." Introduces relevant legal terms and concepts, invites you to evaluate your situation in specific ways, and offers advice on where to go from there, including the specific steps you must take to file your own divorce, Includes suggestions for dealing with special problems, such as not knowing where your spouse is or not being able to afford court costs. Includes ready-to-use forms and the text of especially relevant portions of the Michigan statutes, court rules, and child support guidelines.

Maran, Michael. *The Michigan Divorce Book: A Guide to Doing an Uncontested Divorce Without an Attorney*. 3d ed. East Lansing, MI: Grand River Press, 1993. 1 vol.

This manual comes in two versions, one for divorces that include minor children, the for those that do not. Both present a great deal of information, some of which is fairly technical, but written in an accessible manner for those wishing to obtain a divorce without an attorney. An introductory part examines issues upon which disagreement may occur so that the reader can determine whether an uncontested divorce is really feasible. Included is a checklist of situations that may prove too difficult to handle without help even if the divorce is uncontested (e.g., spouse in military service, temporary relief or bankruptcy needed). A separate chapter covers the actual steps to be taken in getting the divorce, from start to finish. Appendices include blank, tear-out forms.

New York

Bernard, Clyne. *New York Divorce Book: Step-by-Step Guide with Forms*. Mt. Kisco, NY: Moyer Bell Ltd., 1993. 1 vol.

Raggio, Grier H. *How to Divorce In New York: Negotiating Your Divorce Settlement Without Tears or Trial*. New York, NY: St. Martin's Press, 1993. 254p.

North Carolina

Stanley, Jacqueline D. and Edward A. Haman. *How to File for Divorce in North Carolina*. Clearwater, FL: Sphinx Publishing, 1994. 148p.

A guide to divorce, with a good deal of space devoted to the realities of divorce beyond the textbook legal procedures. For example, one chapter is entitled "Do you really want a divorce?" and another section is "The legal system: theory vs. reality." Introduces relevant legal terms and concepts, invites you to evaluate your situation in specific ways, and offers advice on where to go from there, including the specific steps you must take to file your own divorce, Includes suggestions for dealing with special problems, such as not knowing where your spouse is or not being able to afford court costs. Includes ready-to-use forms and the text of especially relevant portions of the North Carolina statutes and child support guidelines.

Oregon

Baldwin, Richard C. *Divorce Guide for Oregon.* 5th ed. Seattle, WA: International Self-Counsel Press, 1993. 1 vol.

Designed to assist the individual seeking to obtain their own divorce without hiring a lawyer, this book explains the divorce laws of Oregon in non-technical language and provides instructions and a step-by-step procedure to follow. An introductory chapter helps readers to decide whether to do their own divorce or employ an attorney. Subsequent chapters explore children and spousal support, property division, and various issues pertaining to the beginning of the divorce process. Sample filled-in forms are provided throughout the text; checklists summarizing steps to follow in different situations are given in the final chapter, "Divorce Forms for Oregon." Kits with ready-to-use forms for petitioners or co-petitioners are available from the same publisher.

Weisser, Herb. *Divorce Guide for Oregon: Step-by-Step Guide for Obtaining Your Own Divorce.* 5th ed. Bellingham, WA: Self-Counsel Press, 1993. 216p.

Designed to assist the individual seeking to obtain their own divorce without hiring a lawyer, this book explains the divorce laws of Oregon in non-technical language and provides instructions and a step-by-step procedure to follow. An introductory chapter helps readers to decide whether to do their own divorce or employ an attorney. Subsequent chapters explore children and spousal support, property division, and various issues pertaining to the beginning of the divorce process. Sample filled-in forms are provided throughout the text; checklists summarizing steps to follow in different situations are given in the final chapter, "Divorce Forms for Oregon." Kits with ready-to-use forms for petitioners or co-petitioners are available from the same publisher.

South Carolina

Cullen, Thomas P. and Edward A. Haman. *How to File for Divorce in South Carolina.* Clearwater, FL: Sphinx Publishing, 1994. 144p.

A guide to divorce, with a good deal of space devoted to the realities of divorce beyond the textbook legal procedures. For example, one chapter is entitled "Do you really want a divorce?" and another section is "The legal system: theory vs. reality." Introduces relevant legal terms and concepts, invites you to evaluate your situation in specific ways, and offers advice on where to go from there, including the specific steps you must take to file your own divorce, Includes suggestions for dealing with special problems, such as not knowing where your spouse is or not being able to afford court costs. Includes ready-to-use forms and the text of especially relevant portions of South Carolina laws.

Texas

Rolcik, Karen Ann and Edward A. Haman. *How to File for Divorce in Texas.* Clearwater, FL: Sphinx Publishing, 1994. 146p.

A guide to divorce, with a good deal of space devoted to the realities of divorce beyond the textbook legal procedures. For example, one chapter is entitled "Do you really want a divorce?" and another section is "The legal system: theory vs. reality." Introduces relevant legal terms and concepts, invites you to evaluate your situation in specific ways, and offers advice on where to go from there, including the specific steps you must take to file your own divorce, Includes suggestions for dealing with special problems, such as not knowing where your spouse is or not being able to afford court costs. Includes ready-to-use forms and the text of especially relevant portions of the Texas Family Code.

Virginia

Kalenik, Sandra. *How to Get a Divorce: A Practical Guide for the Residents of the District of Columbia, Maryland & Virginia Who Are Contemplating Divorce.* Washington Book Trading Co. 1991. 1 vol.

Washington

Patterson, Mark. *Divorce Guide for Washington: Step-by-step Guide for Obtaining Your Own Divorce.* 9th ed. Bellingham, WA: Self-Counsel Press, 1994. 143p.

Designed to assist the individual seeking to obtain their own divorce without hiring a lawyer, this book explains the divorce laws of Washington in non-technical language and provides instructions and a step-by-step procedure to follow. An introductory chapter reviews doing one's own divorce; another explores child custody and support, matrimonial property, and tax aspects of divorce. Sample filled-in forms are provided throughout the text. A checklist of steps to follow in different situations is given in the Appendix. Preprinted forms sets are also available: Divorce Forms for Washington and Complete Forms Necessary to Obtain Your Own Divorce, intended for use with the *Guide*.

Wechsler, Mary. *Marriage, Separation, Divorce, and Your Rights: For Wives, Husbands, Children, and Cohabitating Couples in Washington*. Bellingham, WA: Self-Counsel Press, 1994. 207p.

A guide to family law in Washington, with a focus on preventative measures you can take to minimize the legal troubles that often stem from family troubles. Gives basic and general legal information on the legal issues involved in marriage and cohabitating, separation, divorce, and parent-child problems, and samples of legal documents commonly involved. The authors emphasize that their intent is to give information to help readers spot and plan to avoid potential legal difficulties, and that a lawyer should be consulted for existing serious legal problems.

Washington D.C.

Kalenik, Sandra. *How to Get a Divorce: A Practical Guide for the Residents of the District of Columbia, Maryland & Virginia Who Are Contemplating Divorce*. Washington Book Trading Co. 1991. 1 vol.

FRANCHISES

Keup, Erwin J. *Franchise Bible: Complete Guide to Franchising with Updated UFOC Guidelines*. 3rd ed. Grant's Pass, OR: Oasis Press, 1995. 314p.

A manual written for two types of people with an interest in franchising: the prospective business owner who wants to determine whether buying a franchise is a better approach than starting a business from scratch or buying an ongoing operation; and the successful business owner wondering whether to expand by franchising the business. For both situations, the book explains in detail what franchising entails and the precise benefits it offers. A significant inclusion is a sample offering circular which shows the typical types of terms and conditions a franchisee will face and also what should be included from the franchisor's point of view. A variety of other sample documents are included (e.g., franchise lease guarantee, territory development agreement) along with reproducible franchisor evaluation forms, a directory of state franchising statutes, and interview checklists to help a franchisee rate potential franchisors.

Purvin, Robert L. *Franchise Fraud: How to Protect Yourself Before and After You Invest*. New York, NY: J. Wiley, 1994. 1 vol.

An exposé of the franchise industry and tips on how to take advantage of the benefits of franchising without becoming a victim. Explains the various scams franchisors commonly use to draw in unwary investors, and how to "separate the wheat from the chaff" when selecting a franchise. Also discusses existing legal protections for franchisers and how franchisers can organize to bring about a fairer balance of power with franchisors.

GAMBLING

Rose, I. Nelson. *Gambling and the Law*. Hollywood, CA: Gambling Times, 1986. 304p.

Although this first major work about gambling and the law is written by a law professor and experienced attorney, it is not intended as a scholarly legal treatise but rather as a practical guide for the gambler who wishes to know how the law affects his activities. It answers many questions that the gambler is likely to confront, or ought to at least consider, such as how to collect gambling debts, how to deduct losses on taxes, how to determine if gambling activities are legal (including a chapter specifically addressing "How to Find the Law"), and the rights of a gambler in a casino (e.g., to count cards, stop payment on a check, or avoid blacklisting). The author uses actual cases to demonstrate the operation of the law in this field, but strongly recommends consulting an attorney "if your money or freedom is at stake."

GAY AND LESBIAN RIGHTS

Curry, Hayden and Denis Clifford. *A Legal Guide for Lesbian and Gay Couples.* 8th ed. Berkeley, CA: Nolo Press, 1991. 384p.

A practical book designed to help lesbian and gay couples understand the laws that affect them and to take charge of the legal aspects of their lives. Oriented toward the financial, practical, and legal aspects of a relationship and the consequences which can result from a failure to work out the legal ramifications of that relationship. Includes sample legal documents (e.g., living-together agreements, wills, co-parenting agreements) as well as discussion on a wide variety of topics: contracts; housing arrangements; marriage, children and divorce; adoption; estate planning; and separations.

Hunter, Nan D., Sherryl E. Michaelson, and Thomas B. Stoddard. *The Rights of Lesbians and Gay Men: The Basic ACLU Guide to a Gay Person's Rights.* 3rd ed. Carbondale, IL: Southern Illinois University Press, 1992. 220p.

GUARDIANSHIP AND CONSERVATORSHIP

California

Goldoftas, Lisa and Carolyn Farren. *The Conservatorship Book.* 2nd ed. Berkeley, CA: Nolo Press, 1994. 288p.

After explaining the role of a conservator (to oversee the personal care or financial matters of an incapacitated adult) and the legal consequences of such an arrangement, this book examines considerations in deciding whether to seek a conservatorship and whether someone should accept the position of conservator. It also offers detailed chapters on establishing, maintaining, and ending a conservatorship in California, including sample filled-in examples of the documents used throughout the process (blank, tear-out forms ready for actual use are also provided). The duties and liabilities of a conservator of the person and a conservator of the estate, as established by California law, are identified, including the use of bond or other financial guarantees required for the protection of the estate.

Goldoftas, Lisa and David Brown. *The Guardianship Book: How to Become a Child's Guardian in California.* 2nd ed. Berkeley, CA: Nolo Press, 1995. 304p.

Directed to an adult who is planning to become a guardian, this book begins with an overview of the purpose of guardianships: establishing legal recognition that an adult is responsible for taking care of a minor's physical needs, financial assets, or both. It reviews California's laws pertaining to the legal responsibilities of a guardian and offers ideas on how to determine whether to seek a legal guardianship, including the exploration of alternative methods to assist and protect a minor. Once the decision to become a guardian is made, this book can guide you through the entire process, since it provides detailed instructions on getting started (identifying the documents and information which are needed), providing notice and obtaining consents, preparing forms (samples and ready-to-use, tear-out forms are included), filing and serving papers, participating in the guardianship investigation and subsequent hearing, and ending the guardianship.

Florida

Nickel, Gudrun M. *How to File a Guardianship in Florida.* Clearwater, FL: Sphinx Publishing, 1993. 122p.

HEALTH LAW

Annas, George J. *The Rights of Patients: The Basic ACLU Guide to Patient Rights.* 2nd ed. Carbondale, IL: Southern Illinois University Press, 1989. 312p.

Premised on the idea that patients have rights that "are not automatically forfeited on entering a health care facility or a doctor-patient relationship," this book is designed to "encourage patients to exercise their rights and to help health care professionals recognize and respect these rights." As with other ACLU guides, the information is presented in a question-and-answer format, with individual chapters focusing on particular areas of interest. For example, after reviewing the general rules hospitals must follow (e.g., what is the American Hospital Association's Bill of Rights), the author considers questions relating to such topics as emergency medicine, informed consent, surgery, pregnancy and birth, medical records, privacy and confidentiality, care of the dying, and organ donation. Appendices include the Patient Bill of Rights, a sample living will and durable power of attorney, and instruction on how to use law and medical libraries.

Murphy, Susan Schuerman. *Legal Handbook for Texas Nurses*. Austin, TX: University of Texas Press, 1995. 256p.

Sigman, Robert. *Medical Malpractice*. Altamonte Springs, FL: Legovac, 1990. Audio

DuBoff, Leonard D. *The Law (In Plain English) for Health Care Professionals*. New York, NY: John Wiley & Sons, 1993. 206p.

Designed to help health care professionals understand the legal issues the face in their businesses, and to enable them to take advantage of the legal protections available to them. It focuses on: avoiding potential legal problems in business proceedings; organizing and financing your business; advertising; keeping records; tax considerations; and the like. Malpractice liability is also discussed, at less length. The author intends the book to be used as an aid to understanding and planning for legal issues, and not as a substitute for a lawyer, and a chapter on finding a good lawyer and accountant is included.

Issacs, Stephen L. *The Consumer's Legal Guide to Today's Health Care: Your Medical Rights and How to Assert Them*. Boston, MA: Houghton Mifflin, 1992. 362p.

This book is intended to empower consumers to take charge and avoid being victimized by a health care system they don't understand, so that they can get the health care they need or seek redress for harm already done to them. One chapter deals with "seven paths to patient power," explaining your right to informed consent, and control of your own treatment, how to break the code of silence in the health care professions, get access to your own records, and complain effectively. Contact information for state departments of health and other potentially helpful organizations and agencies are included.

IMMIGRATION AND CITIZENSHIP

Baldwin, Carl R. *Immigration Questions and Answers.* New York, NY: Allworth Press, 1995. 175p.

According to the preface, this book is intended to give a step-by-step description of what you need to do to solve your immigration problems. There are no forms included, however, and the question-and-answer format, although easy to read, does not lend itself to ordered instruction. You may have to hunt about a bit to find what you want. Still, the explanations are clear and detailed, and will almost certainly clarify this complicated subject for most people. Covers visas, green cards, job discrimination, eligibility for public benefits, becoming a citizen, help for abuse victims, and other immigration issues. An appendix offers brief suggestions for finding further information and updating information.

Canter, Laurence A. and Martha S. Siegel. *U.S. Immigration Made Easy.* 5th ed. Berkeley, CA: Nolo Press, 1995. 500p.

Divulges the safest and quickest ways to get green cards, visas, and U.S. citizenship. Includes ready-to-use, tear-out forms, with detailed instructions on how to fill them out and file them correctly. INS office addresses and phone numbers are provided. Also includes advice on building the strongest possible case for the INS, information on the tax consequences of relocating yourself or your business to the United States, and a chapter on the special (relaxed) immigration rules for Canadians. Careful explanations of qualifying guidelines should make it possible for a reader to get a good idea of his or her chances of immigrating to the United States.

Carliner, David, Lucas Guttentag, Arthur C. Helton, and Wade J. Henderson. *The Rights of Aliens and Refugees: The Basic ACLU Guide to Alien and Refugee Rights.* 2nd ed. Carbondale, IL: Southern Illinois University Press, 1990. 240p.

Although almost all of the Constitutional protections are written in terms which make them applicable to all, aliens as well as citizens, disparate treatment of aliens has occurred as the result of both state and federal legislation. This book attempts to define the rights of aliens in the United States under existing laws, including interpretations given to them by the courts. It covers a wide range of subjects, from rights pertaining to entry and residency in the country, to those concerning students, working, and owning property. The right of aliens to receive government benefits is also covered. The material is presented in a question-and-answer format. Extensive endnotes for each chapter provide citations to statutes, regulations, and court decisions.

Carrion, Ramon. *Guia de Immigracion a Estados Unidos.* Clearwater, FL: Sphinx Publishing, 1994. 142p.

The *U.S.A. Immigration Guide* described below, translated into Spanish.

Carrion, Ramon. *U.S.A. Immigration Guide.* 2nd ed. Clearwater, FL: Sphinx Publishing, 1994. 144p.

Explains the various ways to enter and stay in the United States legally, and suggests tax and pre-entry planning matters you should attend to. Appendices include contact information for regional INS offices, INS instructions for completing a petition for a nonimmigrant farm worker (form I-29), an INS application for employment authorization, and an INS eligibility form for academic and language students.

Harrington, Patricia, editor. *This Land Is Your Land: Preparation for Amnesty Legalization and Citizenship.* Glenview, IL.: Scott, Foresman and Co., 1990. 121p.

A workbook designed to help individuals prepare to become citizens and for applying for permanent residency under the amnesty program. It covers the U.S. government and history content required by the INS. The book provides practice using both multiple-choice and oral format tests. Key vocabulary are defined in context when they first appear in the book and also in the appended glossary. "Interview Practice" pages provide practice in answering the one hundred standard questions formulated by the INS. The book uses large type and is extensively illustrated.

Kimmel, Barbara Brooks. *Immigration Made Simple: An Easy to Read Guide to the U.S. Immigration Process.* New Decade Marketing & Advertising, 1990. 196p.

Designed to provide a basic understanding of the rules and regulations concerning immigration procedure, though not meant to replace or substitute for advice given by lawyers. Language is straightforward, presentation promotes readability. Commonly asked questions are answered in one chapter, others provide a clear overview of the immigration procedure. Blank forms are provided and an appendix includes addresses of the INS and Department of Labor offices, various schedules, and common filing fees.

Lewis, Loida Nicolas and Len T. Madlansacay. *Como Obtener la Tarjeta Verde: Maneras Legistimas de Permanecer en los Estados Unidos.* 1st ed. Berkeley, CA: Nolo Press, 1994. 225p.

Lewis, Loida Nicolas and Len T. Madlansacay. *How to Get a Green Card: Legal Ways to Stay in the U.S.A.* 2nd ed. Berkeley, CA: Nolo Press, 1993. 400p.

Canada

Segal, Gary L. *Immigrating to Canada: Who Is Allowed? What Is Required? How to Do It!* 9th Bellingham, WA: Self-Counsel Press, 1994. 223p.

Designed to explain the rules regulating immigration to Canada, this book offers a straightforward explanation of the process you must follow to immigrate, study, visit, or set up business in Canada. The particular requirements of the Quebec province are also examined. The various immigration classes are described, as are independent applications and the sophisticated selection system for business people. The point system used to grade applicants for admission to Canada is also described. The book is replete with sample filled-in forms and documents used in the Canadian immigration process, making it useful not only as an explanation of the law but also as a "how-to-do-it" manual.

INDEPENDENT CONTRACTORS

Fishman, Stephen. *Hiring Independent Contractors: A Legal Guide for Employers.* 1st ed. Berkeley, CA: Nolo Press, 1993. 1 vol.

INSURANCE

Bailard, Biehl & Kaiser, Inc. *How to Buy the Right Insurance at the Right Price.* Homewood, IL: Irwin Publishing, 1995. 134p.

How to get the best liability, auto, health, property, or life insurance for your needs for the best price. The author contends that about 80% of Americans buy the wrong kind of insurance for their needs. Includes checklists and guidelines for each type of insurance to help you determine your insurance needs and to pick a policy. The author examines emotions involved in insurance issues and offers suggestions on recognizing your own emotional style and dealing logically with insurance choices without falling into emotional traps.

Matthews, Joseph L. *How to Win Your Personal Injury Claim.* 1st ed. Berkeley, CA: Nolo Press, 1992. 224p.

The "claim" in the title refers to insurance claims. An attorney tells you how to gauge how much your claim is worth, and gives step-by step instructions on obtaining a settlement without paying a lawyer or enduring an insurance company runaround. The author explains how to protect your rights after an accident, how to prepare a claim and negotiate a settlement, and how to manage your case if you do hire a lawyer. Includes sample letters to an insurance company, and checklists and worksheets for the claims process.

INTERNET

Kurz, Raymond A. *Internet and the Law.* Rockville, MD: Government Institutes, Inc., 1996. 1 vol.

INVENTIONS AND INVENTORS

Battersby, Gregory J. and Charles W. Grimes. *The Toy and Game Inventor's Guide for Selling Product (sic) Into the Toy and Game Industry.* Stanford, CT: Kent Press, 1995. 1 vol.

Grissom, Fred and David Pressman. *The Inventor's Notebook.* 1st ed. Berkeley, CA: Nolo Press, 1989. 240p.

Addresses the documentation and process an inventor must follow to have an invention patented, and explains why a patent is vital to financial success. The book is designed to help you create and organize the documentation you need to successfully build, test, market, finance, and legally protect your invention. Much of the book consists of worksheets for the inventor to use in compiling appropriate documentation and reaching sound decisions. Contains a bibliography of recommended reading, 10 copies of a Proprietary Materials Agreement (for use when you disclose significant details about your unpatented invention to potential investors and the like), five copies of a form to use to evaluate your product, and a tear-out "potential user survey," rather impressively named considering it has only 19 words of text. The book does not explain details of patent law, but provides cross-references to the same publisher's *Patent It Yourself,* also annotated in this bibliography (in the Copyrights, Patents, and Trademarks section).

LABOR

Bernbach, Jeffrey and Rae Lindsay. *Job Discrimination: How to Fight, How to Win.* New York, NY: Crown Trade Paperbacks, 1996. 224p.

Elias, Stephen. *Nolo's Law Form Kit: Hiring Child Care and Household Help.* 1st ed. Berkeley, CA: Nolo Press, 1994. 96p.

Hartnett, John. *OSHA in the Real World: Cutting Through the Regulatory Knot: Taking Control Series.* 1st ed. Berkeley, CA: Nolo Press, 1995. 352p.

Jackson, Gordon E. and Stephen L. Shields. *How to Defend and Win Labor and Employment Cases.* Englewood Cliffs, NJ: Prentice-Hall, 1992. 1 vol.

Jacobs, R. and C. Koch. *Legal Compliance Guide to Personnel Management.* Englewood Cliffs, NJ: Prentice-Hall, 1993. 562p.

Offers guidance on all aspects of the personnel management, with specific suggestions for how to avoid legal difficulties and how to handle them if they do arise. Includes numerous sample policies and forms designed to avoid or minimize liability. Suggestions for adapting forms to fit specific organizations are given. A veritable sea of legislation under various acronyms is explained, including: OSHA, COBRA, IRCA, FLSA, ERISA, NLRA, WARN. Packed with information, but easily accessible despite its considerable bulk, this book is well-organized and thoroughly indexed.

Joel, Lewin G. *Every Employee's Guide to the Law: Everything You Need to Know About Your Rights in the Workplace, and What to Do If They Are Violated.* 2nd ed. New York, NY: Pantheon Books, 1993. 414p.

This book explains more than 100 employment-related laws, focusing on helping the reader/employee decide if he or she has a potentially valid claim against an employer for violating one of them. Attention is also given to recognizing invalid waivers and authorization forms employers often use to convince you that you have no recourse against them on these points. The author then outlines options for the wronged employee, with step-by-step instructions for filing a claim and practical advice for other approaches. The potential risks of each course of action are discussed. Includes an appendix of relevant state and federal agencies with addresses and phone numbers, and a summary of federal labor laws with citations so you can look up the full text of the laws yourself.

Ramey, Ardella and Carl R.J. Sniffen. *A Company Policy & Personnel Workbook.* Grant's Pass, OR: Oasis Press, 1991. 330p.

Model policies for more than 65 issues, with alternatives and suggestions for modifications to suit your specific business. Topics covered include: hiring practices; employee benefits; employee expenses; compensation; and dress codes. Also includes sample organization chart, position description, grievance forms, and suggestions on developing and maintaining your own policy manual.

Repa, Kate. *Your Rights in the Workplace.* 2nd ed. Berkeley, CA: Nolo Press, 1994. 480p.

A guide to employee's rights in the workplace, including wages, hours, overtime, maternity and parental leave, safety, discrimination, and worker's comp, as well as unemployment and disability insurance. Offers general advice for all employees, and specific pointers for employees in particular states. In addition to explaining what rights employees have, the author offers advice on challenging infringements of these rights.

Sack, Steven Mitchell. *The Employee Rights Handbook: Answers to Legal Questions From Interview to Pink Slip.* New York, NY: Facts on File, 1991. 223p.

Offers practical advice and numerous preventive steps to take to help avoid employment-related problems. Although the author's initial focus in the labor law field was on the rights of terminated workers (e.g., recovering compensation and other benefits "lost" when the employee is fired), a major part of this book is devoted to learning "how to be hired properly" so as to reduce the chances for exploitation later. It also covers on-the-job rights (i.e., union rights, privacy rights, health and safety, sexual harassment, age and racial discrimination) and the obligations of employers to deal fairly with long-time workers. Charts, checklists (e.g., Key Negotiating Points to Cover During Hiring Interview), strategy lists, and sample forms are effectively used throughout the book to clarify points made in the text.

Stay Out of Court: The Manager's Guide to Preventing Employee Lawsuits. Englewood Cliffs, NJ: Prentice-Hall, 1993. 1 vol.

Walsh, James. *Mastering Diversity: Managing Your Workforce Under ADA and Other Anti-Discrimination Laws.* 1st ed. Berkeley, CA: Nolo Press, 1995. 350p.

Walsh, James. *Rightful Termination: Defensive Strategies for Hiring and Firing In the Lawsuit-Happy 90's.* 1st ed. Berkeley, CA: Nolo Press, 1994. 300p.

Weiss, Donald H. *Fair, Square and Legal: Safe Hiring, Managing and Firing Practices to Keep You and Your Company Out of Court.* Rev. ed. New York, NY: American Management Association, 1995. 358p.

Intended to help managers stay out of legal trouble in the "Age of Litigation," and to help them establish defensible positions in case they end up in court anyway. The focus is on fair and consistent policies that prevent problems before they arise, and on enabling business to operate effectively, without being hampered either by unfounded fear of legal infractions which prevents them from taking reasonable actions, or from suffering the ramifications of unknowingly violating actual legal requirements. Divided into three sections: safe hiring practices; safe management practices; and safe firing practices, with a 50-page appendix of civil rights laws and regulations.

Zgarelli, Michael A. *Can They Do That?: A Guide to Your Rights on the Job.* New York, NY: Lexington Books, 1994. 191p.

Practical information on issues of employment law from an employee perspective. Organized into sections dealing with discrimination and discharge, employee privacy, wages and hours, benefits, and worker safety and health. Includes government agency phone numbers and a list of important statutes and cases organized by subject.

Florida

Vail, Jason. *Employee/Employer Rights in Florida: a Practical, Easy to Understand Guide.* Bellingham, WA: Self-Counsel Press, 1993. 256p.

Answers many common questions about Florida employment law, including unions, wages and hours, safety standards, worker's compensation, employment contracts, retirement, special hiring practices for state government jobs, unemployment compensation, and other employment-related issues. The author stresses that this is "not a litigation handbook on which you should rely if you decide to act as your own lawyer, a practice that is not recommended anymore than self-surgery . . . the best use you can make of this guide is in ordering your daily work activities, heading off problems before they reach critical mass, and spotting issues so that you'll know when to seek the help of an attorney."

Washington

Phillabaum, Stephen D. *Employee/Employer Rights: The Complete Guide for the Washington Work Force.* 2nd ed. Bellingham, WA: Self-Counsel Press, 1992. 112p.

A brief overview of the rights and obligations of both employers and employees under Washington and federal law. Written in layperson's terms, the book reviews such common questions as: When can an employer fire a worker? Can veterans be given preferences? What are the requirements of an employment contract? What protection exists against sexual harassment? What regulations affect workplace safety? What can an employee do about unfair labor practices? Separate chapters consider wages, hours, workplace standards, civil rights, and ending the employment relationship. Supplemental government programs such as industrial insurance and unemployment insurance are presented. Briefly reviewed are unions and collective bargaining.

LANDLORD AND TENANT

Eviction Forms Creator Software for Windows.™ El Cerrito, CA: ExPress
Publishing, 1994. Computer software

Easy-to-use software for creating eviction forms. Includes 24-page manual.
For information on how and when to use the forms, see *The Eviction Book
for California*, also published by ExPress. Works by itself, or with data from
Pushbutton Landlording program files (also by ExPress). Updates are available at a reduced price.

LANDLORDING™ (The Forms Diskette). El Cerrito, CA: ExPress Publishing, 1994. Computer software

Pushbutton Landlording. El Cerrito, CA: ExPress Publishing, 1993. Computer software

Robinson, Leigh. *Landlording: A Handymanual for Scrupulous Landlords and Landladies Who Do It Themselves.* 7th ed. El Cerrito,
CA: ExPress Publishing, 1995. 430p.

Detailed but easy-to-read (humorous cartoons lighten up the text) examination of the rights and obligations of owners of residential real estate
property. The basics of "do-it-yourself" landholding are covered in the initial
chapters, followed by chapters which address specific issues (e.g., getting
good tenants; keeping good tenants; dealing with problem tenants; insurance; providing for security and safety; records; and taxes). Sample filled-in
forms are presented throughout the text with a variety of blank, ready-to-
use forms included in the appendix. A final chapter explains how a personal
computer may be used by a landlord to improve efficiency. A diskette with
word processing forms and a template is available for separate purchase.

Stewart, Marcia, Ralph Warner, and David Brown. *Every Landlord's
Legal Guide.* 1st ed. Berkeley, CA: Nolo Press, 1995. 384p.

Warda, Mark. *How to Negotiate Real Estate Leases.* Clearwater, FL:
Sphinx Publishing, 1994. 120p.

Warner, Ralph and Marcia Stewart. *Nolo's Law Form Kit: Leases and
Rental Agreements.* 1st ed. Berkeley, CA: Nolo Press, 1994.
96p.

California

Brown, David and Ralph Warner. *The Landlord's Law Book, Vol. 1: Rights and Responsibilities*. 4th ed. Berkeley, CA: Nolo Press, 1994. 384p.

A concise guide for California landlords, focusing on the legal rules covering most aspects of renting and managing residential real property (excluding coverage of mobile homes, condominiums, and hotels). Includes information on leases, rental agreements, deposits, managers, credit checks, discrimination, invasion of privacy, the landlord's duty to maintain the premises, and ending a tenancy. Landlord "no-no's" such as self-help evictions, utility terminations, and taking a tenant's property are also discussed. Filled-in sample forms are provided throughout the text, including various notices, letters, and agreements. The appendix includes tear-out forms ready for actual use. A "Landlord-Tenant Checklist" designed to improve communication between the parties and minimize disputes is particularly helpful.

Brown, David. *The Landlord's Law Book, Vol. 2: Evictions*. 5th ed. Berkeley, CA: Nolo Press, 1994. 368p.

The second volume in a two-volume legal guide for California landlords, this book is intended specifically to serve as a "do-it-yourself" eviction manual. It shows the steps required to file and conduct an uncontested eviction lawsuit against a residential tenant (excluding coverage of a hotel guest or tenant in a mobile home park). The author explains all the grounds for an eviction (e.g., nonpayment of rent, lease violations, damaging property, or making a nuisance) and the uses of either a 30-day or 3-day notice. Eviction without notice is also reviewed. Completed forms are offered as samples for use in filling out the tear-out forms provided in the appendix. Instructions on preparing and serving the tenant with proper legal notice, filing an unlawful detainer (eviction) lawsuit, and collecting a money judgment are given in straightforward language. Checklists (including what to do and when to do it) are provided for many elements in the eviction process.

Moskovitz, Myron and Ralph Warner. *California Tenants' Handbook: Tenants' Rights*. 12th ed. Berkeley, CA: Nolo Press, 1994. 288p.

A detailed guide for residential tenants designed to explain the complex subject of California landlord-tenant law as simply as possible and to suggest how this information can be used to anticipate and, where possible, avoid legal problems. Thus, while the authors explain the rights of a tenant and the remedies available if those rights are violated, they also emphasize the importance of developing a positive relationship with the landlord to resolve problems in a way that both parties can accept. Recognizing that some landlords are neglectful and hostile toward their tenants, however, they do provide detailed information for dealing with improper conduct, including discrimination, invasion of the tenant's privacy, substandard living conditions, and abuse of security deposits. Introductory chapters cover the mechanics of finding and renting a home, sharing a home, and rights concerning rent. Sample forms are included in the text for illustrative purposes; tear-out, ready-to-use forms are provided in the appendix.

Robinson, Leigh. *The Eviction Book for California.* 7th ed. El Cerrito, CA: ExPress Publishing, 1995. 254p.

A companion volume to the author's *Landlording* (a book national in scope), this work seeks to explain the legal and practical aspects of using the remedy of eviction in California to deal with recalcitrant tenants. As part of the author's emphasis on saving as much time and money as possible, the first chapters explore how to avoid the necessity of using evictions. Subsequent chapters review methods for handling evictions in a variety of situations (e.g., nonpayment of rent, breech of contract, nuisance, failure to vacate). Handling a contested case and collecting on a judgement are also considered. A variety of reproducible blank forms are offered at the end of the book while filled-in examples are presented throughout the text.

Florida

Badgley, Richard. *Real Estate Buying/Selling Guide for Florida.* Bellingham, WA: Self-Counsel Press, 1992. 176p.

This book is full of things you may really regret not having known before you bought or sold a house in Florida; things to help you decide whether to get into the whole shebang, and what you can do to make your life easier (and taxes lower) once the deal is done. Includes information on condominiums and cooperatives as well as traditional single-family homes. Includes information on financing, tips for sellers, brokers, insurance, and (shudder) foreclosure. Sample contracts, amortization schedules, and a checklist of things to examine before you sign anything are included.

Clark, William D. *Landlord/Tenant Rights in Florida.* Bellingham, WA: Self-Counsel Press, 1993. 144p.

Explains the rights and duties of landlords and tenants in Florida under the Florida Residential Landlord and Tenant Act and various Fair Housing

Laws, and the remedies available when something goes wrong. Includes ready-to-use forms for terminating a lease, withholding rent, and noting the condition of property before and after a lease, and three types of lease forms approved by the Florida Supreme Court. An appendix includes the text of the Florida Residential Landlord and Tenant Act.

Warda, Mark. *Landlords' Rights and Duties in Florida*. 5th ed. Clearwater, FL: Sphinx Publishing, 1994. 146p.

A guide for landlords trying to protect their investment and maximize their income. Explains how to avoid potential substantial liability to tenants for failing to follow proper procedures, with forms and advice on how to do everything by the book from the outset. Covers all aspects of landlord/tenant law, from taking applications to evicting and suing for back rent, and including maintenance rules and security deposits.

Oregon

Marcus, Michael. *Landlord/Tenant Rights in Oregon*. 4th ed. Bellingham, WA: Self-Counsel Press, 1994. 328p.

The author offers an explanation of the Oregon Residential Landlord and Tenant Act, reviewing the rights and remedies of both parties in a rental situation. While the focus is on practical problems and solutions, the legal theory involved in landlord/tenant relations is also discussed. Important areas of coverage include rental agreements and rules, repairs, and evictions. The author admits in the beginning that the primary audience is tenants and that his goal is to educate them sufficiently so that they can assert their rights as consumers of rental housing, either with the assistance of an attorney (especially if a dispute is likely to reach court) or on their own. Appendices include relevant Oregon laws and many sample forms are provided in the text. A separate rental forms kit is available.

Texas

Brown, William R. and Mark Warda. *Landlords' Rights and Duties in Texas*. Clearwater, FL: Sphinx Publishing, 1994. 130p.

A guide for landlords trying to protect their investment and maximize their income. Explains how to avoid potential substantial liability to tenants for failing to follow proper procedures, with forms and advice on how to do everything by the book from the outset. Covers all aspects of landlord/

tenant law, from taking applications to evicting and suing for back rent, and including maintenance rules and security deposits.

Washington

Isenhour, Barbara A., James E. Fearn, and Steve Fredrickson. *Tenants' Rights: A Guide for Washington State*. 1991 ed. Seattle, WA: University of Washington Press, 1991. 158p.

Directed toward residents of Washington who rent or lease a place to live, this book is designed to acquaint readers with their rights and responsibilities under the Residential Landlord-Tenant Act of 1973 (reproduced in the Appendix), though not necessarily to serve as a substitute for a lawyer. It covers a variety of areas (e.g., moving in; deposits; landlord duties; tenant duties; dealing with repair problems; right to privacy; evictions; and moving out), many of which are complex and confusing. The authors hope to provide enough information that the reader can intelligently decide whether a lawyer should be consulted. Examples of documents which a tenant may receive or be required to send are included, as well as a model rental agreement and deposit checklist. These can be consulted before signing any written agreement presented by a landlord.

Strong, Sidney J. *Landlord/Tenant Rights for Washington*. 7th ed. Bellingham, WA: Self-Counsel Press, 1993. 136p.

Written in clear language, this short book explores the components of the landlord-tenant relationship in Washington. It seeks to answer the most common questions of both parties. The uses and abuses of rental agreements are considered, along with the duties and remedies of both landlords and tenants. Issues such as security and damage deposits, eviction by lockout, withholding of rent, termination of a month-to-month rental agreement, repairs, and requisite notice for various actions are all reviewed. Practice assistance is provided in the form of sample forms and checklists throughout the text. The final chapter, "Answers to Your Questions," considers some of the most common questions about landlord/tenant rights.

LEGAL RESEARCH

Elias, Stephen and Susan Levinkind. *Legal Research: How to Find and Understand the Law.* 4th ed. Berkeley, CA: Nolo Press, 1995. 304p.

Designed for use by either a beginner to legal research or one who has had some experience but wants guidance on a particular aspect or phase of research. Emphasizes a functional rather than scholarly approach, offering a simple yet effective method for doing legal research. Begins with overviews of legal research, the law, and how the law is organized, then covers background legal resources; statutes, regulations, and ordinances; judicial procedure; and case law. A separate chapter presents the usage of *Shepard's Citations.* Two practical examples of doing legal research are provided for illustrative purposes. "Fast Tracks" are interspersed throughout, offering specific detailed instructions on how to do specific research tasks (e.g., finding recent cases).

Herskowitz, Susan. *Legal Research Made Easy.* Clearwater, FL: Sphinx Publishing, 1995. 124p.

A legal research guide for non-lawyers, explaining what you are looking for and why, and how to find it. This book presumes nothing—it starts with where to find a law library you can use, and goes through the various research materials available (even includes an explanation of using a card catalog) to "putting it all together." Includes a sample research problem.

McKnight, Jean Sinclair. *The LEXIS Companion: A Concise Guide to Effective Searching.* Reading, MA: Addison-Wesley Publishing Co., 1995. 256p.

Nolo Press and Legal Star Communications. *Legal Research Made Easy: A Roadmap Through the Law Library Maze.* 1st ed. Berkeley, CA: Nolo Press, 1990. 40-page booklet, 2½-hr. video

A video and booklet covering the basics of legal research for the layperson. Explains how to use basic legal research tools to find state and federal statutes, cases, and regulations as well as how to use legal encyclopedias and find legal periodical articles. Also explains the process and importance of updating your research, including the use of *Shepard's Citators* and the *Federal Register.* The accompanying booklets lists research resources and outlines the contents of the tape. It also offers a short, annotated lists of books to read for more information on legal research.

Libel and Slander

Rosini, Neil J. *The Practical Guide to Libel Law.* New York, NY: Praeger, 1991. 229p.

Directed to media professionals with the intention of establishing and explaining a three-step process to avoid potential problems before a defamatory piece is published. The emphasis is on practical approaches to coping with the complexities of the libel law rather than an analysis of the law applicable to any particular state. The book is organized around the steps suggested for limiting the risk of being sued: Step 1. "What to Look For" (identifies practical ways of identifying a potential problem); Step 2. "How Much Proof" (shows how to gather sufficient factual support); Step 3. "What to Write" (demonstrates how to write a story so as to take advantage of available legal defenses). The book includes numerous case illustrations which clarify the text along with a help appendix of "Quick Questions and Short Answers" for ready reference. A list of 17 simple "do's and don'ts" is also provided.

Mail Order

Keup, Erwin J. *Mail Order Legal Guide: A Comprehensive Guide Through the Legal Maze of Mail Order.* Grant's Pass, OR: Oasis Press, 1993. 332p.

Explains federal, state, and local laws which mail-order businesses need to be aware of to avoid civil and criminal liability. Keup offers a simple checklist of questions for mail-order businesses to use to insure compliance with applicable rules and regulations, and the information you need to understand and answer those questions, which deal with advertising, taxes, location, licenses and permits, and whether your particular product or service invokes special requirements or limitations. Specific state laws are noted by state.

MEDIA LAW

Holsinger, Ralph L. *Media Law*. 2nd ed. Blue Ridge Summit, PA: Tab
    Books, 1991. 1 vol.

A textbook for journalism, broadcasting, advertising, public relations, and
corporate communications students, to help them recognize and avoid legal
pitfalls in media work. Divided into three parts: freedom of speech and freedom of the press; news media and the law; and legal regulation of the
media. Includes a glossary and an appendix of very basic information on
the workings of the U.S. legal system.

NAMES

California

Loeb, David and David Brown. *How to Change Your Name*. 6th ed.
    Berkeley, CA: Nolo Press, 1994. 144p.

Rather than paying several hundred dollars to an attorney for assistance in
changing your name, this book explains in detail the two methods to legally
change a name in California: the usage method, and the court petition
method. These may be used to change a name after divorce, marriage, or
annulment; where children are involved; to return to an original family
name which was abandoned when immigrating to the United States; for
lifestyle or convenience reasons; or to reflect religious or political beliefs.
Restrictions on new names are explained. A separate chapter describes the
specific steps needed to change a name by court petition, including sample
filled-out documents to use as examples for completing the tear-out forms
provided at the end of the book.

Florida

Warda, Mark. *How to Change Your Name in Florida*. 3rd ed. Clear-
    water, FL: Sphinx Publishing, 1995. 105p.

How to change your name, your children's names, or your whole family's
names; register a fictitious name; and change a birth certificate. Includes
ready-to-use forms with instructions and flowcharts to clarify the process.
Also lists the records you'll need to have changed after your legal name

change is complete, with tips on how to go about it, from school records, driver's licenses and voter registration, to utility companies and charge accounts (and many more).

New York

Anosike, Benji O. *How to Legally Change Your Name Without a Lawyer.* New York, NY: Do-It-Yourself Legal Publishers, 1991. 107p.

Although the author asserts that "broad similarities in rules and procedures among states" makes this book applicable to one wishing to change a name in any of the 50 states, the focus here is primarily on the name changing procedures in the state of New York. The sample filled-in forms and step-by-step checklists are oriented to New York. A short chapter on filing for change of name in any state is provided, however, as well as an appendix briefly summarizing state-specific information. Background information on name changes, both generally and for specific situations, is provided, including discussion of the common reasons for changing a name and the two basic methods to do so (i.e., by common usage and by court order).

NEIGHBOR LAW

Warda, Mark. *Neighbor vs. Neighbor: Legal Rights of Neighbors in Dispute.* 1st ed. Clearwater, FL: Sphinx Publishing, 1991. 229p.

This book is divided into five parts: general principles of neighbor law; specific problems of neighbor law (noise, obnoxious behaviors, etc); how to solve a neighbor problem without going to court; how to solve a neighbor problem in court; and how to research your case further. Points are illustrated with "war stories" which are summaries of actual cases and outcomes.

California

Jordan, Cora. *Neighbor Law: Fences, Trees, Boundaries and Noise.* 2nd ed. Berkeley, CA: Nolo Press, 1994. 1 vol.

Subtitled *Resolve Neighbor Disputes,* this book addresses the relatively few basic issues which typically arise, such as who must maintain a fence on a boundary line, or who can trim a tree which hangs over a neighbor's property. Other common questions pertaining to trees, fences, boundaries, and

noise are explored, as the author shows how to find the law on these subjects and resolve conflicts without resorting to contentious litigation.

PARALEGALS

Warner, Ralph. *Getting Started as an Independent Paralegal.* 2nd
    ed. Berkeley, CA: Nolo Press, 1992. Two audio tapes, 120 min.

An edited audiotape of a seminar at the Nolo Press offices on setting up
your own paralegal business, focusing on avoiding the unauthorized practice of law, and marketing your services.

Warner, Ralph. *The Independent Paralegal's Handbook.* 3rd ed.
    Berkeley, CA: Nolo Press, 1994. 300p.

A guide for those considering a career as an independent paralegal, emphasizing the paralegal movement's potential for positive social change. Discusses
the nature and availability of paralegal work and where to get necessary
training. For qualified paralegals, the author offers suggestions on starting your
own business, from what to name it to what to charge and how to market it.
Strategies for avoiding being charged with the unauthorized practice of law
are enumerated, and suggestions for taking full advantage of computerization
are included. The last quarter of the book is devoted to interviews with
"eleven important figures in the independent paralegal movement."

PERSONAL INJURY

Koff, Gail J. *The Jacoby & Meyers Practical Guide to Personal Injury.*
    New York, NY: Simon and Schuster, 1991. 225p.

Written by a founding partner of the Jacoby & Meyers law firm known
nationally for its focus on representing the average citizen, this book
explains to individuals involved in accidents "how personal injury law and
the legal system pertaining to it work." Doesn't include forms or checklists;
intended to create informed clients who are better able to assist their
attorneys. Thus it provides general information on personal injury law,
followed by illustrations on how the law works in specific kinds of accidents

(e.g., motor vehicles, product defects, medical malpractice). It offers real case histories with verdict and settlement estimates.

PHOTOGRAPHY

Crawford, Tad. *Business and Legal Forms for Photographers.* New York, NY: Allworth Press, 1991. 205p.

Forms available on diskette for Mac or PC. Includes 24 complete forms dealing with the most important business transactions with which a photographer is likely to be involved (e.g., assignment estimate/confirmation/invoice, permission form; licensing agreement; copyright registration or transfer, model release; consignment agreement, contracts with book designers, printers, distributors, merchandisers). Each form is accompanied by an explanation of its use and purpose, as well as a negotiation checklist designed to assist the author in making effective use of the form, clarifying what changes would be desirable from the author's point of view. Extra copies of each form are provided so they may be removed from the book for copying purposes. Forms available on diskette for Mac or PC.

Crawford, Tad. *Protecting Your Rights and Increasing Your Income: A Guide for Authors, Graphic Designers, Illustrators, and Photographers.* New York, NY: Allworth Press, 1990. Audio, 60 min.

DuBoff, Leonard. *The Law (in Plain English) for Photographers.* New York, NY: Allworth Press, 1995. 207p.

Discusses legal issues faced by professional photographers including: contracts and remedies (sample contracts are included); copyright; defamation and libel; privacy rights; censorship; business organization; taxes; and agency law. Includes a chapter on how to find a good lawyer. Appendices contain the ASMP code of ethics, a table of relevant cases, organizations that offer help to photographers, and recommended books.

Duvernet, Christopher. *Photography and the Law: A Guide for Amateur and Professional Photographers.* 2nd ed. Bellingham, WA: Self-Counsel Press, 1991. 176p.

The basic focus of this book is the "tension that exists between people who want to take photographs and those who do not want them taken." Thus, the author concentrates on "what can be photographed, how a photograph can be taken, and how and when it can be used." Negligence, trespassing, harassment, and the right to privacy are all discussed in relation to how and when a photo can be taken. Another section considers restrictions on the use of photos in specific situations, such as advertisements, judicial proceedings, photographic contests, and by the news media. Releases are also discussed (and a sample form is included), as well as how to secure copyright protection for your photographic efforts. The author, a Canadian attorney, discusses relevant law in both Canada and the United States in an easy-to-read style that is suitable for his intended audience of amateur and professional photographers.

Canada

Duvernet, Christopher. *Photography and the Law: A Guide for Amateur and Professional Photographers.* 2nd ed. Bellingham, WA: Self-Counsel Press, 1991. 176p.

The basic focus of this book is the "tension that exists between people who want to take photographs and those who do not want them taken." Thus, the author concentrates on "what can be photographed, how a photograph can be taken, and how and when it can be used." Negligence, trespassing, harassment, and the right to privacy are all discussed in relation to how and when a photo can be taken. Another section considers restrictions on the use of photos in specific situations, such as advertisements, judicial proceedings, photographic contests, and by the news media. Releases are also discussed (and a sample form is included), as well as how to secure copyright protection for your photographic efforts. The author, a Canadian attorney, discusses relevant law in both Canada and the United States in an easy-to-read style that is suitable for his intended audience of amateur and professional photographers.

POWER OF ATTORNEY

Clifford, Denis. *The Power of Attorney Book.* 4th ed. Berkeley, CA: Nolo Press, 1991. 288p.

A power of attorney is a document in which one person gives another legal authority to act on his/her behalf. This book provides the information, forms (for all states), and instructions necessary to create conventional and durable (for finances or health care) powers of attorney. Guidelines help the reader decide whether to consult a lawyer. Separate chapters explain how each type of power of attorney works and options available to an individual. Two introductory chapters provide background information for the principal and the attorney; a final chapter explains how to revoke a power of attorney. Sample forms are included.

Clifford, Denis, Mary Randolfph, and Lisa Goldoftas. *Nolo's Law Form Kit: Power of Attorney.* 1st ed. Berkeley, CA: Nolo Press, 1993. 80p.

Haman, Edward A. *The Power of Attorney Handbook.* Clearwater, FL: Sphinx Publishing, 1994. 144p.

Florida

Haman, Edward A. *Florida Power of Attorney Handbook.* Clearwater, FL: Sphinx Publishing, 1994. 90p.

Explains what a power of attorney is and why you would want to write one, and also describes a living will. Covers special powers of attorney for health care, child care, real estate, or general purposes, and how to revoke an existing power of attorney. Discusses how to decide if you really need a lawyer and how to select one if you do. Includes all the forms and instructions you need to write any of these documents, with sample completed forms and text of selected statutes.

Michigan

Maran, Michael. *The Michigan Power of Attorney Book: A Guide to Making Financial, Health Care and Custodial Powers of Attorney Without a Lawyer.* East Lansing, MI: Grand River Press, 1991. 140p.

For more than a decade, Michigan has authorized the use of powers of attorney for financial management duties which last during a physical or mental incapacity. It has also provided for "custodial" powers of attorney by which parents can transfer custody of their minor children to agents for up to six months. In 1990, Michigan became one of the few states to use the power of attorney as the method for incapacitated patients to control their health care, including handling the issue of terminating life-sustaining treatment. With this background, the author explains what powers of attorney are and how they work, and compares them with their alternatives (i.e., living wills, guardianship, conservatorship). He provides the information, instructions, and forms necessary to create financial, custodial, and health care powers of attorney.

PRIVACY

Hendricks, Evan, Trudy Hayden, and Jack D. Novik. *Your Right to Privacy: A Basic Guide to Legal Rights in an Information Society.* 2nd ed. Carbondale, IL: Southern Illinois University Press, 1990. 186p.

Issued as part of a continuing series of handbooks published in cooperation with the American Civil Liberties Union, this book sets forth the rights of individuals "in relation to information about them that is circulating throughout society." Modern technology and an increased demand for special services has led to the development of data networks that can maintain and distribute personal information in large quantities at incredibly high speed. Consequent to this development has been a growing concern that such information not be circulated in circumstances outside the control of the individual in question. This book addresses how information is collected, accessed, and controlled both by government agencies and in the private sector. Record keeping is explored in areas such as criminal justice, social services, social security, schools, credit and consumer transactions, tax, and medical and insurance. The lack of an index makes access a little difficult but the question-and-answer format utilized is easy to follow.

PROPERTY

Hughes, Theodore E. *Own It and Keep It.* New York, NY: Facts on File, 1995. 174p.

The best ways to handle all your assets and protect yourself from avoidable tax consequences and losses. Focuses on vehicles, real estate, small businesses and bank accounts, and the ownership implications of divorce, single parenthood, second marriages, and ownership by minors. Considerable attention is given to planning for probate and death taxes and the disposition of assets after death. Includes: tables outlining the elements of a trust agreement; income and gift tax liability for jointly held property; state probate requirements; assets exempted by SSI and Medicaid; selected state laws governing incorporation; and the legal consequences of various forms of ownership. Also includes some sample documents and basic information about making needed legal arrangements.

REAL ESTATE

American Bar Association. *The American Bar Association Guide to Home Ownership: The Complete and Easy Guide to All the Law Every Home Owner Should Know*. New York, NY: Times Books, 1995. 193p.

This book contains advice on the hundreds of legal pitfalls lying in wait for homeowners. Includes tips on: property rights and restrictions; home improvements; security; environmental hazards; financing (and refinancing and re-refinancing); lowering your taxes; neighbor troubles; condos; co-ops; and planned communities. Lots of good information to be aware of before the trouble starts, but probably a little thin on details for dealing with an existing problem. The ABA probably wouldn't be horrified if you hired an attorney for your profitable, or rather, major legal difficulties, but you still have to appreciate the gesture of offering this legal information in a book you can get for the library for free rather than hiring one of them.

Gadlow, Sandy. *How to Buy the Brooklyn Bridge and Have the Last Laugh*. 5th ed. El Cerrito, CA: ExPress Publishing, 1993. 222p.

Lohmar, Cecil. *Buy More for Less: How to Make Sure You Get Your Money's Worth*. Kila, MT: Kessinger Publishing Co., 1990. 120p

A realistic portrayal of the housing market offering a frank appraisal of the legal and economic issues confronting the prospective home buyer who is acting without the assistance of a real estate agent. The author takes the buyer through house-hunting strategies, and provides techniques for negotiating a successful purchase and for gathering information from professionals outside the real estate field (e.g., bankers, lawyers, accountants).

Milko, George. *Real Estate: The Legal Side to Buying a House, Condo, or Co-op, A Step-by-Step Guide.* New York, NY: Random House, 1990. 165p.

Written for the home buyer who wishes to work with real estate professionals in an informed way, this book introduces the parties involved in the selling and buying of homes and what role they play. It prepares the home buyer to participate in the process by briefly defining legal concepts such as forms of ownership, reviewing how to househunt (e.g., explaining multiple listing services, use of agents, and inspections), and describing what is involved in the actual purchase. The latter encompasses chapters on mortgages, types of lenders, applying for a loan, title, and closing a deal. Appendices include a list of items to check during an inspection, a glossary of terms, and a bibliography of related books. Forms are not included.

Smith, Jeremy D. *Homeseller Strategies in a Soft Market.* Dobbs Ferry, NY: Oceana Publications, 1991. 160p.

This book discusses things sellers can do to make their houses more attractive to buyers, and ways to cope with lengthy periods of time on the market. After a chapter on fixing up a house to appeal to buyers, most of the book deals with taxes, financing, leases. Monthly payment tables, loan reduction tables, and effect of monthly prepayments tables are appendices. The final chapter considers the benefits of brokers versus the "for sale by owner" approach, and selling techniques.

Warda, Mark. *How to Negotiate Real Estate Contracts.* Clearwater, FL: Sphinx Publishing, 1993. 1 vol. 124p.

Warda, Mark. *How to Negotiate Real Estate Leases.* Clearwater, FL: Sphinx Publishing, 1994. 120p.

Weaver, Jefferson Hane. *The Compact Guide to Property Law: A Civilized Approach to the Law.* St. Paul, MN: West Pub. Co., 1992. 235p.

Provides the general reader with a broad overview of the basic principles of property law. Humorous examples are included to make the concepts more accessible, and the author has sought to present the subject in as clear and concise a manner as possible. General topics treated are estates in land; leasehold estates; future interests; easements, covenants, and equitable servitudes; and other property law concepts such as zoning, eminent domain, adverse possession, and real property transactions.

California

Randolph, Mary. *The Deeds Book: How to Transfer Title to Real Estate.* 3rd ed. Berkeley, CA: Nolo Press, 1994. 208p.

Designed for simple title changes and transfers of California real property, this book explains how to distinguish between and choose the right kind of deed to achieve a particular purpose (e.g., transfer title to a relative or friend or to or from a trust; add or delete a spouse's name on the title; make real estate security for a loan; or give up any legal claims of ownership). An overview of real property transfers, including definitions of basic terminology, is followed by chapters discussing: who must sign a deed; how new owners should take title; how to prepare a deed; and how to record a deed. Sample forms are included to clarify the text, and the appendix provides a series of tear-out, ready-to-use deed forms.

Warner, Ralph, Charles Sherman, and Toni Ihara. *Homestead Your House.* 8th ed. Berkeley, CA: Nolo Press, 1992. 96p.

The California Constitution provides a mechanism by which homeowners may protect their equity (the amount over and above what is owed on the house) if creditors file against the home. Complete, easy-to-follow instructions are provided for the preparation and filing of a Declaration of Homestead; tear-out forms are also included. It also offers background information on homestead protection, explaining how it works to protect equity against creditors. A separate chapter reviews what to do if a judgment creditor tries to force the sale of the debtor's house. A glossary of real estate law terms is included.

Warner, Ralph, Ira Serkes, and George Devine. *How to Buy a House in California.* 3rd ed. Berkeley, CA: Nolo Press, 1994. 336p.

Recognizing the unique aspects of the California real estate market, this book provides a thorough, practical discussion of the steps in finding and financing the purchase of a starter, middle-market, luxury, or new house in California (note: condominiums are not covered). This book prepares the reader to make informed decisions on many issues which plague all buyers, but especially the first-timer, such as: choosing an agent; determining the size of a down payment; acquiring the best kind of mortgage; getting a house inspected; bargaining for the best price; and taking title. Strategies to handle these and other problems are presented throughout the text, along with a variety of checklists, charts, graphic displays, and other devices which help clarify what is often a murky subject to the average citizen. The appendices include much helpful information: California facts and figures; other sources to consult; moving checklists; and a variety of reproducible forms.

Oregon

Granata, Fred A. *Real Estate Buying/Selling Guide for Oregon.* 2nd ed. Bellingham, WA: Self-Counsel Press, 1990. 111p.

Offered as a concise explanation of how a real estate transaction works in Oregon, this book is intended more to provide insight into the process for a buyer or seller rather than as a guide on "how to do it yourself." The author contends that it is better to use a professional who will approach the subject with objective judgment and experience. It explains the various stages in buying or selling a house and explains the responsibilities of the seller, buyer, agent, and lawyer. A variety of issues are covered, including: what down payment is required; how to arrange a mortgage; what an earnest money agreement is used for; how to make a counteroffer; how to close a deal; and how title is taken. Sample forms are provided throughout the text of the book.

Washington

Corvello, Charles, J. *Real Estate Buying/Selling Guide for Washington.* 4th ed. Bellingham, WA: Self-Counsel Press, 1991. 96p.

This book seeks to provide both home buyers and sellers with basic information about the potential problems and complexities involved in real estate transactions. Armed with such information, the individual can better judge when professional advice should be sought and when it is possible to proceed without it. Topics covered include how to look for a house, the nature and use of real estate contracts, methods of paying for a house, negotiating a purchase and the use of an earnest money agreement, the role and use of an escrow agent, and foreclosure. A final chapter considers condominiums, cooperative apartments, and mobile homes. Filled-in forms are offered throughout the book as examples to work from.

RECORD KEEPING

Kruse, Ann. *Keeping Track: An Organizer for Your Legal, Business, and Personal Records*. Bellingham, WA: Self-Counsel Press, 1991. 88p.

A book on organizing legal, business and personal records with explanations of what information you need to keep and why. Discusses keeping track of assets, debts and liabilities, and personal information, and storing your documents. Significant space is devoted to planning for disability or death. Forms are distributed throughout the book (intended to be filled in and kept in the book), to help you keep the information you need close at hand and readily accessible, and to help your family administer your affairs if you should die or become incapacitated. Includes a short chapter on what to do when a death occurs.

RELIGION

Lynn, Barry. *The Right to Religious Freedom*. Carbondale, IL: Southern Illinois University Press, 1995. 1 vol.

Staver, Matthew D. *Faith and Freedom: A Complete Handbook for Defending Your Religious Rights*. Wheaton, IL: Crossway Books, 1995. 240p.

A general explanation of the rights of Christians written from the perspective of a pastor/lawyer who argues that the courts have gone much farther toward restricting the rights of Christians than the "founding fathers" ever intended. Chapters include: "Religion: an endangered species"; students' and teachers' rights; door-to-door witnessing; religious displays on public property; religious discrimination in employment; and "Religion and the Future of America." Appendices contain school board and club sample policies, selected statutes, and the Bill of Rights. Contrary to the impression created by the subtitle of this book, specific instructions for defending your religious rights are few and far between, but information on what the courts have interpreted those rights to be is plentiful.

Whitehead, John W. *The Rights of Religious Persons.* Revised ed. Wheaton, IL: Crossway Books, 1994. 379p.

In the course of building his case for "accommodating religious expression in public education" author John Whitehead (founder of the Rutherford Institute) offers a detailed examination of the current state of the law on the rights on religious persons in public explanation. Many citations to legal sources are included. Divided into seven parts: problems; accommodation; rights; equal access; excusal and parents' rights; holidays and graduation prayers; and the marketplace of ideas. Includes extensive notes, a substantial bibliography, a general index, and an index of cases.

RETIREMENT AND PENSIONS

Cleary, David and Virginia Cleary. *Retire Smart: Sound Advice to Help You Make Your Retirement Years Happy, Healthy and Active.* New York, NY: Allworth Press, 1993. 223p.

Advice on making retirement a joy, and making the many changes and decisions it involves wisely. While the focus of this book is not on law, the legal implications of various decisions are explained, and basic information about law that retirees need to consider are given, with references for further reading. Pleasant reading, full of helpful ideas to enhance health and happiness in retirement years (many are appealing in the just dreaming-of-retirement years as well).

Warner, Ralph. *Get a Life: You Don't Need a Million to Retire Well.* 1st ed. Berkely, CA: Nolo Press, 1996. 250p.

Get a Life is intended to help readers "beat the anxiety surrounding retirement and develop a plan that will ensure that the years after age 65 will really be the best years of their lives." The author claims that the conventional wisdom that it is necessary to put away huge sums of money to have a comfortable old age is false, and that the keys to a happy retirement are sensible savings (advice on how to realistically calculate how much you will need and the best ways to secure it is included), maintaining good health, lots of friends, a close family, and varied interests and activities. The author outlines specific things you can do in midlife to protect your health, cultivate close relationships with friends and family, and develop and maintain vital interests and activity levels.

SENIORS

Battle, Carl W. *Senior Counsel: Legal and Financial Strategies for Age 50 and Beyond.* New York, NY: Allworth Press, 1993. 256p.

Basic information on legal issues of special interest to "seniors" (I can just hear those cries of "over fifty doesn't make me a senior!"). Discusses attaining self-fulfillment; health care insurance; Medicare; Medicaid; social security; pensions; financial and estate planning; credit; life insurance; avoiding crime and consumer fraud; planning for disability; handling age discrimination; wills; taxes; and travel. Appendices contain contact information for Better Business Bureaus, consumer protection offices, relevant federal and state agencies, sources of assistance in employment, EEOC offices, and U.S. Government bookstore locations.

Planning for Incapacity: A Self-Help Guide. Washington, DC: Legal Counsel for the Elderly, 1992–1994.

A series of state-specific guides (one for each state) dealing with powers of attorney, the right to die, medical care decision making, and the physician and patient relationship. Includes advance directive forms. Sponsored by the American Association of Retired People.

Sloan, Irving J. *Rights and Remedies for Senior Citizens.* Dobbs Ferry, NY: Oceana Publications, 1992. 149p.

Part of the publisher's *Law for the Layperson—Legal Almanacs* series, this book provides a brief overview of a wide variety of subjects of concern to senior citizens. Both substantive law and procedure are examined, though often not in great depth. Topics covered are: age discrimination; social security; Medicare and Medicaid; nursing homes; incapacity and protective services; making a will; and elderly abuse protection. The discussions are brief and written primarily in non-legal terms without citation to legal authorities. Nearly one third of the book is devoted to appendices which list the names and addresses of local and national agencies and organizations that offer assistance to the elderly.

Smith, Wesley J. *Legal Rights for Seniors: A Guide to Health Care, Income Benefits & Senior Legal Services.* Washington, DC: HALT, 1993. 215p.

Describes rights and protections available to seniors, as well as the benefits they are entitled to and how to claim them. Covers: Medicare, Medicaid, and

Medigap; Social Security and Supplemental Security Income; living wills; pensions and other retirement plans; life insurance; estate planning and trusts; guardianships; nursing homes; veteran's benefits; tapping your home for income; age discrimination; and death and funeral expenses. Includes a glossary and bibliography, and contact information for Medicare peer organizations, Medicare carriers, state agencies on aging, national organizations, and Medicare supplemental insurance counseling.

Florida

Phillips, Elwood. *Florida Retirees' Handbook: Answers to Your Legal and Financial Questions.* 3rd ed. Sarasota, FL: Pineapple Press, 1993. 230p.

Designed as an "orientation guide for the Florida retiree," especially one new to the state, this book provides general background on Florida law and financial matters. It uses a question-and-answer format throughout, following the purpose of alerting the retiree to a possible problem area rather than serving as a "do-it-yourself" book. As such, the answers given are relatively short, easy to understand, and often provide references to other sources. Areas covered are: real property law (e.g., buying and selling a home, condominiums, mobile homes, and renting); consumer protection; medical and health; social security; taxes; and estate planning. The appendix provides an extensive list of useful addresses and phone numbers.

SEXUAL HARASSMENT

Lynch, Francis. *Draw the Line: Developing a Sexual Harassment-Free Workplace.* Grant's Pass, OR: Oasis Press, 1995. 150p.

A guide for business owners and managers who want to create a sexual harassment-free workplace avoid sexual harassment lawsuits. Explains what sort of remarks and behavior are illegal, and offers a model sexual harassment policy with complaint forms and disciplinary letters. Also offers suggestions for curbing harassment of employees by clients or vendors, in keeping with court holdings that a company may be liable for harassment of its employees by people the employees are forced to work with even if those people are not employed by the company.

Petrocelli, William and Barbara Kate Repa. *Sexual Harassment on the Job: What It Is and How to Stop It.* 2nd ed. Berkeley, CA: Nolo Press, 1994. 336p.

SMALL CLAIMS COURT

Koff, Gail J. *The Jacoby and Meyers Guide to Small Claims Litigation.* 1st ed. New York, NY: Henry Holt, 1991. 1 vol.

Sigman, Robert. *Small Claims Court.* Altamonte Springs, FL: Legovac, 1990. Audio

Warner, Ralph. *Everybody's Guide to Small Claims Court.* 6th ed. Berkeley, CA: Nolo Press, 1995. 386p.

Although the small claims court procedures may vary slightly from state to state, the basic approach necessary to prepare and present a case remains the same for all jurisdictions. The author thoroughly discusses both the procedural and practical/tactical aspects of bringing a case, covering such questions as: Do you have a case? Can you recover if you win? How much can you sue for? Who can sue and be sued? How do you settle? Later chapters review specific types of cases, including vehicle repair and purchases, vehicle accidents, and landlord-tenant problems. The final chapter explains how to collect on a judgment when it is in your favor. A separate appendix includes the small claims rules for each of the 50 states.

Warner, Ralph and Joanne Greene. *Winning in Small Claims Court.* 1st ed. Berkeley, CA: Nolo Press, 1993. Audio

Wilber, W. Kelsea. *Small Claims Court Without a Lawyer.* Naperville, IL: Sourcebooks, Inc., 1991. 212p.

Step-by-step instructions on how to file a lawsuit, serve a summons, garnish a defendant's wages or non-wage holdings, or place a lien on a debtor's property. Details for each state are included: the name of the court; dollar limitation on amount in controversy; whether attorneys are allowed; filing fees; statutes of limitations; methods of serving process; wage garnishment; homestead and personal property exemptions; and miscellaneous notes. Guides the reader through each step of the trial, with advice on what to

expect and what to say. Includes a glossary of legal terms and sample letters
and forms.

California

Warner, Ralph. *Everybody's Guide to Small Claims Court in California.*
12th ed. Berkeley, CA: Nolo Press, 1995. 336p.

This book offers practical advice on how to use the small claims court
system in California to resolve disputes involving small amounts of money
($5,000 or less), without long delays and using relatively simple procedures.
Tactical guidance is provided, such as how to decide whether you have a
winning or losing case, along with step-by-step information on how to
initiate and proceed with an action. For instance, separate chapters explain
how to: file court papers; serve papers; respond if you are sued; deal with
witnesses (including the use of subpoenas); and present a case to the judge.
Sample forms are included throughout the book.

Florida

Brown, Luke S. *Small Claims Court Guide for Florida.* Bellingham, WA:
Self-Counsel Press, 1993. 240p.

For plaintiffs or defendants, this book walks the reader through the Florida
small claims court processes from filing a complaint to collecting or appealing
a judgment. Includes suggestions on resolving disputes without going to court,
and predicting the costs of going the court route. Includes both sample copies
of filled-in forms and blank, ready-to-use forms that are commonly needed,
and a list of addresses and phone numbers of county courthouses in Florida.

Warda, Mark. *How to Win Small Claims Court in Florida.* 5th ed. Clearwater, FL: Sphinx Publishing, 1994. 124p.

Explains how to negotiate the small claims process, from filing your case to
collecting your judgment or appealing the judgement against you. Includes
checklists for plaintiff and defendant, the text of the Florida small claims
rules, and 43 forms.

Texas

Brown, William R. *How to Win in Small Claims Court in Texas.* Clearwater, FL: Sphinx Publishing, 1995. 124p.

Explains how to negotiate the small claims process, from filing your case to collecting your judgment or appealing the judgement against you. Includes checklists for plaintiff and defendant, the text of selected Texas statues and court rules.

Washington

Stuart, Donald D. *Small Claims Court Guide for Washington: How to Win Your Case!* 3rd ed. Bellingham, WA: Self-Counsel Press, 1989. 168p.

Even though the purpose of small claims court is to shortcut the complex procedures of larger cases and make it possible for a non-lawyer to come to court and settle a dispute, the successful utilization of this system requires an understanding of how it functions. This book tries to unlock the mysteries of the small claims proceedings in Washington, providing a step-by-step guide for either suing or defending a case. It begins by examining the powers and jurisdiction of small claims courts and considering how to decide whether to sue or defend an action. Practical chapters divulge how to start or respond to a lawsuit, how to prepare for trial, what to expect at trial, and how to collect on judgments. Filled-in samples are used to illustrate suggested actions.

SOCIAL SECURITY AND MEDICARE

Bove, Alexander A. *The Medicaid Planning Handbook: A Guide to Protecting Your Family's Assets from Nursing Home Costs.* 2nd ed. Boston, MA: Little, Brown, 1996. 1 vol.

Designed to help family members cope with the economic problems that so often accompany serious illness. The author uses case studies to show how to protect assets, offering a variety of strategies such as gifts, trusts, and paying relatives for services rendered. He explains how a trust works and covers the differences between a revocable and irrevocable trust. Also covered is the use of a durable power of attorney, long-term care insurance, and guardianships for incompetent persons. Procedural aspects of Medicaid are explained, including eligibility and appeals of a denial of benefits or to increase a spousal allowance. Appendices identify differences in state laws relating to the treatment of a home as a Medicaid asset and limits on income for Medicaid purposes, as well as providing a list of state Medicaid offices.

Matthews, Joseph L. and Dorothy Matthews Berman. *Social Security, Medicare and Pensions: The Sourcebook for Older Americans.* 6th ed. Berkeley, CA: Nolo Press, 1995. 288p.

Provides basic information about benefits available to older Americans and how to collect them. Explains how much you can receive, how and when to file claims, and how to make plans so that you can receive benefits income while continuing to work during retirement years. Also explains both government programs and private health insurance supplements. Each chapter explains a different benefits program (e.g., retirement, disability, dependents' and survivors', Medicare, Medicaid) and begins with a highlights section, followed by information presented in a question-and-answer format (e.g., what services does Medicaid pay for?).

TAXATION

Aczel, Amir D. *How to Beat the I.R.S. at Its Own Game: Strategies to Avoid—and Fight—an Audit.* New York, NY: Four Walls Eight Windows, 1995. 1 vol.

Berg, Adriane G. *Keys to Avoiding Probate and Reducing Estate Taxes.* Hauppauge, NY: Barron's Educational Series, 1992. 171p.

Contains 50 "key concepts" for avoiding probate, saving estate taxes, choosing trustees and attorneys, and saving the family business. Written in clear terms with particular attention to correcting common myths and misperceptions about good estate planning. Also includes a short question-and-answer section (mostly showing why you would bother taking the recommended steps), and a glossary.

Daily, Frederick W. *Stand Up to the IRS*. 2nd ed. Berkeley, CA: Nolo
Press, 1992. 368p.

The author purports to provide everything you need to know to successfully
defend yourself in an audit, challenge an incorrect tax bill, or represent
yourself in tax court. Explains how to keep or gather records to support your
deductions, petition for the removal of a penalty, lien, or wage attachment.
The book also includes "confidential forms, unavailable to taxpayers, used
by the IRS during audits and collection interviews," so you can see how the
other half thinks.

Daily, Frederick W. *Tax Savvy for Small Business*. 1st ed. Berkeley, CA:
Nolo Press, 1995. 320p.

Hanlon, R. Brendan. *The New Tax Guide for Performers, Writers, Directors, Designers, and Other Show Biz Folk*. Rev. ed. New York,
NY: Limelight Editions, 1994. 128p.

The author warns that "This book is not a do-it-yourself manual enabling
you to prepare your own tax return. If your return is at all complicated, it is
well worth the costs of having it prepared by a competent tax person who
knows the performing arts." The book is mostly dedicated to the funda-
mentals of good record keeping, aimed at enabling you to claim the lowest
honest tax liability you can and to avoid additional liability in the unhappy
event of an audit.

Koenig, R. Harry. *How to Lower Your Property Taxes*. Old Tappan, NJ:
Simon & Schuster, 1991. 1 vol.

Kraemer, Sandy F. *Sixty Minute Estate Planner: Fast & Easy Illustrated
Plans to Save Taxes, Avoid Probate and Maximize Inheritance*.
Englewood Cliffs, NJ: Prentice Hall, 1994. 279p.

The Price Waterhouse Personal Tax Advisor. Burr Ridge, IL: Irwin
Professional Publishing, 1994. 347p.

Roberson, Cliff. *The McGraw-Hill Personal Tax Advisor*. 2nd ed. New
York, NY: McGraw-Hill, 1992. 220p.

All manner of information to help you comply with the tax code and keep
your tax liability as low as possible. Includes suggestions on how to keep
your vital tax records adequately and efficiently, and how to deal with the

dreaded IRS audit. A chapter of significant court decisions helps to clarify the meaning and scope of various tax law provisions.

Sydlaske, Janet M. and Richard K. Millcroft. *The Only Tax Audit Guide You'll Ever Need.* New York, NY: John Wiley & Sons, 1990. 326p.

Written for those being audited and those who want to minimize their chances of such a dreadful thing happening to them. The author notes that it is for careful taxpayers who filed honest returns but are being audited anyway, and who want to represent themselves because the amount of tax at issue is not enough to justify the cost of retaining a professional, or for those who have hired a professional but want to understand the process and play an active role. Part I deals with avoiding being selected for an audit, and Part II describes what the audit process is like, how to handle it, and what to do if it doesn't come out in your favor.

Your Guide to Living Trusts & Other Trusts: How Trust Can Help You Avoid Probate & Taxes. Washington, DC: HALT, 1994. 214p.

TRAFFIC COURT

California

Brown, David. *Fight Your Ticket . . . and Win!* 6th ed. Berkeley, CA: Nolo Press, 1995. 368p.

Directed to the California driver who receives a traffic citation which he or she perceives to be unfair, this book shows how to handle a case in traffic court, get the right kind of hearing, and maximize the chances of avoiding a traffic conviction. It provides legal strategies to combat tickets for speeding and drunk driving; also to deal with license suspension. Appealing a conviction is also considered.

Florida

Adkins, John C. *Winning in Florida Traffic Court.* Clearwater, FL: Sphinx Publishing, 1994. 134p.

A guide to defending yourself against charges of driving while impaired, speeding, driving with a suspended licence, speeding, running a red light or stop sign, and other traffic offenses. Explains how to file motions and what to expect in traffic court, what possible penalties you face. Suggests effective defenses. Appendices include: commonly asked traffic questions; traffic violations classifications; points and statutes; and selected rules of practice and procedure for traffic courts. With glossary and sample forms.

UNEMPLOYMENT

Schuyler, Nina. *The Unemployment Survival Book.* New York, NY: Allworth Press, 1993. 144p.

Advice on handling the financial and emotional crises that unemployment often brings, and negotiating the unemployment benefits system. Schuyler explains how to determine if you are eligible for benefits, how much those benefits would be, and how to fill out the necessary forms for the best chance of having benefits granted. Also discusses how to appeal if benefits are denied, and how to start your job search without inadvertently causing your benefits to be cut before you find work. Covers all 50 states, but includes sample forms only for California.

VEHICLES

Faglio, Andrew A. *Lemonaid!: A Layperson's Guide to the Automotive Lemon Laws.* Dobbs Ferry, NY: Oceana Publications, 1991. 1 vol.

Written for automobile owners who feel that they are stuck with a "lemon," and who are willing to go the distance to see to it that the manufacturer is made to bear the financial burden caused by its incompetence. The author stresses that this can be a lengthy and trying process, but offers information and advice that he says will be enough for most consumers to win and obtain a refund without a lawyer. A "Fifty State Lemon Law Master Matrix" is included, along with chapters on preparing your case and negotiating arbitration and small claims court. For the faint of heart there is a chapter on finding the right lawyer. The book is intended for consumers in all states, but most examples and detailed examinations of particular laws are specific to New York.

Richard L. Kaye. *Lemon Aid: Exercising Your Rights Under the Consumer Lemon Law*. Northbrook, IL: TeleTravel Network, 1991. 126p.

"Lemon Law" legislation, enacted in nearly all states, provides consumers with specific rights and remedies if they experience continuing problems within the first 12 to 24 months of purchasing a new automobile. This book introduces the reader to those rights and remedies, including specifying how to complain and to whom to direct a complaint. It also explains how to determine if one's problem qualifies for recourse under a state's Lemon Law. The general Lemon Law process is outlined. A lengthy appendix details the Lemon Laws of each individual state, providing information on coverage, consumer procedure, available awards if the consumer prevails, and which office to contact for assistance or to initiate a claim. Another appendix gives contact information for most major automotive manufacturers.

Sigman, Robert. *Automobile Accidents*. Altamonte Springs, FL: Legovac, 1990. Audio

WILLS, TRUSTS, AND PROBATE

American Bar Association. *The American Bar Association Guide to Wills and Estates*. 1st ed. New York, NY: Times Books/Random House, 1995. 1 vol.

Appel, Jens C. and F. Bruce Gentry. *The Complete Probate Kit*. New York, NY: Wiley, 1991. 1 vol.

Berg, Adriane G. *Keys to Avoiding Probate and Reducing Estate Taxes*. Hauppauge, NY: Barron's Educational Series, 1992. 171p.

Contains 50 "key concepts" for avoiding probate, saving estate taxes, choosing trustees and attorneys, and saving the family business. Written in clear terms with particular attention to correcting common myths and misperceptions about good estate planning. Also includes a short question-and-answer section (mostly showing why you would bother taking the recommended steps), and a glossary.

Christianson, Stephen G. *How to Administer an Estate: A Step-by-Step Guide for Families and Friends.* Seacaucus, N.J.: Citadel Press, 1993. 139p.

The author begins with the assumption that most people will plan to handle an estate without a lawyer, and proceeds to note "red flags" for problem estates and situations in which you really should call an accountant or lawyer. After a discussion about things to consider before you decide to become an executor at all, the author offers orderly instructions for each step of the process, including example situations, checklists, a glossary, summaries of legal requirements in all fifty states, and a few illustrative sample forms.

Clifford, Denis. *Make Your Own Living Trust.* 1st ed. Berkeley, CA: Nolo Press, 1993. 336p.

Clifford, Denis. *Nolo's Simple Will Book.* 2nd ed. Berkeley, CA: Nolo Press, 1989. 256p.

A practical, step-by-step guide designed to enable the reader to prepare a will valid in every state but Louisiana. Provides the necessary background to understand the process of making a will (e.g., overview of wills, choosing an executor, identifying property to pass by a will, deciding who gets what), followed by individual chapters on the actual preparation of a will. The latter contains sample complete will forms, sample clauses, and checklists. The formalities of preparing the will, including requirements for signing and witnessing, are also covered Although it is largely devoid of technical terms, a glossary is included.

Clifford, Denis. *The Quick and Legal Will Book.* Berkeley, CA: Nolo Press, 1996. 280p.

Clifford, Denis and Lisa Goldoftas. *Nolo's Law Form Kit: Wills.* 1st ed. Berkeley, CA: Nolo Press, 1993. 80p.

Colen, B.D. *The Essential Guide to a Living Will: How to Protect Your Right to Refuse Medical Treatment.* Old Tappan, NJ: Prentice-Hall, 1991. 146p.

Starting from the view that "having a well-drawn Living Will will provide physicians, hospital administrators, or judges with greater certainty of what you yourself would be requesting were you competent to make the request," this book shows how such a document can be used to try to guarantee that the right one has as a competent individual to refuse or agree to medical treatment is preserved even when one is no longer competent. After reviewing the role of the doctor and of technology in such situations, sample living will forms conforming to the requirements of the 38 states (as of January 1, 1987) with a living will law are presented. Practical steps of to effectuate a Living Will are then discussed, including preparation of a written document and a videotape.

The Easy Way to Probate: A Step-by-Step Guide to Settling an Estate. Washington, DC: HALT, 1994. 173p.

Esperti, Robert A. *The Loving Trust Workbook: How to Initiate, Create, Design, and Fund Your Living Trust.* Bergenfield, NJ: Penguin Books, 1995. 1 vol.

Goodart, Nan L. *The Truth About Living Trusts.* Chicago, IL: Dearborn Financial Publishing, 1995. 157p.

Hughes, Theodore E. *The Executor's Handbook: A Step-by-Step Guide to Settling an Estate for Personal Representatives and Administrators.* New York, NY: Facts on File, 1994. 235p.

Clear instructions on all aspects of the often bewildering process of settling an estate, for estate executor's and personal representatives. No knowledge of legal terms is presumed. Includes sample documents, letters, flowcharts and checklists. Somewhat surprisingly, considering its title, almost one-quarter of the book dealing with planning strategies before death. Throughout, attention is given to recognizing hidden expenses and controlling costs. An excellent book.

Koff, Gail J. *The Jacoby and Meyers Guide to Wills and Estates.* 1st ed. New York, NY: Henry Holt, 1991. 1 vol.

Living Trust Maker, version 2.0. Berkeley, CA: Nolo Press, 1996. Computer software

Outerbridge, David E. and Alan R. Hersh. *Easing the Passage: A Guide for Prearranging and Ensuring a Pain-Free and Tranquil Death Via a Living Will, Personal Medical Mandate, and Other Medical, Legal and Ethical Resources.* New York, NY: HarperCollins Publishers, 1991. 162p.

Plotnick, Charles K. and Stephan R. Leimberg. *How to Settle an Estate: A Manual for Executors and Trustees.* Rev. ed. Yonkers, NY: Consumers Union, 1991. 324p.

Intended to inform the individual lay executor what is required to properly handle the affairs of a deceased person. Recognizing the widespread use of revocable living trusts, it also includes a chapter on the duties of a trustee. The authors cover almost every facet of handling an estate that a personal representative might encounter, but they also discuss how to select and when to use professionals for estate settlement (e.g., attorney, accountant, appraiser, etc.). Practical and easy-to-use checklists (e.g., executor's primary duties) are provided to minimize the possibility of neglecting an essential step. It also includes a variety of sample forms and worksheets, and a lengthy glossary to assist the reader in understanding the text.

Rolcik, Karen Ann. *Living Trusts and Simple Ways to Avoid Probate.* Clearwater, FL: Sphinx Publishing, 1996. 140p.

Discusses ways to insure that your property passes to your heirs without expense or delay. Includes forms and instructions you need to follow the authors suggestions. Describes the probate process and explains why it is such a good thing to avoid. Explains how to set up a living trust so that your property will go where you want it to in the event of your death or in-capacity, and how to take advantage of additional probate alternatives such as joint tenancy, life insurance, and retirement plans.

Sigman, Robert. *Wills, Trusts, and Estate Planning.* Altamonte Springs, FL: Legovac, 1990. Audio

Sitarz, Daniel. *Prepare Your Own Will: The National Will Kit.* 4th ed. Carbondale, IL: Nova Publishing Co., 1994. 246p.

Designed to serve as a guide and explanation of the processes and legal techniques required in preparing a valid will without the aspects of the law of wills, though it suggests the assistance of an attorney where complex personal or business property holdings are involved. Procedures involved in the administration of an estate are outlined. Practical aids included are a step-by-step outline of how to draft a will, a detailed personal question-naire, sample fill-in-the-blank will clauses, and an actual sample will.

Sloan, Irving J. *Wills & Trusts*. Rev. ed. Dobbs Ferry, NY: Oceana Publications, 1992. 194p.

Part of the publisher's popular *Law for the Layperson* legal almanac series, this volume offers basic background information to the lay reader on wills (including chapters on "The Historical Development of Wills" and "General Principles of Wills") and trusts ("The Trust Alternative to a Will"). More specific chapters deal with requirements pertaining to execution and revocation, holographic and noncupative (i.e., not written) wills, and federal and state taxation issues. The consequences of dying without a will are explored, as is the use of a "living" will. Sample forms are included throughout the text and are prominently featured in a chapter on "Will Clauses"; forms of complete wills and a trust indenture are included in appendices. A glossary of legal terms is also provided.

Smith, Bradley E. and Jess M. Brallier. *Write Your Own Living Wills*. Westminster, MD: Crown Publishers, 1991. 97p.

Instructions and forms you need to create a simple living will without a lawyer. The author points out that anyone who does not want to be kept alive by artificial means in the event of an accident or illness that results in a terminal condition needs a Living Will. Includes ready-to-use living will forms for every state.

Warner, Ralph and Joanne Greene. *5 Ways to Avoid Probate*. 1st ed. Berkeley, CA: Nolo Press, 1993. Audio

Warner, Ralph and Joanne Greene. *Write Your Will*. 1st ed. Berkeley, CA: Nolo Press, 1993. Audio

Weber, Doron. *The Complete Guide to Living Wills: How to Safeguard Your Treatment Choices*. New York, NY: Bantam Books, 1991. 1 vol.

Wills: A Do-It-Yourself Guide. Washington, DC: HALT, 1992. 256p.

Williamson, Gordon. *Your Living Trust: How to Protect Your Estate from Probate, Taxes, and Lawyers*. New York, NY: Perigree Books, 1992. 208p.

WillMaker, version 6.0. Berkeley, CA: Nolo Press, 1995. Computer software

Your Guide to Living Trusts & Other Trusts: How Trust Can Help You Avoid Probate & Taxes. Washington, DC: HALT, 1994. 214p.

Alabama

Benjamin, Nancy, H, and Mark Warda. *How to Make an Alabama Will.* Clearwater, FL: Sphinx Publishing, 1993. 97p.

Instructions, information, and forms needed to make a simple will and to appoint a guardian for minor children without a lawyer's help. Explains basic concepts and terms you need to understand, and step-by-step instructions on how to make, sign, and execute a simple will, make a living will, or make anatomical gifts. Includes both ready-to-use forms and sample filled-in forms.

California

Nissley, Julia. *How to Probate an Estate.* 8th ed. Berkeley, CA: Nolo Press, 1994. 416p.

The author explains in simple, mostly non-technical terms (a glossary is included), how to probate a routine or uncomplicated California estate (e.g., assets clearly defined and no disputes by inheritors). An important part of the book is the detailed instructions on how to conduct a simple probate court proceeding entirely by mail, including sample illustrative forms. It also explains how to: transfer and clear title to property owned in joint tenancy by the decedent; transfer property to a surviving spouse with an abbreviated court proceeding; transfer securities, real property, motor vehicles, and other property to the heirs; and file income and estate tax returns. Introductory chapters cover the first steps in settling an estate, determining what makes up an estate, and preparing a schedule of assets and debts. The appendices include a large variety of tear-out forms that can be filled out according to directions in the book and actually used to probate a simple California estate.

Canada

Botnick, David I. *Probate Guide for Ontario: A Step-by-Step Guide to Probating an Estate.* 6th ed. Seattle, WA: International Self-Counsel Press, 1991. 84p.

Wong, Steven G. *Wills for British Columbia: How to Make Your Own Will.* 14th ed. Bellingham, WA: Self-Counsel Press, 1990. 99p.

Florida

Herskowitz, Susan. *Wills for Florida: How to Make Your Own Will (Includes Forms)*. Bellingham, WA: Self-Counsel Press, 1992. 240p.

Herskowitz explains why you need a will and how to make one valid. Offers guidelines for deciding whether you need a lawyer and how much you can reasonably expect to pay one. Explains legal concepts and terms involved and includes tear-out forms with instructions. Also covers living wills, guardians for children, power of attorney arrangements, trusts, and health care surrogates.

Nickel, Gudrun M. *How to Probate an Estate in Florida*. 2nd ed. Clearwater, FL: Sphinx Publishing, 1995. 140p.

Describes the four types of probate in Florida, and explains when you need an attorney and when you probably can get by without one. Includes instructions, forms, checklists, and text of selected statutes. Also contains a brief glossary of legal terms.

Warda, Mark. *How to Make a Florida Will*. 4th ed. Clearwater, FL: Sphinx Publishing, 1995. 93p.

Instructions, information, and forms needed to make a simple will and appoint a guardian for minor children without a lawyer's help. Explains basic concepts and terms you need to understand, and step-by-step instructions on how to make, sign, and execute a simple will, make a living will, or make anatomical gifts. Includes both ready-to-use forms and sample filled-in forms.

Warda, Mark. *Land Trusts in Florida*. 4th ed. Clearwater, FL: Sphinx Publishing, 1995. 142p.

You can use land trusts in Florida for all sorts of unsavory-sounding purposes (and a few savory ones as well), and Mark Warda shows you how. However, "since no book can be expected to answer all questions regarding each particular case and because some of the material is technical, readers who are not attorneys are urged to consult an attorney before setting up a land trust." A few of the things land trusts can be used to do include keeping your assets secret, keeping liens of your property, keeping your spouse from getting an otherwise mandated share of your property when you die, avoiding litigation and liability and, as they say on television, "much, much more."

Georgia

Moses, Edward P. and Mark Warda. *How to Make a Georgia Will.*
  Clearwater, FL: Sphinx Publishing, 1996. 95p.

Instructions, information, and forms needed to make a simple will and appoint a guardian for minor children without a lawyer's help. Explains basic concepts and terms you need to understand, and step-by-step instructions on how to make, sign, and execute a simple will, make a living will, or make anatomical gifts. Includes both ready-to-use forms and sample filled-in forms.

Michigan

Haman, Edward A. and Mark Warda. *How to Make a Michigan Will.*
  Clearwater, FL: Sphinx Publishing, 1995. 92p.

Instructions, information, and forms needed to make a simple will and appoint a guardian for minor children without a lawyer's help. Explains basic concepts and terms you need to understand, and step-by-step instructions on how to make, sign, and execute a simple will, make a living will, or make anatomical gifts. Includes both ready-to-use forms and sample filled-in forms.

North Carolina

Naylor, Wanda and Mark Warda. *How to Make a North Carolina Will.*
  Clearwater, FL: Sphinx Publishing, 1994. 94p.

Instructions, information, and forms needed to make a simple will and appoint a guardian for minor children without a lawyer's help. Explains basic concepts and terms you need to understand, and step-by-step instructions on how to make, sign, and execute a simple will, make a living will, or make anatomical gifts. Includes both ready-to-use forms and sample filled-in forms.

Oregon

Johnson, Rees C. *Wills and Estate Planning Handbook for Oregon.* 4th
  ed. Bellingham, WA: Self-Counsel Press, 1990. 196p.

The primary purpose of this book is to assist the non-attorney in planning and writing a will. To do so, the author explains the legal requirements for a valid will in Oregon, what happens when a person dies without a will, the effect of marriage on a will, and methods for making gifts to minors. A sample simple will is provided. It also offers a general guide to estate planning in simple, non-technical language, with the goal of making it easier for

the layperson to deal with professional advisors. A guide to probate administration (e.g., how to start probate proceedings, required notices, claims
against the estate) is provided, as well as a discussion of federal estate and
Oregon inheritance taxes. Finally, anatomical gifts and living wills are
discussed. Preprinted will forms are available from the publisher.

South Carolina

Cullen, Thomas P. and Mark Warda. *How to Make a South Carolina
    Will.* Clearwater, FL: Sphinx Publishing, 1993. 96p.

Instructions, information, and forms needed to make a simple will and appoint
a guardian for minor children without a lawyer's help. Explains basic concepts
and terms you need to understand, and step-by-step instructions on how to
make, sign, and execute a simple will, make a living will, or make anatomical
gifts. Includes both ready-to-use forms and sample filled-in forms.

Texas

Rolcik, Karen Ann and Mark Warda. *How to Make a Texas Will.*
    Clearwater, FL: Sphinx Publishing, 1994. 95p.

Instructions, information and forms needed to make a simple will and appoint
a guardian for minor children without a lawyer's help. Explains basic concepts
and terms you need to understand, and provides step-by-step instructions on
how to make, sign, and execute a simple will, make a living will, or make
anatomical gifts. Includes both ready-to-use forms and sample filled-in forms.

Rolcik, Karen Ann. *How to Probate an Estate in Texas.* Clearwater, FL:
    Sphinx Publishing, 1995. 124p.

Describes the seven types of probate in Texas, and explains when you need
an attorney (and how to find a good one) and when you can probably get
by without one. Includes instructions, forms, checklists, tax advice, and text
of selected statutes. Also contains a brief glossary of legal terms.

Washington

Fredenberg, D. Van. *Wills for Washington.* 5th ed. Bellingham, WA:
    Self-Counsel Press, 1992. 82p.

After a brief introductory chapter presenting reasons for having a will and the
feasibility of writing one without the assistance of a lawyer, the bulk of this
concise book is taken up with detailed chapters on drafting a will and

community property agreements in the state of Washington. In addition to basic provisions, the book presents many of special clauses that might be used in a will (e.g., naming an executor; alternative beneficiaries; handling personal effects; use of percentages; funeral arrangements; and a living will clause). The text analyzes who can utilize a community property agreement, what it can accomplish, and its advantages and disadvantages. Ten sample filled-in forms are provided throughout the book; a short legal glossary is also included. Pre-printed will forms are available from the publisher.

Have You Made Your Will?: Will and Estate Planning Kit for Washington and Oregon. Bellingham, WA: Self-Counsel Press, 1994.

Thom, Phillip L. *Probate Guide for Washington: A Step-by-Step Guide to Probating an Estate.* 4th ed. Bellingham, WA: Self-Counsel Press, 1991. 112p.

Complete instructions for probating an estate without a lawyer. Includes 42 sample forms for probating an uncomplicated estate. Tells you what to expect and what to say in court, and how to manage family support and other responsibilities while the estate is in probate. With tax table and glossary. Pre-printed, ready-to-use probate forms may be ordered from the publisher for an additional charge.

WOMEN'S RIGHTS

Ross, Susan Deller and Ann Barcher. *The Rights of Women.* Carbondale, IL: Southern Illinois University Press, 1993. 1 vol.

Florida

Collins, Gale Forman. *Women's Legal Rights in Florida.* Clearwater, FL: Sphinx Publishing, 1993. 172p.

Lists legal rights of women in Florida in very concise outline form. Covers such topics as: reproductive rights; marriage; divorce; inheritance; violence against women; sexually transmissible diseases and AIDS; employment discrimination; motherhood; adoption; child abuse; and finding a lawyer. Includes contact information for crisis hotlines, legal referral services, legal aid offices, legal service organizations, and Florida courts.

WORKERS' COMPENSATION

Ball, Christopher A. *How to Handle Your Workers' Compensation Claim: A Complete Guide for Employees.* 1st ed. Berkeley, CA: Nolo Press, 1995. 400p.

Walsh, James. *Workers' Comp for Employers: How to Cut Claims, Reduce Premiums, and Stay Out of Trouble.* 2nd ed. Berkeley, CA: Nolo Press, 1994. 325p.

WRITERS

Blue, Martha. *By the Book: Legal ABCs for the Printed Word.* Flagstaff, AZ: Northland Publishing Co., 1990. 431p.

The goal of this text is to educate the publisher regarding legal business matters, thereby expediting the handling of legal problems and reducing lawyer's fees (though consultation with a lawyer is highly recommended, especially in adopting the forms provided for a particular use). Information and forms are provided for publishers of many types of materials: books; magazines; newspapers; catalogues and brochures; and journals. Several chapters are devoted to a wide variety of book contract concerns; others concentrate on copyright issues and production (e.g., manufacturing, marketing). Checklists and sample forms are provided throughout the text.

Breimer, Stephen F. *Clause by Clause: The Screenwriter's Legal Guide.* New York, NY: Dell Trade Paperback, 1995. 1 vol.

Bunnin, Brad and Peter Beren. *The Writer's Legal Companion.* Reading, MA: Addison-Wesley Publishing Co., 1988. 340p.

Directed to anyone involved in producing material for print publishing, this book offers a thorough grounding in the many legal issues and relationships (e.g., writer and agent; writer and publisher; writer and subject) which are likely to arise. Subjects treated vary from copyright to libel, and taxes to collaborations. A basic subject, that of the publishing contract, is dealt with in an extensive chapter covering the many nuances of such agreements and including many sample clauses. While this book would serve the writer well as a basic reference tool, it also tells how to obtain further assistance, providing a chapter on "Legal Resources for the Writer" and a "Resource

Directory" which lists many books, individuals, and organizations to consult. Appendices include a glossary of publishing terms and several complete sample publishing agreements.

Crawford, Tad. *Business & Legal Forms for Authors & Self-Publishers.* New York, NY: Allworth Press, 1990. 176p.

Includes 17 complete forms dealing with the most important business transactions with which an author is likely to be involved (e.g., author-agent contract; book publishing contract; licensing agreement; lecture contract; privacy release; contracts with book designers, printers, and distributors). Each form is accompanied by an explanation of its use and purpose, as well as a negotiation checklist designed to assist the author in making effective use of the form, clarifying what changes would be desirable from the author's point of view. Extra copies of each form are provided so they may be removed from the book for copying purposes.

Crawford, Tad. *Protecting Your Rights and Increasing Your Income: A Guide for Authors, Graphic Designers, Illustrators, and Photographers.* New York, NY: Allworth Press, 1990. Audio, 60 min.

Klavens, Kent J. *Protecting Your Songs & Yourself.* Cincinnati, OH: Writer's Digest Books, 1989. 112p.

Provides a basic legal background for songwriters, covering the fundamental laws and business principles that affect the craft of songwriting. Begins with an analysis of copyright law since this provides the basis for all rights, agreements, and other legal issues that relate to protecting one's songs. Other chapters examine limits on song creation (e.g., parody, libel, right of publicity), co-writers, song contests, and transfers of publishing rights.

Levine, Mark L. *Negotiating a Book Contract: A Guide for Authors, Agents and Lawyers.* Mt. Kisco, NY: Moyer Bell Limited, 1988. 90p.

Recognizing that most publishing contracts are written by publishers' lawyers seeking to protect the interests of their clients, the author has attempted here to alert authors, their agents, and lawyers to many issues which are either omitted entirely from the standard agreement or are treated in a way favorable only to the publisher. Since most publishers will change a standard contract when asked to do so by an author, it behooves the latter to be familiar with troublesome areas that need to be negotiated, rather than simply accepted. The book is organized to match the main areas dealt with in a typical contract, thus, it considers issues relating to: the grant of rights; the manu-script; publication (e.g., changes in manuscript, title approval); copyright; advances; royalties; subsidiary rights; options; "next book" clauses; and revised editions. The focus is on listing points to watch out for in these and the other areas discussed, rather than a thorough presentation of legal require-ments. Sample clauses are sprinkled throughout the text.

Norwick, Kenneth P., Jerry Simon Chasen, and Henry B. Kaufman. *The Rights of Authors, Artists, and Other Creative People.* Carbondale, IL: Southern Illinois University Press, 1992. 1 vol.

Author Index

Aczel, Amir D.
How to Beat the I.R.S. at Its Own Game. (Taxation)

Adkins, John C.
Winning in Florida Traffic Court. (Traffic Court, Florida)

Agran, Libbie
The Economics of Divorce. (Family Law)

Allen, Jeffrey G.
Complying with the ADA. (ADA and Disability)

American Bar Association
The American Bar Association Family Legal Guide. (General/Comprehensive Works)
The American Bar Association Guide to Home Ownership. (Real Estate)
The American Bar Association Guide to Wills and Estates. (Wills, Trusts, and Probate)
Your Legal Guide to Consumer Credit. (Debtor and Creditor)

American Lawyer (see Court TV)

Amernick, Burton A.
Patent Law for the Nonlawyer. (Copyrights, Patents, and Trademarks)

Anderson, Keith & Roy MacSkimming
On Your Own Again. (Family Law)

Annas, George J.
The Rights of Patients. (Health Law)

Anosike, Benji O.
How to Legally Change Your Name Without a Lawyer. (Names, New York)

APPEL, JENS C. & F. BRUCE GENTRY
The Complete Probate Kit. (Wills, Trusts, and Probate)

AVERY, MICHAEL
Do Your Own Divorce in Connecticut. (Family Law, Connecticut)

AVERY, MICHAEL, DIANE POLAN & SARAH D. ELDRICH
Do Your Own Divorce in Connecticut. (Family Law, Connecticut)

BADGLEY, RICHARD
Real Estate Buying/Selling Guide for Florida. (Landlord and Tenant, Florida)

BAILARD, BIEHL & KAISER, INC.
How to Buy the Right Insurance at the Right Price. (Insurance)

BAKER, STEPHEN
How to Survive a Lawyer. (Attorney and Client)

BALDWIN, CARL R.
Immigration Questions and Answers. (Immigration and Citizenship)

BALDWIN, RICHARD C.
Divorce Guide for Oregon. (Family Law, Oregon)

BALL, CHRISTOPHER A.
How to Handle Your Workers' Compensation Claim. (Workers' Compensation)

BARBER, HOYT L.
Copyrights, Patents and Trademarks. (Copyrights, Patents, and Trademarks)

BARCHER, ANN (see ROSS, SUSAN DELLER)

BARRET, E.T.
Write Your Own Business Contracts. (Contracts)

BATTERSBY, GREGORY J. & CHARLES W. GRIMES
The Toy and Game Inventor's Guide for Selling Products. (Inventions and Inventors; Copyrights, Patents, and Trademarks)

BATTLE, CARL W.
Legal-Wise. (General/Comprehensive Works)
Senior Counsel. (Seniors)

BENJAMIN, NANCY H. & MARK WARDA
How to Make an Alabama Will. (Wills, Trusts, and Probate, Alabama)

BENZEL, RICK
Legal Services on Your Home-Based PC. (Computers and Computer Software)

BEREN, PETER (see BUNNIN, BRAD)

BERG, ADRIANE G.
Keys to Avoiding Probate and Reducing Estate Taxes. (Taxation; Wills, Trusts, and Probate)

BERGMAN, PAUL & SARA J. BERMAN-BARRETT
Represent Yourself in Court. (Courts)

BERMAN, DOROTHY MATTHEWS (see MATTHEWS, JOSEPH L.)

BERMAN-BARRETT, SARA J. (see BERGMAN, PAUL)

BERNARD, CLYNE
New York Divorce Book. (Family Law, New York)

BERNBACH, JEFFREY & RAE LINDSAY
Job Discrimination. (Labor)

BERTEAU, JOHN
Estate Planning in Florida. (Estate Planning, Florida)

BIANCHINA, PAUL
How to Hire the Right Contractor. (Construction and Construction Liens)

BIRACREE, TOM
How to Protect Your Spousal Rights. (Family Law)

BLAKEMAN, M.C. (see MANN, STEPHANIE; WOODHOUSE, VIOLET)

BLUE, MARTHA
By the Book. (Writers)

BOTNICK, DAVID I.
Probate Guide For Ontario. (Wills, Trusts, and Probate, Canada)

BOVE, ALEXANDER A.
The Medicaid Planning Handbook. (Social Security and Medicare)

BRALLIER, JESS M. (see SMITH, BRADLEY E.)

BREIMER, STEPHEN F.
Clause by Clause. (Writers)

BRONSTEIN, ALVIN J. (see RUDOVSKY, DAVID)

BROWN, DAVID (see also GOLDOFTAS, LISA; LOEB, DAVID; STEWARD, MARCIA)
Fight Your Ticket . . . and Win! (Criminal Law, California)
The Landlord's Law Book, Vol. 2: Evictions. (Landlord and Tenant, California)

BROWN, DAVID & RALPH WARNER
The Landlord's Law Book, Vol. 1: Rights and Responsibilities. (Landlord and Tenant, California)

BROWN, LUKE S.
Small Claims Court Guide for Florida. (Small Claims Court, Florida)

BROWN, W. DEAN
Incorporating in Alabama. (Business, Alabama)
Incorporating in Arizona. (Business, Arizona)
Incorporating in Arkansas. (Business, Arkansas)
Incorporating in California. (Business, California)
Incorporating in Colorado. (Business, Colorado)
Incorporating in Connecticut. (Business, Connecticut)
Incorporating in Florida. (Business, Florida)
Incorporating in Georgia. (Business, Georgia)
Incorporating in Illinois. (Business, Illinois)
Incorporating in Indiana. (Business, Indiana)
Incorporating in Kansas. (Business, Kansas)
Incorporating in Kentucky. (Business, Kentucky)
Incorporating in Maryland. (Business, Maryland)
Incorporating in Massachusetts. (Business, Massachusetts)
Incorporating in Michigan. (Business, Michigan)
Incorporating in Minnesota. (Business, Minnesota)
Incorporating in Mississippi. (Business, Mississippi)
Incorporating in Missouri. (Business, Missouri)
Incorporating in Nevada. (Business, Nevada)
Incorporating in New Jersey. (Business, New Jersey)
Incorporating in New York. (Business, New York)
Incorporating in North Carolina. (Business, North Carolina)
Incorporating in Ohio. (Business, Ohio)
Incorporating in Oklahoma. (Business, Oklahoma)
Incorporating in Oregon. (Business, Oregon)

Incorporating in Pennsylvania. (Business, Pennsylvania)
Incorporating in Tennessee. (Business, Tennessee)
Incorporating in Texas. (Business, Texas)
Incorporating in Utah. (Business, Utah)
Incorporating in Virginia. (Business, Virginia)
Incorporating in Washington. (Business, Washington)
Incorporating in Wisconsin. (Business, Wisconsin)

BROWN, WILLIAM R.
How to Win in Small Claims Court in Texas. (Small Claims Court, Texas)

BROWN, WILLIAM R. & MARK WARDA
How to Start a Business in Texas. (Business, Texas)
Landlords' Rights and Duties in Texas. (Landlord and Tenant, Texas)

BROWNSON, ANN L.
Judicial Staff Directory. (Directories)

BRUCK, EVA DOMAN (see CRAWFORD, TAD)

BUNNIN, BRAD & PETER BEREN
The Writer's Legal Companion. (Writers)

BURSHTEIN, SHELDON
Patent Your Own Invention in Canada. (Copyrights, Patents, and Trademarks)

CADE, JULIA D. (see RUDOVSKY, DAVID)

CANTER, LAURENCE A. & MARTHA S. SIEGEL
U.S. Immigration Made Easy. (Immigration and Citizenship)

CARLINER, DAVID, LUCAS GUTTENTAG, ARTHUR C. HELTON & WADE J. HENDERSON
The Rights of Aliens and Refugees. (Immigration and Citizenship)

CARRION, RAMON
Guia de Inmigracion a Estados Unidos. (Immigration and Citizenship)
U.S.A. Immigration Guide. (Immigration and Citizenship)

CARROLL, NICHOLAS
Dancing with Lawyers. (Attorney and Client)

CASTELLANO, LUCINDA A. WITH RANDY CHAPMAN & THE LEGAL CENTER
Prentice Hall ADA Compliance Advisor. (ADA and Disability)

CHAMBERS, CAROLE A.
Child Support. (Family Law)

CHAPMAN, RANDY (see CASTELLANO, LUCINDA A.)

CHASEN, JERRY SIMON (see NORWICK, KENNETH P.)

CHRISTIANSON, STEPHEN G.
100 Ways to Avoid Common Legal Pitfalls Without a Lawyer. (General/
     Comprehensive Works)
How to Administer an Estate. (Wills, Trusts, and Probate)

CLARK, WILLIAM D.
Landord/Tenant Rights in Florida. (Landlord and Tenant, Florida)

CLEARY, DAVID & VIRGINIA CLEARY
Retire Smart. (Retirement and Pensions)

CLEARY, VIRGINIA (see CLEARY, DAVID)

CLIFFORD, DENIS (see also CURRY, HAYDEN)
Make Your Own Living Trust. (Wills, Trusts, and Probate)
Nolo's Simple Will Book. (Wills, Trusts, and Probate)
The Partnership Book. (Business; Corporations and Partnerships)
The Power of Attorney Book. (Power of Attorney)
The Quick and Legal Will Book. (Wills, Trusts, and Probate)

CLIFFORD, DENIS & CORA JORDAN
Plan Your Estate. (Estate Planning)

CLIFFORD, DENIS & LISA GOLDOFTAS
Nolo's Law Form Kit: Wills. (Wills, Trusts, and Probate)

CLIFFORD, DENIS, MARY RANDOLPH & LISA GOLDOFTAS
Nolo's Law Form Kit: Power of Attorney. (Power of Attorney)

COLEN, B.D.
The Essential Guide to a Living Will. (Wills, Trusts, and Probate)

COLLINS, GALE FORMAN
Women's Legal Rights in Florida. (Women's Rights, Florida)

COLLINS, VICTORIA F. (see WOODHOUSE, VIOLET)

DAVIS, THOMAS C.
Incorporation and Business Guide for Oregon. (Corporations and Partner-
      ships, Oregon)

DERAMUS, STERLING & EDWARD A. HAMAN
How to File for Divorce in Alabama. (Family Law, Alabama)

DEVINE, GEORGE (see WARNER, RALPH)

DORAN, KENNETH J.
Personal Bankruptcy and Debt Adjustment. (Bankruptcy)

DOWD, MERLE E.
Estate Planning Made Simple. (Estate Planning)

DUBOFF, LEONARD D.
Business Forms and Contracts (in Plain English) for Craftspeople. (Artists
      and Craftspeople)
The Law (in Plain English) for Health Care Professionals. (Health Law)
The Law (in Plain English) for Photographers. (Photography)
The Law (in Plain English) for Small Businesses. (Business)

DUFFY, JAMES P. (see REICH, LAWRENCE P.)

DUNCAN, RODERIC
Everybody's Guide to Municipal Court. (Courts, California)

DUNCAN, RODERIC & WARREN SIEGEL
How to Raise or Lower Child Support in California. (Family Law, California)

DUNLEAVY, PATRICIA GODWIN & MARK WARDA
How to Start and Run a Georgia Business. (Business, Georgia)

DUVERNET, CHRISTOPHER
Photography and the Law. (Photography)

ELDRICH, SARAH D. (see AVERY, MICHAEL)

ELIAS, STEPHEN (SEE ALSO LEONARD, ROBIN; MCGRATH, KATE; WARNER, RALPH)
Nolo's Law Form Kit: Hiring Child Care and Household Help. (Labor)
Patent, Copyright and Trademark. (Copyrights, Patents, and Trademarks)

ELIAS, STEPHEN, ALBIN RENAUER & ROBIN LEONARD
How to File for Bankruptcy. (Bankruptcy)

ELIAS, STEPHEN, ALBIN RENAUER, ROBIN LEONARD & LISA GOLDOFTAS
Nolo's Law Form Kit: Personal Bankruptcy. (Bankruptcy)

ELIAS, STEPHEN & LISA GOLDOFTAS
Nolo's Law Form Kit: Buy & Sell Contracts. (Contracts)

ELIAS, STEPHEN & MARCIA STEWART
Simple Contracts for Personal Use. (Contracts)

ELIAS, STEPHEN & SUSAN LEVINKIND
Legal Research. (Legal Research)

ELIAS, STEPHEN, MARCIA STEWART & LISA GOLDOFTAS
Nolo's Law Form Kit: Loan Agreements. (Debtor and Creditor)

ESPERTI, ROBERT A.
The Loving Trust Workbook. (Wills, Trusts, and Probate)

FAGLIO, ANDREW A.
Lemonaid!: A Layperson's Guide to the Automotive Lemon Laws. (Vehicles)

FARON, FAY
A Private Eye's Guide to Collecting a Bad Dept. (Debtor and Creditor)

FARREN, CAROLYN (see GOLDOFTAS, LISA)

FEARN, JAMES E. (see ISENHOUR, BARBARA A.)

FISHMAN, STEPHEN
The Copyright Handbook. (Copyrights, Patents, and Trademarks)
Copyright Your Software. (Computers and Computer Software)
Hiring Independent Contractors. (Independent Contractors)
Software Development. (Computers and Computer Software)

FOLBERG, JAY
Joint Custody and Shared Parenting. (Family Law)

FRASIER, LYNN ANN
The Small Business Legal Guide. (Business)

FREDENBERG, D. VAN
Wills for Washington. (Wills, Trusts, and Probate, Washington)

FREDRICKSON, STEVE (see ISENHOUR, BARBARA A.)

FREIDMAN, GARY
Taking Charge of Your Own Divorce. (Arbitration; Family Law)

FRIEDMAN, SCOTT E.
Forming Your Own Limited Liability Company. (Corporations and Partnerships)

GADLOW, SANDY
How to Buy the Brooklyn Bridge and Have the Last Laugh. (Real Estate)

GENTRY, F. BRUCE (see APPEL, JENS C.)

GIFIS, STEVEN
Dictionary of Legal Terms. (Dictionaries)

GIMA, PATTI (see GUERIN, LISA)

GINSBURG, WILLIAM L.
Victims' Rights. (Crime and Crime Victims)

GOLDOFTAS, LISA (see also CLIFFORD, DENIS; ELIAS, STEPHEN)

GOLDOFTAS, LISA & CAROLYN FARREN
The Conservatorship Book. (Guardianship and Conservatorship, California)

GOLDOFTAS, LISA & DAVID BROWN
The Guardianship Book. (Guardianship and Conservatorship, California)

GOLDSTEIN, ARNOLD S. & ROBERT L. DAVIDSON
Starting Your Subchapter "S" Corporation. (Corporations and Partnerships)

GOLDSTEIN, PAUL
Copyright's Highway. (Copyrights, Patents, and Trademarks)

GOODART, NAN L.
The Truth About Living Trusts. (Wills, Trusts, and Probate)

GRANATA, FRED A.
Real Estate Buying/Selling Guide for Oregon. (Real Estate, Oregon)

GREENE, JOANNE (see WARNER, RALPH)

GRIMES, CHARLES W. (see BATTERSBY, GREGORY J.)

GRISSOM, FRED & DAVID PRESSMAN
The Inventor's Notebook. (Inventions and Inventors)

GUERIN, LISA & PATTI GIMA
Nolo's Pocket Guide to California Law. (General/Comprehensive Works, California)

GUGGENHEIM, MARTIN
The Rights of Families. (Family Law)

GUTTENTAG, LUCAS (see CARLINER, DAVID)

HAAS, CAROL
The Consumer Reports Law Book. (General/Comprehensive Works)

HAMAN, EDWARD A. (see also CULLEN, THOMAS P.; DERAMUS, STERLING; ROBERTSON, CHARLES T.; ROLCIK, KAREN ANN; STANLEY, JACQUELINE D.)
Florida Power of Attorney Handbook. (Power of Attorney, Florida)
How to File for Divorce in Florida. (Family Law, Florida)
How to File for Divorce in Michigan. (Family Law, Michigan)
How to File Your Own Bankruptcy. (Bankruptcy)
How to File Your Own Divorce. (Family Law)
How to Form Your Own Partnership. (Corporations and Partnerships, Alabama, Florida, Georgia, Louisiana)
How to Modify Your Florida Divorce Judgment. (Family Law, Florida)
How to Write Your Own Premarital Agreement. (Family Law)
The Power of Attorney Handbook. (Power of Attorney)

HAMAN, EDWARD A. & MARK WARDA
How to Make a Michigan Will. (Wills, Trusts, and Probate, Michigan)

HANCOCK, WILLIAM A.
The Small Business Legal Advisor. (Business)

HANLON, R. BRENDAN
The New Tax Guide for Performers, Writers, Directors, Designers, and Other Show Biz Folk. (Taxation)

HARRINGTON, PATRICIA
This Land Is Your Land. (Immigration and Citizenship)

HARTNETT, JOHN
OSHA in the Real World. (Labor)

HAUSER, THOMAS
The Family Legal Companion. (General/Comprehensive Works)

HAYDEN, TRUDY (see HENDRICKS, EVAN)

HAYES, J. MICHAEL
Help Your Lawyer Win Your Case. (Attorney and Client)

HEDGLON, MEAD
How to Get the Best Legal Help for Your Business. (Attorney and Client; Business)

HELTON, ARTHUR C. (see CARLINER, DAVID)

HENDERSON, WADE J. (see CARLINER, DAVID)

HENDRICKS, EVAN, TRUDY HAYDEN & JACK D. NOVIK
Your Right to Privacy. (Privacy)

HERMAN, PETER J.
A Practical Guide to Divorce in Hawaii. (Family Law, Hawaii)

HERSH, ALAN R. (see OUTERBRIDGE, DAVID E.)

HERSKOWITZ, SUSAN
Legal Research Made Easy. (Legal Research)
Wills for Florida. (Wills, Trusts, and Probate, Florida)

HOLSINGER, RALPH L.
Media Law. (Media Law)

HOWELL, JOHN C.
Forming Corporations and Partnerships. (Corporations and Partnerships)

HUGHES, THEODORE E.
The Executor's Handbook. (Wills, Trusts, and Probate)
Own It and Keep It. (Property)

HUNTER, NAN D., SHERRYL E. MICHAELSON & THOMAS B. STODDARD
The Rights of Lesbians and Gay Men. (Gay and Lesbian Rights)

IHARA, TONI (see ALSO WARNER, RALPH)

IHARA, TONI & RALPH WARNER
The Living Together Kit. (Family Law)

ISENHOUR, BARBARA A., JAMES E. FEARN & STEVE FREDRICKSON
Tenants' Rights. (Landlord and Tenant, Washington)

ISSACS, STEPHEN L.
The Consumer's Legal Guide to Today's Health Care. (Health Law)

JACKSON, GORDON E. & STEPHEN L. SHIELDS
How to Defend and Win Labor and Employment Cases. (Labor)

JACOBS, R. & C. KOCH
Legal Compliance Guide to Personnel Management. (Labor)

JENKINS, MICHAEL D. (see SHAW, KAREN A.)

JOEL, LEWIN G.
Every Employee's Guide to the Law. (Labor)

JOHNSON, REES C.
Wills and Estate Planning Handbook for Oregon. (Wills, Trusts, and Probate, Oregon)

JORDAN, CORA (see also CLIFFORD, DENIS)
Neighbor Law. (Neighbor Law, California)

KALENIK, SANDRA
How to Get a Divorce. (Family Law, Maryland, Virginia, Washington, D.C.)

KALMANSON, BARRY
How to File a Florida Construction Lien. (Construction and Construction Liens, Florida)

KAMOROFF, BERNARD
Small Time Operator. (Business)

KAPLIN, WILLIAM A. & BARBARA A. LEE
The Law of Higher Education. (Education)

KAUFMAN, BARBARA
Nolo's Pocket Guide to Consumer's Rights. (Consumer Law, California)

KAUFMAN, HENRY B. (see NORWICK, KENNETH P.)

KAYE, RICHARD L.
Lemon Aid. (Vehicles)

KEMERER, FRANK R. & JIM WALSH
The Educator's Guide to Texas School Law. (Education, Texas)

KEUP, ERWIN J.
*Franchise Bible: Complete Guide to Franchising with Updated UFOC
        Guidelines.* (Franchises)
Mail Order Legal Guide. (Mail Order)

KIMMEL, BARBARA BROOKS
Immigration Made Simple. (Immigration and Citizenship)

KIRK, JOHN
Incorporating Your Business. (Corporations and Partnerships)

KLAVENS, KENT J.
Protecting Your Songs & Yourself. (Copyrights, Patents, and Trademarks;
        Writers)

KLEIN, RAYMOND
Putting a Lid on Legal Fees: How to Deal Effectively with Lawyers.
        (Attorney and Client)

KOCH, C. (see JACOBS, R.)

KOENIG, R. HARRY
How to Lower Your Property Taxes. (Taxation)

KOFF, GAIL J.
The Jacoby and Meyers Guide to Personal Bankruptcy. (Bankruptcy)
The Jacoby and Meyers Guide to Small Claims Litigation. (Small Claims
        Court)
The Jacoby and Meyers Guide to Wills and Estates. (Wills, Trusts, and
        Probate)
The Jacoby & Meyers Practical Guide to Personal Injury. (Personal Injury)

KOREN, EDWARD I. (see RUDOVSKY, DAVID)

KRAEMER, SANDY F.
Sixty Minute Estate Planner. (Taxation)

KRUSE, ANN
Keeping Track. (Record Keeping)

KURZ, RAYMOND A.
Internet and the Law. (Internet)

LEAVY, ROBERT M.
The Rights of Mentally Disabled People. (ADA and Disability)

LEE, BARBARA A. (see KAPLIN, WILLIAM A.)

LEE, ROBERT E.
A Copyright Guide for Authors. (Copyrights, Patents, and Trademarks)

LEEDS, DOROTHY
Smart Questions to Ask Your Lawyer. (Attorney and Client)

LEGAL STAR COMMUNICATIONS (see NOLO PRESS)

LEIMBERG, STEPHAN R. (see PLOTNICK, CHARLES K.)

LELAND, CARYN R.
Licensing, Art and Design. (Artists and Craftspeople)

LEONARD, ROBIN (see ALSO ELIAS, STEPHEN)
Chapter 13 Bankruptcy. (Bankruptcy)
Money Troubles. (Debtor and Creditor)
Nolo's Law Form Kit: Rebuild Your Credit. (Debtor and Creditor)

LEONARD, ROBIN & STEPHEN ELIAS
Nolo's Pocket Guide to Family Law. (Family Law)

LeVALLIANT, TED & MARCEL THEROUX
What's the Verdict? (Courts)

LEVINE, MARK L.
Negotiating a Book Contract. (Writers)

LEVINKIND, SUSAN (see ELIAN, STEPHEN)

LEVY, RICHARD C.
Inventing and Patenting Sourcebook. (Copyrights, Patents, and Trademarks)

LEWIS, LOIDA NICOLAS & LEN T. MADLANSACAY
Como Obtener la Tarjeta Verde. (Immigration and Citizenship)
How to Get a Green Card. (Immigration and Citizenship)

LINDSAY, RAE (see BERNBACH, JEFFREY)

LOEB, DAVID & DAVID BROWN
How to Change Your Name. (Names, California)

LOHMAR, CECIL
Buy More for Less. (Real Estate)

LOVENHEIM, PETER
How to Mediate Your Dispute. (Arbitration and Mediation)

LYNCH, FRANCIS
Draw the Line. (Sexual Harassment)

LYNN, BARRY
The Right to Religious Freedom. (Religion)

MACKEY, PHILIP ENGLISH
The Giver's Guide. (Charities)

MACKIE, SAM A.
How to Form a Nonprofit Corporation in Florida. (Corporations and Partnerships, Florida)

MACSKIMMING, ROY (see ANDERSON, KEITH)

MADLANSACAY, LEN T. (see LEWIS, LOIDA NICOLAS)

MANCUSO, ANTHONY
California Nonprofit Corporation Handbook. (Corporations and Partnerships, California)
California Professional Corporation Handbook. (Corporations and Partnerships, California)
Form Your Own Limited Liability Company. (Corporations and Partnerships)
How to Form a Nonprofit Corporation. (Corporations and Partnerships)

How to Form Your Own California Corporation. (Corporations and Partnerships, California)

How to Form Your Own Florida Corporation. (Corporations and Partnerships, Florida)

How to Form Your Own New York Corporation. (Corporations and Partnerships, New York)

How to Form Your Own Texas Corporation. (Corporations and Partnerships, Texas)

Taking Care of Your Corporation, Vol. 1: Director and Shareholder Meetings Made Easy. (Corporations and Partnerships)

Taking Care of Your Corporation, Vol. 2: Key Corporate Decisions Made Easy. (Corporations and Partnerships)

MANN, STEPHANIE & M.C. BLAKEMAN
Safe Homes, Safe Neighborhoods. (Crime and Crime Victims)

MARAN, MICHAEL
Landlord/Tenant Rights in Oregon. (Landlord and Tenant, Oregon)
The Michigan Divorce Book. (Family Law, Michigan)
The Michigan Power of Attorney Book. (Power of Attorney, Michigan)

MATTHEWS, JOSEPH L.
How to Win Your Personal Injury Claim. (Insurance)

MATTHEWS, JOSEPH L. & DOROTHY MATTHEWS BERMAN
Social Security, Medicare and Pensions. (Social Security and Medicare)

McCORMACK, THOMAS P.
The AIDS Benefits Handbook. (AIDS)

McGRATH, KATE, STEPHEN ELIAS & SARAH SHENA
Trademark. (Copyrights, Patents, and Trademarks)

McGREGOR, RONALD J.
Buying a Business. (Business)

McKEEVER, MIKE
How to Write a Business Plan. (Business)

McKNIGHT, JEAN SINCLAIR
The LEXIS Companion. (Legal Research)

MEYRIC, SANDRA J.
Divorce Guide for Ontario. (Family Law, Canada)

MICHAELSON, SHERRYL E. (see HUNTER, NAN D.)

MIERZWA, JOSEPH
The 21st Century Family Legal Guide. (General/Comprehensive Works)

MILANO, CAROL
Hers: The Wise Woman's Guide to Starting a Business on $2,000 or Less. (Business)

MILKO, GEORGE
Real Estate: The Legal Side to Buying a House, Condo, or Co-op. (Real Estate)

MILKO, GEORGE, KAY OSTBERG & THERESA RUDY
Everyday Contracts. (Contracts)

MILLCROFT, RICHARD K. (see SYDLASKE, JANET M.)

MILTON, JAY WITH GINITA WALL
Cover Your Assets: Lawsuit Protection. (General/Comprehensive Works)

MOSES, EDWARD P. & MARK WARDA
How to Make a Georgia Will. (Wills, Trusts, and Probate, Georgia)

MOSKOVITZ, MYRON & RALPH WARNER
California Tenants' Handbook. (Landlord and Tenant, California)
Tenants' Rights. (Landlord and Tenants, California)

MUNNA, RAYMOND J.
Legal Power for Small Business Owners and Managers. (Business)

MURPHY, SUSAN SCHUERMAN
Legal Handbook for Texas Nurses. (Health Law, Texas)

NAYLOR, WANDA & MARK WARDA
How to Make a North Carolina Will. (Wills, Trusts, and Probate, North Carolina)
How to Start a Business in North Carolina. (Business, North Carolina)

NICHOLAS, TED
How to Form Your Own Corporation without a Lawyer for Under $75.00.
(Corporations and Partnerships)
How to Form Your Own "S" Corporation and Avoid Double Taxation.
(Corporations and Partnerships, Taxation)

NICKEL, GUDRUN M.
Debtors' Rights. (Debtor and Creditor)
How to File a Guardianship in Florida. (Guardianship and Conservator-
ship, Florida)
How to File an Adoption in Florida. (Adoption, Florida)
How to Probate an Estate in Florida. (Wills, Trusts, and Probate, Florida)

NIGITO, DANIEL G.
Avoiding the Estate Tax Trap. (Estate Planning)

NISSLEY, JULIA P.
How to Probate An Estate. (Wills, Trusts, and Probate, California)

NOLO PRESS
Nolo's Partnership Maker. (Corporations and Partnerships)

NOLO PRESS & LEGAL STAR COMMUNICATIONS
Legal Research Made Easy. (Legal Research)

NORWICK, KENNETH P., JERRY SIMON CHASEN & HENRY B. KAUFMAN
The Rights of Authors, Artists, and Other Creative People. (Artists and
Craftspeople)

NOVIK, JACK D. (see HENDRICKS, EVAN)

OSTBERG, KAY (see also MILKO, GEORGE)
Using a Lawyer . . . And What to Do If Things Go Wrong. (Attorney and
Client)

OSTBERG, KAY & THERESA MEEHAN RUDY
If You Want to Sue a Lawyer. (Attorney and Client)

OUTERBRIDGE, DAVID E. & ALAN R. HERSH
Easing the Passage. (Wills, Trusts, and Probate)

PATTERSON, MARK
Divorce Guide for Washington. (Family Law, Washington)

PETROCELLI, WILLIAM & BARBARA KATE REPA
Sexual Harassment on the Job. (Sexual Harassment)

PHILLABAUM, STEPHEN D.
Employee/Employer Rights. (Labor, Washington)

PHILLIPS, ELWOOD
Florida Retirees' Handbook. (Seniors, Florida)

PHILLIPS, PATRICIA
Divorce: A Guide for Women. (Family Law)

PINE TREE LEGAL ASSISTANCE INC. STAFF
Do Your Own Divorce in Maine. (Family Law, Maine)

PLATT, HARVEY J.
Your Living Trust and Estate Plan. (Estate Planning)

PLOTNICK, CHARLES K. & STEPHAN R. LEIMBERG
How to Settle an Estate. (Wills, Trusts, and Probate)

POLAN, DIANE (see AVERY, MICHAEL)

PRESSMAN, DAVID (see also GRISSOM, FRED)
Patent It Yourself. (Copyrights, Patents, and Trademarks)

PURVIN, ROBERT L.
Franchise Fraud. (Franchises)

QUITTNER, MARVIN (see SCHACHNER, ROBERT W.)

RAGGIO, GRIER H.
How to Divorce in New York. (Family Law, New York)

RAMEY, ARDELLA & CARL R.J. SNIFFEN
A Company Policy & Personnel Workbook. (Labor)

RANDOLPH, MARY (see also CLIFFORD, DENIS; ZAGONE, FRANK)
Deeds Book. (Real Estate, California)

Dog Law. (Animals)

RAY, JAMES C.
The Most Valuable Business Forms You'll Ever Need. (Business)

REICH, LAWRENCE R. & JAMES P. DUFFY
You Can Go Bankrupt Without Going Broke. (Bankruptcy)

RENAUER, ALBIN (see ELIAS, STEPHEN)

REPA, KATE (see also PETROCELLI, WILLIAM)
Your Rights in the Workplace. (Labor)

ROBERSON, CLIFF
The McGraw-Hill Personal Tax Advisor. (Taxation)

ROBERTSON, CHARLES T. & EDWARD A. HAMAN
How to File for Divorce in Georgia. (Family Law, Georgia)

ROBINSON, LEIGH
Eviction Book for California. (Landlord and Tenant, California)
Landlording. (Landlord and Tenant)

ROLCIK, KAREN ANN
How to Probate an Estate in Texas. (Wills, Trusts, and Probate, Texas)
Living Trusts and Simple Ways to Avoid Probate. (Wills, Trusts, and Probate)

ROLCIK, KAREN ANN & EDWARD A. HAMAN
How to File for Divorce in Texas. (Family Law, Texas)

ROLCIK, KAREN ANN & MARK WARDA
How to Form a Simple Corporation in Texas. (Corporations and Partnerships, Texas)
How to Make a Texas Will. (Wills, Trusts, and Probate, Texas)

ROSE, I. NELSON
Gambling and the Law. (Gambling)

ROSINI, NEIL J.
The Practical Guide to Libel Law. (Libel and Slander)

ROSS, SUSAN DELLER & ANN BARCHER
The Rights of Women. (Women's Rights)

RUDOVSKY, DAVID, ALVIN J. BRONSTEIN, EDWARD I. KOREN & JULIA D. CADE
The Rights of Prisoners. (Criminal Law)

RUDY, THERESA (see MILKO, GEORGE; OSTBERG, KAY)

RUEBENSTEIN, WILLIAM
The Rights of HIV-Positive People. (AIDS)

SACK, STEVEN MITCHELL
The Employee Rights Handbook. (Labor)

SANDERSON, STEPHEN L.P.
Standard Legal Forms and Agreements for Small Business. (Business)

SARTORIUS III, ARTHUR G. (see WILBUR, W. KELSEA)

SCHACHNER, ROBERT W. & MARVIN QUITTNER
How and When to Be Your Own Lawyer. (General/Comprehensive Works)

SCHUYLER, NINA
The Unemployment Survival Book. (Unemployment)

SCOTT, GINI GRAHAM
Collect Your Court Judgment. (Debtor and Creditor, California; Courts, California)

SEGAL, GARY L.
Immigrating to Canada. (Immigration and Citizenship, Canada)

SERKES, IRA (see WARNER, RALPH)

SHAW, KAREN A., MICHAEL D. JENKINS & ANTHONY J. WALTERS
Starting and Operating a Business in Alabama. (Business, Alabama)
Starting and Operating a Business in Alaska. (Business, Alaska)
Starting and Operating a Business in Arizona. (Business, Arizona)
Starting and Operating a Business in Arkansas. (Business, Arkansas)
Starting and Operating a Business in California. (Business, California)
Starting and Operating a Business in Colorado. (Business, Colorado)
Starting and Operating a Business in Connecticut. (Business, Connecticut)
Starting and Operating a Business in Delaware. (Business, Delaware)
Starting and Operating a Business in Florida. (Business, Florida)
Starting and Operating a Business in Georgia. (Business, Georgia)
Starting and Operating a Business in Hawaii. (Business, Hawaii)
Starting and Operating a Business in Idaho. (Business, Idaho)
Starting and Operating a Business in Illinois. (Business, Illinois)
Starting and Operating a Business in Indiana. (Business, Indiana)

Starting and Operating a Business in Washington, D.C. (Business, Washington, D.C.)
Starting and Operating a Business in West Virginia. (Business, West Virginia)
Starting and Operating a Business in Wisconsin. (Business, Wisconsin)
Starting and Operating a Business in Wyoming. (Business, Wyoming)

SHENA, SARAH (see McGRATH, KATE)

SHERMAN, CHARLES EDWARD (see also WARNER, RALPH)
Practical Divorce Solutions. (Family Law, California)

SHIELDS, STEPHEN L. (see JACKSON, GORDON E.)

SIEGEL, MARTHA J. (see CANTER, LAURENCE A.)

SIEGEL, WARREN (see also DUNCAN, RODERIC)
The Criminal Records Book. (Criminal Law, California)

SIGMAN, ROBERT
Automobile Accidents. (Vehicles)
Bankruptcy. (Bankruptcy)
Collecting Child Support and Alimony. (Family Law)
Contracts. (Contracts)
Family Violence and the Law. (Domestic Violence)
Legal Malpractice. (Attorney and Client)
Medical Malpractice. (Health Law)
Small Claims Court. (Small Claims Court)
Waging Custody Battles. (Family Law)
Wills, Trusts, and Estate Planning. (Wills, Trusts, and Probate)

SITARZ, DANIEL
Complete Book of Personal Legal Forms. (General/Comprehensive Works)
Complete Book of Small Business Legal Forms. (Business)
Debt Free. (Bankruptcy)
Divorce Yourself. (Family Law)
Incorporate Your Business. (Corporations and Partnerships)
Prepare Your Own Will. (Wills, Trusts, and Probate)
Simplified Small Business Accounting. (Business)

SLOAN, IRVING J.
More Everyday Legal Forms. (General/Comprehensive Works)
Rights and Remedies for Senior Citizens. (Seniors)
Wills & Trusts. (Wills, Trusts, and Probate)

SYDLASKE, JANET M. & RICHARD K. MILLCROFT
The Only Tax Audit Guide You'll Ever Need. (Taxation)

TERRY, BRENT
The Complete Idiot's Guide to Protecting Yourself from Everyday Legal Hassles. (General/Comprehensive Works)

THEROUX, MARCEL (see LeVALLIANT, TED)

THOM, PHILLIP L.
Probate Guide for Washington. (Wills, Trusts, and Probate, Washington)

TRULY, TRACI
Grandparents' Rights. (Family Law)

TULLER, LAWRENCE W.
Tap the Hidden Wealth in Your Business. (Business; Corporations and Partnerships)

ULLIAN, LEONARD
In Debt? Help Is on the Way. (Bankruptcy)

VAIL, JASON
Employee/Employer Rights in Florida. (Labor, Florida)

VAN HOF, VICTORIA
Incorporation and Business Guide for Washington. (Corporations and Partnerships)

VENTURA, JOHN
The Bankruptcy Kit. (Bankruptcy)

VICTOROFF, GREGORY T.
The Visual Artist's Business and Legal Guide. (Artists and Craftspeople)

WALL, GINITA (see MILTON, JAY)

WALLACE, L. JEAN

What Every 18-Year-Old Needs to Know About California Law. (General/Comprehensive Works, California)

What Every 18-Year-Old Needs to Know About Texas Law. (General/Comprehensive Works, Texas)

WALSH, JAMES (see also KEMERER, FRANK R.)

Mastering Diversity. (ADA and Disability; Labor)

Rightful Termination. (Labor)

Workers' Comp for Employers. (Workers' Compensation)

WALTERS, ANTHONY J. (see SHAW, KAREN A.)

WARDA, MARK (see also BENJAMIN, NANCY H.; BROWN, WILLIAM R.; CULLEN, THOMAS P.; DUNLEAVY, PATRICIA GODWIN; HAMAN, EDWARD A.; MOSES, EDWARD P.; ROLCIK, KAREN ANN; STANKO, GARY G.)

How to Change Your Name in Florida. (Names, Florida)

How to Form a Simple Corporation in Florida. (Corporations and Partnerships, Florida)

How to Make a Florida Will. (Wills, Trusts, and Probate, Florida)

How to Negotiate Real Estate Contracts. (Real Estate)

How to Negotiate Real Estate Leases. (Real Estate; Landlord and Tenant)

How to Register Your Own Copyright. (Copyrights, Patents, and Trademarks)

How to Register Your Own Trademark. (Copyrights, Patents, and Trademarks)

How to Start a Business in Florida. (Business, Florida)

How to Win in Small Claims Court in Florida. (Small Claims Court, Florida)

Land Trusts in Florida. (Wills, Trusts, and Probate, Florida)

Landlords' Rights and Duties in Florida. (Landlord and Tenant, Florida)

Neighbor vs. Neighbor. (Neighbor Law)

Simple Ways to Protect Yourself from Lawsuits. (General/Comprehensive Works)

WARNER, RALPH (see also BROWN, DAVID; IHARA, TONI; MOSKOVITZ, MYRON; NAYLOR, WANDA; STEWART, MARCIA)

California Marriage & Divorce Law. (Family Law, California)

Everybody's Guide to Small Claims Court. (Small Claims Court)

Everybody's Guide to Small Claims Court in California. (Courts, California)

Get a Life. (Retirement and Pensions)

Getting Started as an Independent Paralegal. (Paralegals)

The Independent Paralegal's Handbook. (Paralegals)

WARNER, RALPH & JOANNE GREENE
5 Ways to Avoid Probate. (Wills, Trusts, and Probate)
How to Start Your Own Business: Small Business Law. (Business)
Winning in Small Claims Court. (Small Claims Court)
Write Your Will. (Wills, Trusts, and Probate)

WARNER, RALPH & MARCIA STEWART
Nolo's Law Form Kit: Leases and Rental Agreements. (Landlord and Tenant)

WARNER, RALPH & STEVEN ELIAS
Fed Up with the Legal System. (General/ Comprehensive Works)

WARNER, RALPH, CHARLES SHERMAN & TONI IHARA
Homestead Your House. (Real Estate, California)

WARNER, RALPH, IRA SERKES & GEORGE DEVINE
How to Buy a House in California. (Real Estate, California)

WATERS, ROBERT C.
Corporation. (Business, Florida; Corporations and Partnerships, Florida)
Divorce Guide for Florida. (Family Law, Florida)
Incorporation and Business Guide for Florida. (Corporations and Parner-
        ships, Florida)
Kids, the Law, and You. (Children)

WEAVER, JEFFERSON HANE
The Compact Guide to Property Law. (Real Estate)

WEBER, DORON
The Complete Guide to Living Wills. (Wills, Trusts, and Probate)

WECHSLER, MARY
Marriage, Separation, Divorce, and Your Rights. (Family Law, Washington)

WEISS, DONALD H.
Fair, Square and Legal: Safe Hiring, Managing and Firing Practices. (Labor)

WEISSER, HERB
Divorce Guide for Oregon. (Family Law, Oregon)

WHITEHEAD, JOHN W.
The Rights of Religious Persons. (Religion)

WHITTINGHAM, NIKKI
Do-It-Yourself Divorce. (Family Law, Illinois)

WILBER, W. KELSEA
Small Claims Court Without a Lawyer. (Small Claims Court)

WILBER, W. KELSEA & ARTHUR G. SARTORIUS III
How to Form Your Own Corporation. (Corporations and Partnerships)

WILLIAMS, PHILLIP G.
How to Form Your Own Indiana Corporation Before the Inc. Dries! (Corporations and Partnerships, Indiana)
How to Form Your Own Missouri Corporation Before the Inc. Dries! (Corporations and Partnerships, Missouri)

WILLIAMSON, GORDON
Your Living Trust. (Wills, Trusts, and Probate)

WILSON, LEE
Make It Legal. (Artists and Craftspeople; Copyrights, Patents, and Trademarks)

WONG, STEVEN G.
Wills for British Columbia. (Wills, Trusts, and Probate, Canada)

WOODHOUSE, VIOLET, VICTORIA F. COLLINS & M.C. BLAKEMAN
Divorce and Money. (Family Law)

ZAGONE, FRANK & MARY RANDOLPH
How to Adopt Your Stepchild in California. (Adoption, California)

ZGARELLI, MICHAEL A.
Can They Do That?: A Guide to Your Rights on the Job. (Labor)

TITLE INDEX

AIDS Benefits Handbook. McCormack, Thomas P. 1990. (AIDS)

American Bar Association Family Legal Guide. American Bar Association. 1994. (General/Comprehensive Works)

American Bar Association Guide to Home Ownership: The Complete and Easy Guide to All the Law Every Home Owner Should Know. American Bar Association. 1995. (Real Estate)

American Bar Association Guide to Wills and Estates. American Bar Association. 1995. (Wills, Trusts, and Probate)

Art, the Art of Community, and the Law: A Legal and Business Guide for Artists, Collectors, Gallery Owners, and Curators. 1994. (Artists and Craftspeople)

Automobile Accidents. Sigman, Robert. 1990. (Vehicles)

Avoiding the Estate Tax Trap. Nigito, Daniel G. 1991. (Estate Planning)

Bankruptcy. Sigman, Robert. 1990. (Bankruptcy)

Bankruptcy Kit. Ventura, John. 1996. (Bankruptcy)

Business and Legal Forms for Authors and Self-Publishers. Crawford, Tad. 1990. (Writers)

Business and Legal Forms for Fine Artists. Crawford, Tad. 1990. (Artists and Craftspeople)

Business and Legal Forms for Graphic Designers. Crawford, Tad & Eva Doman Bruck. 1990. (Artists and Craftspeople)

Business and Legal Forms for Illustrators. Crawford, Tad. 1990. (Illustrators, Artists, and Craftspeople)

Business and Legal Forms for Photographers. Crawford, Tad. 1991. (Photography)

Business Forms and Contracts (in Plain English) for Craftspeople. DuBoff,
Leonard D. 1990. (Artists and Craftspeople)

Buy More for Less: How to Make Sure You Get Your Money's Worth.
Lohmar, Cecil. 1990. (Real Estate)

Buying a Business: A Step-by-Step Guide. McGregor, Ronald J. 1990.
(Business)

By the Book: Legal ABCs for the Printed Word. Blue, Martha. 1990. (Writers)

California Marriage & Divorce Law. Warner, Ralph E. 1992. (Family Law,
California)

California Nonprofit Corporation Handbook. Mancuso, Anthony. 1992.
(Corporations and Partnerships, California)

California Professional Corporation Handbook. Mancuso, Anthony. 1996.
(Corporations and Partnerships, California)

California Tenants' Handbook: Tenants' Rights. Moskovitz, Myron & Ralph
Warner. 1994. (Landlord and Tenant, California)

Can They Do That?: A Guide to Your Rights on the Job. Zgarelli, Michael A.
1994. (Labor)

Chapter 13 Bankruptcy. Leonard, Robin. 1994. (Bankruptcy)

Child Support: How to Get What Your Child Needs and Deserves.
Chambers, Carole A. 1991. (Family Law)

Clause by Clause: The Screenwriter's Legal Guide. Breimer, Stephen F.
1995. (Writers)

Collect Your Court Judgment. Scott, Gini Graham. 1992. (Courts, California; Debtor and Creditor, California)

Collecting Child Support and Alimony. Sigman, Robert. 1990. (Family Law)

*Como Obtener la Tarjeta Verde: Maneras Legistimas de Permanecer en los
Estado Unidos.* Lewis, Loida Nicolas & Len T. Madlansacay. 1994.
(Immigration and Citizenship)

Compact Guide to Property Law: A Civilized Approach to the Law.
Weaver, Jefferson Hane. 1992. (Real Estate)

Company Policy & Personnel Workbook. Ramey, Ardella & Carl R.J.
Sniffen. 1991. (Labor)

Cover Your Assets: Lawsuit Protection; How to Safeguard Yourself, Your Family, and Your Business in the Litigation Jungle. Milton, Jay with Ginita Wall. 1995. (General/Comprehensive Works)

Criminal Records Book. Siegel, Warren. 1995. (Criminal Law, California)

Dancing With Lawyers: How to Take Charge and Get Results. Carroll, Nicholas. 1992. (Attorney and Client)

Debt Free: The National Bankruptcy Kit. Sitarz, Daniel. 1995. (Bankruptcy)

Debtors' Rights: A Legal Self Help Guide with Forms. Nickel, Gudrun M. 1996. (Debtor and Creditor)

Deeds Book: How to Transfer Title to Real Estate. Randolph, Mary. 1994. (Real Estate, California)

Dictionary of Legal Terms. Gifis, Steven. 1993. (Dictionaries)

Divorce and Money: How to Make the Best Financial Decisions During Divorce. Woodhouse, Violet, Victoria F. Collins & M.C. Blakeman. 1992. (Family Law)

Divorce Guide for Florida. Waters, Robert C. 1992. (Family Law, Florida)

Divorce Guide for Ontario: Step-by-Step Guide for Obtaining Your Own Divorce. Meyric, Sandra J. 1995. (Family Law, Canada)

Divorce Guide for Oregon. Baldwin, Richard C. 1993. (Family Law, Oregon)

Divorce Guide for Oregon: Step-by-Step Guide for Obtaining Your Own Divorce. Weisser, Herb. 1993. (Family Law, Oregon)

Divorce Guide for Washington: Step-by-Step Guide for Obtaining Your Own Divorce. Patterson, Mark. 1994. (Family Law, Washington)

Divorce Yourself: The National No-Fault Divorce Kit. Sitarz, Daniel. 1994. (Family Law)

Divorce: A Guide for Women: What Every Woman Needs to Know About Getting a Fair Divorce Even When She Thinks She Doesn't Need to Know It. Phillips, Patricia. 1995. (Family Law)

Do-It-Yourself Divorce: Cook County, Illinois. Whittingham, Nikki. 1990. (Family Law, Illinois)

Do Your Own Divorce in Connecticut. Avery, Michael, Diane Polan & Sarah D. Eldrich. 1991. (Family Law, Connecticut)

Everybody's Guide to Municipal Court. Duncan, Roderic. 1991. (Courts, California)

Everybody's Guide to Municipal Court: Sue and Defend Cases for Up to $25,000. Duncan, Roderic. 1992. (Courts, California)

Everybody's Guide to Small Claims Court. Warner, Ralph. 1995. (Small Claims Court)

Everybody's Guide to Small Claims Court in California. Warner, Ralph. 1995. (Courts, California)

Everyday Contracts: Protecting Your Rights, A Step-by-Step Guide. Milko, George, Kay Ostberg & Theresa Rudy. 1991. (Contracts)

Eviction Book for California. Robinson, Leigh. 1995. (Landlord and Tenant, California)

Eviction Forms Creator Software for Windows. 1994. (Landlord and Tenant)

Executor's Handbook: A Step-by-Step Guide to Settling an Estate for Personal Representatives and Administrators. Hughes, Theodore E. 1994. (Wills, Trusts, and Probate)

Fair, Square and Legal: Safe Hiring, Managing and Firing Practices to Keep You and Your Company Out of Court. Weiss, Donald H. 1995. (Labor)

Faith and Freedom: A Complete Handbook for Defending Your Religious Rights. Staver, Matthew D. 1995. (Religion)

Family Legal Companion. Hauser, Thomas. 1992. (General/Comprehensive Works)

Family Violence and the Law. Sigman, Robert. 1990. (Domestic Violence)

Fed Up with the Legal System: What's Wrong and How to Fix It. Warner, Ralph & Steven Elias. 1994. (General/Comprehensive Works)

Fight Your Ticket . . . and Win! Brown, David. 1995. (Criminal Law, California)

5 Ways to Avoid Probate. 1993. (Wills, Trusts, and Probate)

Florida Power of Attorney Handbook. 1994. (Power of Attorney, Florida)

Florida Retirees' Handbook: Answers to Your Legal and Financial Questions. 1993. (Seniors, Florida)

Homestead Your House. Warner, Ralph, Charles Sherman & Toni Ihara. 1992. (Real Estate, California)

How and When to Be Your Own Lawyer: A Step-by-Step Guide to Effectively Using the Legal System. Schachner, Robert W. & Marvin Quittner. 1993. (General/Comprehensive Works)

How to Administer an Estate: A Step-by-Step Guide for Families and Friends. Christianson, Stephen G. 1993. (Wills, Trusts, and Probate)

How to Adopt Your Stepchild in California. Zagone, Frank & Mary Randolph. 1994. (Adoption, California)

How to Beat the I.R.S. at Its Own Game: Strategies to Avoid—and Fight—an Audit. Aczel, Amir D. 1995. (Taxation)

How to Buy a House in California. Warner, Ralph, Ira Serkes & George Devine. 1994. (Real Estate, California)

How to Buy the Brooklyn Bridge and Have the Last Laugh. Gadlow, Sandy. 1993. (Real Estate)

How to Buy the Right Insurance at the Right Price. (Bailard, Biehl & Kaiser, Inc.) 1995. (Insurance)

How to Change Your Name. Loeb, David & David Brown. 1994. (Names, California)

How to Change Your Name in Florida. Warda, Mark. 1995. (Names, Florida)

How to Defend and Win Labor and Employment Cases. Jackson, Gordon E. & Stephen L. Shields. 1992. (Labor)

How to Divorce in New York: Negotiating Your Divorce Settlement Without Tears or Trial. Raggio, Grier H. 1993. (Family Law, New York)

How to File a Florida Construction Lien (and Collect!). Kalmanson, Barry. 1995. (Construction and Construction Liens, Florida)

How to File a Guardianship in Florida. Nickel, Gudrun M. 1993. (Guardianship and Conservatorship, Florida)

How to File an Adoption in Florida. Nickel, Gudrun M. 1993. (Adoption, Florida)

How to File for Bankruptcy. Elias, Stephen, Albin Renauer & Robin Leonard. 1995. (Bankruptcy)

How to File for Divorce in Alabama. DeRamus, Sterling & Edward A. Haman. 1995. (Family Law, Alabama)

How to Form Your Own Florida Corporation. Mancuso, Anthony. 1991. (Corporations and Partnerships, Florida)

How to Form Your Own Indiana Corporation Before the Inc. Dries! Williams, Phillip G. 1992. (Corporations and Partnerships, Indiana)

How to Form Your Own Missouri Corporation Before the Inc. Dries! Williams, Phillip G. 1992. (Corporations and Partnerships, Missouri)

How to Form Your Own New York Corporation. Mancuso, Anthony. 1994. (Corporations and Partnerships, New York)

How to Form Your Own Partnership. Haman, Edward A. 1995. (Corporations and Partnerships, Alabama, Florida, Georgia, Louisiana, Mississippi, North Carolina, South Carolina, Texas)

How to Form Your Own Texas Corporation. Mancuso, Anthony. 1989. (Corporations and Partnerships, Texas)

How to Get a Divorce: A Practical Guide for the Residents of the District of Columbia, Maryland & Virginia Who Are Contemplating Divorce. Kalenik, Sandra. 1991. (Family Law, Maryland, Virginia, Washington, D.C.)

How to Get a Green Card: Legal Ways to Stay in the U.S.A. Lewis, Loida Nicolas & Len T. Madlansacay. 1993. (Immigration and Citizenship)

How to Get the Best Legal Help for Your Business (At the Lowest Possible Cost). Hedglon, Mead. 1992. (Attorney and Client; Business)

How to Handle Your Workers' Compensation Claim: A Complete Guide for Employees. Ball, Christopher A. 1995. (Workers' Compensation)

How to Hire the Right Contractor: Getting the Right Prices, Workmanship and Scheduling for Home Remodeling. Bianchina, Paul. 1991. (Construction and Construction Liens)

How to Lower Your Property Taxes. Koenig, R. Harry. 1991. (Taxation)

How to Legally Change Your Name Without a Lawyer. Anosike, Benji O. 1991. (Names, New York)

How to Make a Florida Will. Warda, Mark. 1995. (Wills, Trusts, and Probate, Florida)

How to Make a Georgia Will. Moses, Edward P. & Mark Warda. 1996. (Wills, Trusts, and Probate, Georgia)

How to Make a Michigan Will. Haman, Edward A. & Mark Warda. 1995. (Wills, Trusts, and Probate, Michigan)

How to Start a Business in Alabama. Stanko, Gary G. & Mark Warda. 1994. (Business, Alabama)

How to Start a Business in Florida. Warda, Mark. 1995. (Business, Florida)

How to Start a Business in North Carolina. Naylor, Wanda & Mark Warda. 1994. (Business, North Carolina)

How to Start a Business in Texas. Brown, William R. & Mark Warda. 1994. (Business, Texas)

How to Start and Run a Georgia Business. Dunleavy, Patricia Godwin & Mark Warda. 1995. (Business, Georgia)

How to Start Your Own Business: Small Business Law. Warner, Ralph & Joanne Greene. 1993. (Business)

How to Start Your Own Subchapter S Corporation. Cooke, Robert A. 1995. (Corporations and Partnerships)

How to Survive a Lawyer. Baker, Stephen. 1991. (Attorney and Client)

How to Win in Small Claims Court in Florida. Warda, Mark. 1994. (Small Claims Court, Florida)

How to Win in Small Claims Court in Texas. Brown, William R. 1995. (Small Claims Court, Texas)

How to Win Your Personal Injury Claim. Matthews, Joseph L. 1992. (Insurance)

How to Write a Business Plan. McKeever, Mike. 1992. (Business)

How to Write Your Own Premarital Agreement. Haman, Edward A. 1993. (Family Law)

If You Want to Sue a Lawyer—A Directory of Legal Malpractice Attorneys. Ostberg, Kay & Theresa Meehan Rudy. 1995. (Attorney and Client)

Immigrating to Canada: Who Is Allowed? What Is Required? How to Do It! Segal, Gary L. 1994. (Immigration and Citizenship)

Immigration Made Simple: An Easy to Read Guide to the U.S. Immigration Process. Kimmel, Barbara Brooks. 1990. (Immigration and Citizenship)

Immigration Questions and Answers. Baldwin, Carl R. 1995. (Immigration and Citizenship)

In Debt? Help Is on the Way: From Financial Distress to Financial Relief: A Consumer's Guide to Resolving Your Financial Problems,

Understanding the Benefits of Personal Bankruptcy. Ullian, Leonard. 1991. (Bankruptcy)

In Trouble? 104 Legal Ways Out. 1991. (General/Comprehensive Works)

Incorporate Your Business: The National Corporation Kit. Sitarz, Dan. 1995. (Business, Corporations and Partnerships)

Incorporating in Alabama. Brown, W. Dean. 1991. (Business, Alabama)

Incorporating in Arizona. Brown, W. Dean. 1991. (Business, Arizona)

Incorporating in Arkansas. Brown, W. Dean. 1991. (Business, Arkansas)

Incorporating in California. Brown, W. Dean. 1991. (Business, California)

Incorporating in Colorado. Brown, W. Dean. 1991. (Business, Colorado)

Incorporating in Connecticut. Brown, W. Dean. 1991. (Business, Connecticut)

Incorporating in Florida. Brown, W. Dean. 1991. (Business, Florida)

Incorporating in Georgia. Brown, W. Dean. 1991. (Business, Georgia)

Incorporating in Illinois. Brown, W. Dean. 1991. (Business, Illinois)

Incorporating in Indiana. Brown, W. Dean. 1991. (Business, Indiana)

Incorporating in Kansas. Brown, W. Dean. 1991. (Business, Kansas)

Incorporating in Kentucky. Brown, W. Dean. 1991. (Business, Kentucky)

Incorporating in Maryland. Brown, W. Dean. 1991. (Business, Maryland)

Incorporating in Massachusetts. Brown, W. Dean. 1991. (Business, Massachusetts)

Incorporating in Michigan. Brown, W. Dean. 1991. (Business, Michigan)

Incorporating in Minnesota. Brown, W. Dean. 1991. (Business, Minnesota)

Incorporating in Mississippi. Brown, W. Dean. 1991. (Business, Mississippi)

Incorporating in Missouri. Brown, W. Dean. 1991. (Business, Missouri)

Incorporating in Nevada. Brown, W. Dean. 1991. (Business, Nevada)

Incorporating in New Jersey. Brown, W. Dean. 1991. (Business, New Jersey)

Incorporating in New York. Brown, W. Dean. 1991. (Business, New York)

Incorporating in North Carolina. Brown, W. Dean. 1991. (Business, North Carolina)

Incorporating in Ohio. Brown, W. Dean. 1991. (Business, Ohio)

Incorporating in Oklahoma. Brown, W. Dean. 1991. (Business, Oklahoma)

Incorporating in Oregon. Brown, W. Dean. 1991. (Business, Oregon)

Incorporating in Pennsylvania. Brown, W. Dean. 1991. (Business, Pennsylvania)

Incorporating in Tennessee. Brown, W. Dean. 1991. (Business, Tennessee)

Incorporating in Texas. Brown, W. Dean. 1991. (Business, Texas)

Incorporating in Utah. Brown, W. Dean. 1991. (Business, Utah)

Incorporating in Virginia. Brown, W. Dean. 1991. (Business, Virginia)

Incorporating in Washington. Brown, W. Dean. 1991. (Business, Washington)

Incorporating in Wisconsin. Brown, W. Dean. 1991. (Business, Wisconsin)

Incorporating Your Business. Kirk, John. 1994. (Corporations and Partnerships)

Incorporation and Business Guide for Florida: How to Form Your Own Corporation. Waters, Robert C. 1992. (Business, Florida)

Incorporation and Business Guide for Oregon: How to Form Your Own Corporation. Davis, Thomas C. 1992. (Corporations and Partnerships, Oregon)

Incorporation and Business Guide for Washington: How to Form Your Own Corporation. Van Hof, Victoria. 1993. (Corporations and Partnerships)

Independent Paralegal's Handbook. Warner, Ralph. 1994. (Paralegal)

Internet and the Law. Kurz, Raymond A. 1996. (Internet)

Inventing and Patenting Sourcebook: How to Sell and Protect Your Ideas. Levy, Richard C. 1990. (Copyrights, Patents, and Trademarks)

Inventor's Notebook. Grissom, Fred & David Pressman. 1989. (Inventions and Inventors)

Jacoby and Meyers Guide to Personal Bankruptcy. Koff, Gail J. 1991. (Bankruptcy)

Jacoby and Meyers Guide to Small Claims Litigation. Koff, Gail J. 1991. (Small Claims Courts)

Jacoby and Meyers Guide to Wills and Estates. American Bar Association. 1991. (Wills, Trusts, and Probate)

Jacoby & Meyers Practical Guide to Personal Injury. Koff, Gail J. 1991. (Personal Injury)

Job Discrimination: How to Fight, How to Win. Bernbach, Jeffrey & Rae Lindsay. 1996. (Labor)

Joint Custody and Shared Parenting. Folberg, Jay. 1991. (Family Law)

Judicial Staff Directory. Brownson, Ann L. 1996. (Directories)

Keeping Track: An Organizer for Your Legal, Business, and Personal Records. Kruse, Ann. 1991. (Record Keeping)

Keys to Avoiding Probate and Reducing Estate Taxes. Berg, Adriane G. 1992. (Taxation; Wills, Trusts, and Probate)

Kids, the Law, and You. Waters, Robert C. 1994. (Children)

Know Your Rights, and How to Make Them Work for You. 1995. (General/Comprehensive Works)

Land Trusts in Florida. Warda, Mark. 1995. (Wills, Trusts, and Probate, Florida)

Landlord/Tenant Rights for Washington. Strong, Sidney J. 1993. (Landlord and Tenant, Washington)

Landlords' Rights and Duties in Florida. Warda, Mark. 1994. (Landlord and Tenant, Florida)

Landord/Tenant Rights in Florida. Clark, William D. 1993. (Landlord and Tenant, Florida)

Landlord/Tenant Rights in Oregon. Marcus, Michael. 1994. (Landlord and Tenant, Oregon)

Landlord's Law Book, Vol. 1: Rights and Responsibilities. Brown, David & Ralph Warner. 1994. (Landlord and Tenant, California)

Landlord's Law Book, Vol. 2: Evictions. Brown, David. 1994. (Landlord and Tenant, California)

LANDLORDING™ (The Forms Diskette). 1994. (Landlord and Tenant)

Landlording: A Handymanual for Scrupulous Landlords and Landladies Who Do It Themselves. Robinson, Leigh. 1995. (Landlord and Tenant)

Landlords' Rights and Duties in Texas. Brown, William R. & Mark Warda. 1994. (Landlord and Tenant, Texas)

Law (in Plain English) for Health Care Professionals. DuBoff, Leonard D. 1993. (Health Law)

Law (in Plain English) for Photographers. DuBoff, Leonard. 1995. (Photography)

Law (in Plain English) for Small Businesses. DuBoff, Leonard D. 1991. (Business)

Law of Higher Education. Kaplin, William A. & Barbara A. Lee. 1995. (Education)

Legal Breakdown: 40 Ways to Fix Our Legal System. 1990. (General/Comprehensive Works)

Legal Compliance Guide to Personnel Management. Jacobs, R. & C. Koch. 1993. (Labor)

Legal Expense Defense: How to Control Your Business' Legal Costs and Problems. 1995. (Business; Corporations and Partnerships)

Legal Guide for Lesbian and Gay Couples. Curry, Hayden & Denis Clifford. 1991. (Gay and Lesbian Rights)

Legal Guide for Starting and Running a Small Business. Steingold, Fred. 1995. (Business)

Legal Guide for the Visual Artist. Crawford, Tad. 1990. (Artists and Craftspeople)

Legal Handbook for Texas Nurses. Murphy, Susan Schuerman. 1995. (Health Law, Texas)

Legal Malpractice. Sigman, Robert. 1990. (Attorney and Client)

Legal Power for Small Business Owners and Managers. Munna, Raymond J. 1991. (Business)

Legal Research: How to Find and Understand the Law. Elias, Stephen & Susan Levinkind. 1995. (Legal Research)

Legal Research Made Easy. Herskowitz, Susan. 1995. (Legal Research)

Legal Research Made Easy: A Roadmap Through the Law Library Maze. Nolo Press & Legal Star Communications. 1990. (Legal Research)

Legal Rights for Seniors: A Guide to Health Care, Income Benefits & Senior Legal Services. Smith, Wesley J. 1993. (Seniors)

Medicaid Planning Handbook: A Guide to Protecting Your Family's Assets from Nursing Home Costs. Bove, Alexander A. 1996. (Social Security and Medicare)

Medical Malpractice. Sigman, Robert. 1990. (Health Law)

Michigan Divorce Book: A Guide to Doing an Uncontested Divorce Without an Attorney. Maran, Michael. 1993. (Family Law, Michigan)

Michigan Power of Attorney Book: A Guide to Making Financial, Health Care and Custodial Powers of Attorney Without a Lawyer. Maran, Michael. 1991. (Power of Attorney, Michigan)

Money Troubles: Legal Strategies to Cope with Your Debts. Leonard, Robin. 1991. (Debtor and Creditor)

More Everyday Legal Forms. Sloan, Irving J. 1992. (General/Comprehensive Works)

Most Valuable Business Forms You'll Ever Need. Ray, James C. 1996. (Business)

Most Valuable Corporate Forms You'll Ever Need. Ray, James C. 1995. (Corporations and Partnerships)

Negotiating a Book Contract: A Guide for Authors, Agents and Lawyers. Levine, Mark L. 1988. (Writers)

Neighbor Law: Fences, Trees, Boundaries, and Noise. Jordan, Cora. 1994. (Neighbor Law, California)

Neighbor vs. Neighbor: Legal Rights of Neighbors in Dispute. Warda, Mark. 1991. (Neighbor Law)

New Tax Guide for Performers, Writers, Directors, Designers, and Other Show Biz Folk. Hanlon, R. Brendan. 1994. (Taxation)

New York Divorce Book: Step-by-Step Guide with Forms. Bernard, Clyne. 1993. (Family Law, New York)

Nolo's Law Form Kit: Buy & Sell Contracts: Bills of Sale for Cars, Boats, Electronic Equipment and Other Personal Property. Elias, Stephen & Lisa Goldoftas. 1993. (Contracts)

Nolo's Law Form Kit: Hiring Child Care and Household Help. Elias, Stephen. 1994. (Labor)

Nolo's Law Form Kit: Leases and Rental Agreements. Warner, Ralph & Marcia Stewart. 1994. (Landlord and Tenant)

Nolo's Law Form Kit: Loan Agreements: Borrow and Lend Money. Elias, Stephen, Marcia Stewart & Lisa Goldoftas. 1993. (Debtor and Creditor)

Nolo's Law Form Kit: Personal Bankruptcy. Elias, Steve, Albin Renauer, Robin Leonard & Lisa Goldoftas. 1993. (Bankruptcy)

Nolo's Law Form Kit: Power of Attorney. Clifford, Denis, Mary Randolph & Lisa Goldoftas. 1993. (Power of Attorney)

Nolo's Law Form Kit: Rebuild Your Credit: Solve Your Debt Problems. Leonard, Robin. 1993. (Debtor and Creditor)

Nolo's Law Form Kit: Wills. Clifford, Denis & Lisa Goldoftas. 1993. (Wills, Trusts, and Probate)

Nolo's Partnership Maker. Nolo Press. 1994. (Corporations and Partnerships)

Nolo's Pocket Guide to California Law. Guerin, Lisa & Patti Gima. 1994. (General/Comprehensive Works, California)

Nolo's Pocket Guide to Consumer's Rights: A Resource for All Californians. Kaufman, Barbara. 1994. (Consumer Law, California)

Nolo's Pocket Guide to Family Law. Leonard, Robin & Stephen Elias. 1996. (Family Law)

Nolo's Simple Will Book. Clifford, Denis. 1989. (Wills, Trusts, and Probate)

OSHA in the Real World: Cutting Through the Regulatory Knot: Taking Control Series. Hartnett, John. 1995. (Labor)

On Your Own Again: The Down-to-Earth Guide to Getting Through a Divorce or Separation & Getting on with Your Life. Anderson, Keith & Roy MacSkimming. 1992. (Family Law)

100 Ways to Avoid Common Legal Pitfalls Without a Lawyer. Christianson, Stephen G. 1992. (General/Comprehensive Works)

104 Legal Secrets Before You Say I Do. 1991. (Family Law)

Only Tax Audit Guide You'll Ever Need. Sydlaske, Janet M. & Richard K. Millcroft. 1990. (Taxation)

Own It and Keep It. Hughes, Theodore E. 1995. (Property)

Partnership Book: How to Write a Partnership Agreement: Sample Clauses for All Key Issues. Clifford, Denis. 1991. (Business; Corporations and Partnerships)

Patent, Copyright and Trademark: A Desk Reference to Intellectual Property Law. Elias, Stephen. 1996. (Copyrights, Patents, and Trademarks)

Patent It Yourself. Pressman, David. 1991. (Copyrights, Patents, and Trademarks)

Patent Law for the Nonlawyer: A Guide for the Engineer, Technologist, and Manager. Amernick, Burton A. 1991. (Copyrights, Patents, and Trademarks)

Patent Your Own Invention in Canada: A Complete Step-by-Step Guide. Burshtein, Sheldon. 1991. (Copyrights, Patents, and Trademarks)

Personal Bankruptcy and Debt Adjustment: The Fresh Start, A Step-by-Step Guide. Doran, Kenneth J. 1991. (Bankruptcy)

Photography and the Law: A Guide for Amateur and Professional Photographers. Duvernet, Christopher. 1991. (Photography; Photography, Canada)

Plan Your Estate. Clifford, Denis & Cora Jordan. 1994. (Estate Planning)

Planning for Incapacity: A Self-Help Guide. (Seniors)

Power of Attorney Book. Clifford, Denis. 1991. (Power of Attorney)

Power of Attorney Handbook. Haman, Edward A. 1994. (Power of Attorney)

Practical Divorce Solutions. Sherman, Charles Edward. 1994. (Family Law, California)

Practical Guide to Divorce in Hawaii. Herman, Peter J. 1991. (Family Law, Hawaii)

Practical Guide to Libel Law. Rosini, Neil J. 1991. (Libel and Slander)

Prentice Hall ADA Compliance Advisor. Castellano, Lucinda A., Randy Chapman & The Legal Center. 1993. (ADA and Disability)

Prepare Your Own Will: The National Will Kit. Sitarz, Daniel. 1994. (Wills, Trusts, and Probate)

Price Waterhouse Personal Tax Advisor. 1994. (Taxation)

Private Eye's Guide to Collecting a Bad Debt. Faron, Fay. 1991. (Debtor and Creditor)

Probate Guide for Ontario: A Step-by-Step Guide to Probating an Estate. Botnick, David I. 1991. (Wills, Trusts, and Probate, Canada)

Rights of Aliens and Refugees: The Basic ACLU Guide to Alien and Refugee Rights. Carliner, David, Lucas Guttentag, Arthur C. Helton & Wade J. Henderson 1990. (Immigration and Citizenship)

Rights of Authors, Artists, and Other Creative People. Norwick, Kenneth P., Jerry Simon Chasen & Henry B. Kaufman. 1992. (Artists and Craftspeople)

Rights of Families. Guggenheim, Martin. 1996. (Family Law)

Rights of HIV-Positive People. Ruebenstein, William. 1996. (AIDS)

Rights of Lesbians and Gay Men: The Basic ACLU Guide to a Gay Person's Rights. Hunter, Nan D., Sherryl E. Michaelson & Thomas B. Stoddard. 1992. (Gay and Lesbian Rights)

Rights of Mentally Disabled People. Leavy, Robert M. 1996. (ADA and Disability)

Rights of Patients: The Basic ACLU Guide to Patient Rights. Annas, George J. 1989. (Health Law)

Rights of Prisoners: The Basic ACLU Guide to Prisoners' Rights. Rudovsky, David, Alvin J. Bronstein, Edward I. Koren & Julia D. Cade. 1988. (Criminal Law)

Rights of Religious Persons. Whitehead, John W. 1994. (Religion)

Rights of Women. Ross, Susan Deller & Ann Barcher. 1993. (Women's Rights)

Safe Homes, Safe Neighborhoods: Stopping Crime Where You Live. Mann, Stephanie & M.C. Blakeman. 1993. (Crime)

Senior Counsel: Legal and Financial Strategies for Age 50 and Beyond. Battle, Carl W. 1993. (Seniors)

Sexual Harassment on the Job: What It Is and How to Stop It. Petrocelli, William & Barbara Kate Repa. 1994. (Sexual Harassment)

Simple Contracts for Personal Use. Elias, Stephen & Marcia Stewart. 1994. (Contracts)

Simple Ways to Protect Yourself from Lawsuits: A Complete Guide to Asset Protection. Warda, Mark. 1996. (General/Comprehensive Works)

Simplified Small Business Accounting. Sitarz, Daniel. 1995. (Business)

Sixty Minute Estate Planner: Fast & Easy Illustrated Plans to Save Taxes, Avoid Probate and Maximize Inheritance. 1994. (Taxation)

Small Business Legal Advisor. Hancock, William A. 1992. (Business)

Starting and Operating a Business in Connecticut. Shaw, Karen A., Michael D. Jenkins & Anthony Walters. 1996. (Business, Connecticut)

Starting and Operating a Business in Delaware. Shaw, Karen A., Michael D. Jenkins & Anthony Walters. 1996. (Business, Delaware)

Starting and Operating a Business in Florida. Shaw, Karen A., Michael D. Jenkins & Anthony Walters. 1996. (Business, Florida)

Starting and Operating a Business in Georgia. Shaw, Karen A., Michael D. Jenkins & Anthony Walters. 1996. (Business, Georgia)

Starting and Operating a Business in Hawaii. Shaw, Karen A., Michael D. Jenkins & Anthony Walters. 1996. (Business, Hawaii)

Starting and Operating a Business in Idaho. Shaw, Karen A., Michael D. Jenkins & Anthony Walters. 1996. (Business, Idaho)

Starting and Operating a Business in Illinois. Shaw, Karen A., Michael D. Jenkins & Anthony Walters. 1996. (Business, Illinois)

Starting and Operating a Business in Indiana. Shaw, Karen A., Michael D. Jenkins & Anthony Walters. 1996. (Business, Indiana)

Starting and Operating a Business in Iowa. Shaw, Karen A., Michael D. Jenkins & Anthony Walters. 1996. (Business, Iowa)

Starting and Operating a Business in Kansas. Shaw, Karen A., Michael D. Jenkins & Anthony Walters. 1996. (Business, Kansas)

Starting and Operating a Business in Kentucky. Shaw, Karen A., Michael D. Jenkins & Anthony Walters. 1996. (Business, Kentucky)

Starting and Operating a Business in Louisiana. Shaw, Karen A., Michael D. Jenkins & Anthony Walters. 1996. (Business, Louisiana)

Starting and Operating a Business in Maine. Shaw, Karen A., Michael D. Jenkins & Anthony Walters. 1996. (Business, Maine)

Starting and Operating a Business in Maryland. Shaw, Karen A., Michael D. Jenkins & Anthony Walters. 1996. (Business, Maryland)

Starting and Operating a Business in Massachusetts. Shaw, Karen A., Michael D. Jenkins & Anthony Walters. 1996. (Business, Massachusetts)

Starting and Operating a Business in Michigan. Shaw, Karen A., Michael D. Jenkins & Anthony Walters. 1996. (Business, Michigan)

Starting and Operating a Business in Minnesota. Shaw, Karen A., Michael D. Jenkins & Anthony Walters. 1996. (Business, Minnesota)

Starting and Operating a Business in South Carolina. Shaw, Karen A., Michael D. Jenkins & Anthony Walters. 1996. (Business, South Carolina)

Starting and Operating a Business in South Dakota. Shaw, Karen A., Michael D. Jenkins & Anthony Walters. 1996. (Business, South Dakota)

Starting and Operating a Business in Tennessee. Shaw, Karen A., Michael D. Jenkins & Anthony Walters. 1996. (Business, Tennessee)

Starting and Operating a Business in Texas. Shaw, Karen A., Michael D. Jenkins & Anthony Walters. 1996. (Business, Texas)

Starting and Operating a Business in Utah. Shaw, Karen A., Michael D. Jenkins & Anthony Walters. 1996. (Business, Utah)

Starting and Operating a Business in Vermont. Shaw, Karen A., Michael D. Jenkins & Anthony Walters. 1996. (Business, Vermont)

Starting and Operating a Business in Virginia. Shaw, Karen A., Michael D. Jenkins & Anthony Walters. 1996. (Business, Virginia)

Starting and Operating a Business in Washington. Shaw, Karen A., Michael D. Jenkins & Anthony Walters. 1996. (Business, Washington)

Starting and Operating a Business in Washington, D.C. Shaw, Karen A., Michael D. Jenkins & Anthony Walters. 1996. (Business, Washington, D.C.)

Starting and Operating a Business in West Virginia. Shaw, Karen A., Michael D. Jenkins & Anthony Walters. 1996. (Business, West Virginia)

Starting and Operating a Business in Wisconsin. Shaw, Karen A., Michael D. Jenkins & Anthony Walters. 1996. (Business, Wisconsin)

Starting and Operating a Business in Wyoming. Shaw, Karen A., Michael D. Jenkins & Anthony Walters. 1996. (Business, Wyoming)

Starting Your Subchapter "S" Corporation: How to Build a Business the Right Way. Goldstein, Arnold S. & Robert L. Davidson. 1992. (Corporations and Partnerships)

Stay Out of Court: The Manager's Guide to Preventing Employee Lawsuits. 1993. (Labor)

Taking Care of Your Corporation, Vol. 1: Director and Shareholder Meetings Made Easy. Mancuso, Anthony. 1994. (Corporations and Partnerships)

Victims' Rights: The Complete Guide to Crime Victim Compensation. Ginsburg, William L. 1994. (Crime and Crime Victims)

Visual Artist's Business and Legal Guide. Victoroff, Gregory T. 1995. (Artists and Craftspeople)

Waging Custody Battles. Sigman, Robert. 1990. (Family Law)

What Every 18-Year-Old Needs to Know About California Law. Wallace, L. Jean. 1994. (General/Comprehensive Works, California)

What Every 18-Year-Old Needs to Know About Texas Law. Wallace, L. Jean. 1994. (General/Comprehensive Works, Texas)

What's the Verdict?: Real Life Court Cases to Test Your Legal IQ. LeValliant, Ted & Marcel Theroux. 1991. (Courts)

WillMaker. Version 6.0. 1995. (Wills, Trusts, and Probate)

Wills & Trusts. Sloan, Irving J. 1992. (Wills, Trusts, and Probate)

Wills: A Do-It-Yourself Guide. Rudy, Theresa. 1992. (Wills, Trusts, and Probate)

Wills and Estate Planning Handbook for Oregon. Johnson, Rees C. 1990. (Wills, Trusts, and Probate, Oregon)

Wills for British Columbia: How to Make Your Own Will. Wong, Steven G. 1990. (Wills, Trusts, and Probate, Canada)

Wills for Florida: How to Make Your Own Will (Includes Forms). Herskowitz, Susan. 1992. (Wills, Trusts, and Probate, Florida)

Wills for Washington. Fredenberg, D. Van. 1992. (Wills, Trusts, and Probate, Washington)

Wills, Trusts, and Estate Planning. Sigman, Robert. 1990. (Wills, Trusts, and Probate)

Winning in Florida Traffic Court. Adkins, John C. 1994. (Traffic Court, Florida)

Winning in Small Claims Court. Warner, Ralph & Joanne Greene. 1993. (Small Claims Court)

Women's Legal Rights in Florida. Collins, Gale Forman. 1993. (Women's Rights, Florida)

Workers' Comp for Employers: How to Cut Claims, Reduce Premiums, and Stay out of Trouble. Walsh, James. 1994. (Workers' Compensation)

Jurisdiction Index

Alabama

How to File for Divorce in Alabama. DeRamus, Sterling & Edward A. Haman (Family Law, Alabama)

How to Form Your Own Partnership. Haman, Edward A. (Corporations and Partnerships, Alabama)

How to Make an Alabama Will. Benjamin, Nancy H. & Mark Warda (Wills, Trusts, and Probate, Alabama)

How to Start a Business in Alabama. Stanko, Gary G. & Mark Warda (Business, Alabama)

Incorporating in Alabama. Brown, W. Dean (Business, Alabama)

Starting and Operating a Business in Alabama. Shaw, Karen A., Michael D. Jenkins & Anthony J. Walters (Business, Alabama)

Alaska

Starting and Operating a Business in Alaska. Shaw, Karen A., Michael D. Jenkins & Anthony J. Walters (Business, Alaska)

Arizona

Incorporating in Arizona. Brown, W. Dean (Business, Arizona)

Starting and Operating a Business in Arizona. Shaw, Karen A., Michael D. Jenkins & Anthony J. Walters (Business, Arizona)

201

ARKANSAS

Incorporating in Arkansas. Brown, W. Dean (Business, Arkansas)

Starting and Operating a Business in Arkansas. Shaw, Karen A., Michael D. Jenkins & Anthony J. Walters (Business, Arkansas)

CALIFORNIA

California Marriage & Divorce Law. Warner, Ralph E. (Family Law, California)

California Nonprofit Corporation Handbook. Mancuso, Anthony (Corporations and Partnerships, California)

California Professional Corporation Handbook. Mancuso, Anthony (Corporations and Partnerships, California)

California Tenants' Handbook: Tenants' Rights. Moskovitz, Myron & Ralph Warner (Landlord and Tenant, California)

Collect Your Court Judgment. Scott, Gini Graham (Courts, California; Debtor and Creditor, California)

Conservatorship Book. Goldoftas, Lisa & Carolyn Farren (Guardianship and Conservatorship, California)

Criminal Records Book. Siegel, Warren (Criminal Law, California)

Deeds Book: How to Transfer Title to Real Estate. Randolph, Mary (Real Estate, California)

Everybody's Guide to Municipal Court. Duncan, Roderic (Courts, California)

Everybody's Guide to Municipal Court: Sue and Defend Cases for Up to $25,000. Duncan, Roderic (Courts, California)

Everybody's Guide to Small Claims Court in California. Warner, Ralph (Courts, California)

Eviction Book for California. Robinson, Leigh (Landlord and Tenant, California)

Fight Your Ticket . . . and Win! Brown, David (Criminal Law, California)

Guardianship Book: How to Become a Child's Guardian in California. Goldoftas, Lisa & David Brown (Guardianship and Conservatorship, California)

CANADA

Divorce Guide for Ontario: Step-By-Step Guide for Obtaining Your Own Divorce. Meyric, Sandra J. (Family Law, Canada)

Photography and the Law: A Guide for Amateur and Professional Photographers. Duvernet, Christopher (Photography, Canada)

Probate Guide For Ontario: A Step-by-Step Guide to Probating an Estate. Botnick, David I. (Wills, Trusts, and Probate, Canada)

Wills for British Columbia: How to Make Your Own Will. Wong, Steven G. (Wills, Trusts, and Probate, Canada)

COLORADO

Incorporating in Colorado. Brown, W. Dean (Business, Colorado)

Starting and Operating a Business in Colorado. Shaw, Karen A., Michael D. Jenkins & Anthony J. Walters (Business, Colorado)

CONNECTICUT

Do Your Own Divorce in Connecticut. Avery, Michael (Family Law, Connecticut)

Incorporating in Connecticut. Brown, W. Dean (Business, Connecticut)

Starting and Operating a Business in Connecticut. Shaw, Karen A., Michael D. Jenkins & Anthony J. Walters (Business, Connecticut)

DELAWARE

Starting and Operating a Business in Delaware. Shaw, Karen A., Michael D. Jenkins & Anthony J. Walters (Business, Delaware)

FLORIDA

Divorce Guide for Florida. Waters, Robert C. (Family Law, Florida)

Employee/Employer Rights in Florida: A Practical, Easy to Understand Guide. Vail, Jason (Labor, Florida)

Estate Planning in Florida. Berteau, John (Estate Planning, Florida)

Landlords' Rights and Duties in Florida. Warda, Mark (Landlord and Tenant, Florida)

Real Estate Buying/Selling Guide for Florida. Badgley, Richard (Landlord and Tenant, Florida)

Small Claims Court Guide for Florida. Brown, Luke S. (Small Claims Court, Florida)

Starting and Operating a Business in Florida. Shaw, Karen A., Michael D. Jenkins & Anthony J. Walters (Business, Florida)

Wills for Florida: How to Make Your Own Will (Includes Forms). Herskowitz, Susan (Wills, Trusts, and Probate, Florida)

Winning in Florida Traffic Court. Adkins, John C. (Traffic Court, Florida)

Women's Legal Rights in Florida. Collins, Gale Forman (Women's Rights, Florida)

GEORGIA

How to File for Divorce in Georgia. Robertson, Charles T. & Edward A. Haman (Family Law, Georgia)

How to Form Your Own Partnership. Haman, Edward A. (Corporations and Partnerships, Georgia)

How to Make a Georgia Will. Moses, Edward P. & Mark Warda (Wills, Trusts, and Probate, Georgia)

How to Start and Run a Georgia Business. Dunleavy, Patricia Godwin & Mark Warda (Business, Georgia)

Incorporating in Georgia. Brown, W. Dean (Business, Georgia)

Starting and Operating a Business in Georgia. Shaw, Karen A., Michael D. Jenkins & Anthony J. Walters (Business, Georgia)

HAWAII

A Practical Guide to Divorce in Hawaii. Herman, Peter J. (Family Law, Hawaii)

Starting and Operating a Business in Hawaii. Shaw, Karen A., Michael D. Jenkins & Anthony J. Walters (Business, Hawaii)

LOUISIANA

How to Form Your Own Partnership. Haman, Edward A. (Corporations and Partnerships, Louisiana)

Starting and Operating a Business in Louisiana. Shaw, Karen A., Michael D. Jenkins & Anthony J. Walters (Business, Louisiana)

MAINE

Do Your Own Divorce in Maine. Pine Tree Legal Assistance Inc. Staff (Family Law, Maine)

Starting and Operating a Business in Maine. Shaw, Karen A., Michael D. Jenkins & Anthony J. Walters (Business, Maine)

MARYLAND

How to Get a Divorce: A Practical Guide for the Residents of the District of Columbia, Maryland & Virginia Who Are Contemplating Divorce. Kalenik, Sandra. (Family Law, Maryland)

Incorporating in Maryland. Brown, W. Dean (Business, Maryland)

Starting and Operating a Business in Maryland. Shaw, Karen A., Michael D. Jenkins & Anthony J. Walters (Business, Maryland)

MASSACHUSETTS

Incorporating in Massachusetts. Brown, W. Dean (Business, Massachusettes)

Starting and Operating a Business in Massachusetts. Shaw, Karen A., Michael D. Jenkins & Anthony J. Walters (Business, Massachusetts)

MICHIGAN

How to File for Divorce in Michigan. Haman, Edward A. (Family Law, Michigan)

How to Make a Michigan Will. Haman, Edward A. & Mark Warda (Wills, Trusts, and Probate, Michigan)

Incorporating in Michigan. Brown, W. Dean (Business, Michigan)

Michigan Divorce Book: A Guide to Doing an Uncontested Divorce Without an Attorney. Maran, Michael (Family Law, Michigan)

Michigan Power of Attorney Book: A Guide to Making Financial, Health Care and Custodial Powers of Attorney Without a Lawyer. Maran, Michael (Power of Attorney, Michigan)

Starting and Operating a Business in Michigan. Shaw, Karen A., Michael D. Jenkins & Anthony J. Walters (Business, Michigan)

MINNESOTA

Incorporating in Minnesota. Brown, W. Dean (Business, Minnesota)

Starting and Operating a Business in Minnesota. Shaw, Karen A., Michael D. Jenkins & Anthony J. Walters (Business, Minnesota)

MISSISSIPPI

How to Form Your Own Partnership. Haman, Edward A. (Corporations and Partnerships, Mississippi)

Incorporating in Mississippi. Brown, W. Dean (Business, Mississippi)

Starting and Operating a Business in Mississippi. Shaw, Karen A., Michael D. Jenkins & Anthony J. Walters (Business, Mississippi)

MISSOURI

How to Form Your Own Missouri Corporation Before the Inc. Dries! Williams, Phillip G. (Corporations and Partnerships, Missouri)

Incorporating in Missouri. Brown, W. Dean (Business, Missouri)

Starting and Operating a Business in Missouri. Shaw, Karen A., Michael D. Jenkins & Anthony J. Walters (Business, Missouri)

MONTANA

Starting and Operating a Business in Montana. Shaw, Karen A., Michael D. Jenkins & Anthony J. Walters (Business, Montana)

NEBRASKA

Starting and Operating a Business in Nebraska. Shaw, Karen A., Michael D. Jenkins & Anthony J. Walters (Business, Nebraska)

NEVADA

Incorporating in Nevada. Brown, W. Dean (Business, Nevada)

Starting and Operating a Business in Nevada. Shaw, Karen A., Michael D. Jenkins & Anthony J. Walters (Business, Nevada)

NEW HAMPSHIRE

Starting and Operating a Business in New Hampshire. Shaw, Karen A., Michael D. Jenkins & Anthony J. Walters (Business, New Hampshire)

NEW JERSEY

Incorporating in New Jersey. Brown, W. Dean (Business, New Jersey)

Starting and Operating a Business in New Jersey. Shaw, Karen A., Michael D. Jenkins & Anthony J. Walters (Business, New Jersey)

NEW MEXICO

Starting and Operating a Business in New Mexico. Shaw, Karen A., Michael D. Jenkins & Anthony J. Walters (Business, New Mexico)

NEW YORK

How to Divorce in New York: Negotiating Your Divorce Settlement Without Tears or Trial. Raggio, Grier H. (Family Law, New York)

How to Form Your Own New York Corporation. Mancuso, Anthony (Corporations and Partnerships, New York)

How to Legally Change Your Name Without a Lawyer. Anosike, Benji O. (Names, New York)

OKLAHOMA

Incorporating in Oklahoma. Brown, W. Dean (Business, Oklahoma)

Starting and Operating a Business in Oklahoma. Shaw, Karen A., Michael D. Jenkins & Anthony J. Walters (Business, Oklahoma)

OREGON

Divorce Guide for Oregon. Baldwin, Richard C. (Family Law, Oregon)

Divorce Guide for Oregon: Step-by-Step Guide for Obtaining Your Own Divorce. Weisser, Herb (Family Law, Oregon)

Have You Made Your Will?: Will and Estate Planning Kit for Washington and Oregon. (Wills, Trusts, and Probate, Washington)

Incorporating in Oregon. Brown, W. Dean (Business, Oregon)

Incorporation and Business Guide for Oregon: How to Form Your Own Corporation. Davis, Thomas C. (Corporations and Partnerships, Oregon)

Landlord/Tenant Rights in Oregon. Marcus, Michael (Landlord and Tenant, Oregon)

Real Estate Buying/Selling Guide for Oregon. Granata, Fred A. (Real Estate, Oregon)

Starting and Operating a Business in Oregon. Shaw, Karen A., Michael D. Jenkins & Anthony J. Walters (Business, Oregon)

Wills and Estate Planning Handbook for Oregon. Johnson, Rees C. (Wills, Trusts, and Probate, Oregon)

PENNSYLVANIA

Incorporating in Pennsylvania. Brown, W. Dean (Business, Pennsylvania)

Starting and Operating a Business in Pennsylvania. Shaw, Karen A., Michael D. Jenkins & Anthony J. Walters (Business, Pennsylvania)

RHODE ISLAND

Starting and Operating a Business in Rhode Island. Shaw, Karen A., Michael D. Jenkins & Anthony J. Walters (Business, Rhode Island)

SOUTH CAROLINA

How to File for Divorce in South Carolina. Cullen, Thomas P. & Edward A. Haman (Family Law, South Carolina)

How to Form Your Own Partnership. Haman, Edward A. (Corporations and Partnerships, South Carolina)

How to Make a South Carolina Will. Cullen, Thomas P. & Mark Warda (Wills, Trusts, and Probate, South Carolina)

Starting and Operating a Business in South Carolina. Shaw, Karen A., Michael D. Jenkins & Anthony J. Walters (Business, South Carolina)

SOUTH DAKOTA

Starting and Operating a Business in South Dakota. Shaw, Karen A., Michael D. Jenkins & Anthony J. Walters (Business, South Dakota)

TENNESSEE

Incorporating in Tennessee. Brown, W. Dean (Business, Tennessee)

Starting and Operating a Business in Tennessee. Shaw, Karen A., Michael D. Jenkins & Anthony J. Walters (Business, Tennessee)

TEXAS

Educator's Guide to Texas School Law. Kemerer, Frank R. & Jim Walsh (Education, Texas)

How to File for Divorce in Texas. Rolcik, Karen Ann & Edward A. Haman (Family Law, Texas)

How to Form a Simple Corporation in Texas. Rolcik, Karen Ann & Mark Warda (Corporations and Partnerships, Texas)

How to Form Your Own Partnership. Haman, Edward A. (Corporations and Partnerships, Texas)

How to Form Your Own Texas Corporation. Mancuso, Anthony (Corporations and Partnerships, Texas)

How to Make a Texas Will. Rolcik, Karen Ann & Mark Warda (Wills, Trusts, and Probate, Texas)

How to Probate an Estate in Texas. Rolcik, Karen Ann (Wills, Trusts, and Probate, Texas)

How to Start a Business in Texas. Brown, William R. & Mark Warda (Business, Texas)

How to Win in Small Claims Court in Texas. Brown, William R. (Small Claims Court, Texas)

Incorporating in Texas. Brown, W. Dean (Business, Texas)

Landlords' Rights and Duties in Texas. Brown, William R. & Mark Warda (Landlord and Tenant, Texas)

Legal Handbook for Texas Nurses. Murphy, Susan Schuerman (Health Law, Texas)

Starting and Operating a Business in Texas. Shaw, Karen A., Michael D. Jenkins & Anthony J. Walters (Business, Texas)

What Every 18-Year-Old Needs to Know About Texas Law. Wallace, L. Jean (General/Comprehensive Works, Texas)

UTAH

Incorporating in Utah. Brown, W. Dean (Business, Utah)

Starting and Operating a Business in Utah. Shaw, Karen A., Michael D. Jenkins & Anthony J. Walters (Business, Utah)

VERMONT

Starting and Operating a Business in Vermont. Shaw, Karen A., Michael D. Jenkins & Anthony J. Walters (Business, Vermont)

VIRGINIA

How to Get a Divorce: A Practical Guide for the Residents of the District of Columbia, Maryland & Virginia Who Are Contemplating Divorce. Kalenik, Sandra (Family Law, Virginia)

Incorporating in Virginia. Brown, W. Dean (Business, Virginia)

Starting and Operating a Business in Washington, D.C. Shaw, Karen A., Michael D. Jenkins & Anthony J. Walters (Business, Washington, D.C.)

WEST VIRGINIA

Starting and Operating a Business in West Virginia. Shaw, Karen A., Michael D. Jenkins & Anthony J. Walters (Business, West Virginia)

WISCONSIN

Incorporating in Wisconsin. Brown, W. Dean (Business, Wisconsin)

Starting and Operating a Business in Wisconsin. Shaw, Karen A., Michael D. Jenkins & Anthony J. Walters (Business, Wisconsin)

WYOMING

Starting and Operating a Business in Wyoming. Shaw, Karen A., Michael D. Jenkins & Anthony J. Walters (Business, Wyoming)

LIST OF PUBLISHERS

ABA Public Education
750 N. Lake Shore Dr.
Chicago, IL 60611
(800) 285-2221

Addison-Wesley
1 Jacob Way
Reading, MA 01867
(800) 447-2226

Allworth Press
10 East 23rd St.
New York, NY 10010
(212) 777-8395
(800) 283-3572

Alpha Books
201 W. 103rd
Indianapolis, IN 46290
(317) 581-3500
(800) 428-5331

Amacom
135 W. 50th St., 15th Fl.
New York, NY 10020
(800) 262-9699

American Association of Retired Persons
1909 K. St. N.W.
Washington, DC 20049
(202) 872-4700

American Bar Association
750 N. Lake Shore Dr.
Chicago, IL 60611
(312) 988-5000
(800) 285-2221

American Intellectual Property Law Association
2001 Jefferson Davis Hwy.
Suite 203
Arlington, VA 22202
(703) 521-1680

American Library Association
50 E. Huron St.
Chicago, IL 60611
(312) 944-6780
(312) 280-2424
(800) 545-2433

American Management Association
135 W. 50th St.
New York, NY 10020-1201
(212) 586-8100

Anderson Publishing Company
2035 Reading Rd.
Cincinnati, OH 45202
(513) 421-4142
(800) 582-7295

Ann Arbor Book Co.
P.O. Box 8064
Ann Arbor, MI 48107

Arden Press
3122 Woodbury Rd.
Cleveland, OH 44120
(216) 751-5327

Avery Publishing Group, Inc.
120 Old Broadway
Garden City Park, NY 11040
(800) 548-5757

Bailard, Biehl & Kaiser, Inc.
120 Old Broadway
Garden City Park, NY 11040
(603) 922-5105
(800) 282-5413

Bantam Books
1540 Broadway
New York, NY 10036-4096
(800) 223-6834

Barron's Educational Series, Inc.
P.O. Box 8040
250 Wireless Blvd.
Hauppauge, NY 11788
(516) 434-3311
(800) 645-3476

Bell Springs Publishing
Box 640 Bell Springs Rd.
Laytonville, CA 95454
(707) 984-6746

Betterway Publications, Inc.
P.O. Box 219
Crozet, VA 22932

Bicycle Law Books
P.O. Box 1457
Falls Church, VA 22041
(703) 941-0666

Bob Adams, Inc.
260 Center St.
Holbrook, MA 02343-1074
(800) 872-5627

Books by Village Press
15 Summer St.
Freeport, ME
(207) 865-4588

Bureau of National Affairs BNA Books Distribution Center
300 Raritan Center Pkwy.
P.O. Box 7816
Edison, NJ 08818-7816
(201) 225-1900
(800) 372-1033

Callaghan & Co.
50 Broad St. E.
Rochester, NY 14694
(716) 546-1490
(800) 221-9428

Catbird Press
16 Windsor Rd.
North Haven, CT 06473
(800) 360-2391

Charles Scribner's Sons
866 3rd Ave.
New York, NY 10022
(212) 702-2000

Chicago Review Press, Inc.
814 N. Franklin St.
Chicago, IL 60610
(312) 337-0747
Orders Only:
(800) 888-4741

Chilton Book Co.
(Subsidiary of Capital
Cities /ABC, Inc.)
1 Chilton Way
Radnor, PA 19089
(215) 964-4000

Citadel Press
120 Enterprise Ave.
Seacaucus, NJ 07094
(201) 866-4199

Clark Boardman, Co., Ltd.
375 Hudson St.
New York, NY 10014
(212) 929-7500
Customer Service:
(800) 221-9428

Consumer Financial Solutions
P.O. Box 355
Needham, MA 02192-0355
(617) 849-9421

Consumer Publishing, Inc.
9317 Barrington Blvd. S.W.
Knoxville, TN 37922-6210
(615) 539-2412
(800) 677-2462

Consumer Reports Books
101 Truman Ave.
Yonkers, NY 10703
(914) 378-2000

Consumers Union of U.S., Inc.
101 Truman Ave.
Yonkers, NY 10703
(914) 378-2000

Contemporary Books, Inc.
2 Prudential Plaza, Suite 1200
Chicago, II. 60601
(312) 540-4500
(800) 621-1918

**Copyright Information
Services**
P.O. Box 1460
Friday Harbor, WA 98250-1460
(206) 378-5128

Creighton-Morgan Publishing
2200 Beach St., Suite 102
San Francisco, CA 94123
(415) 922-6684

Crossway Books
1300 Crescent St.
Wheaton, IL 60187
(708) 682-4300
Sales only:
(800) 323-3890

Crown Publishers
201 E. 50th St.
New York, NY 10022
(212) 572-6192
(800) 726-0600

**Dearborn Financial
Publishing/Trade**
155 N. Wacker Dr.
Chicago, IL 60606-1719
(312) 836-4400
(800) 621-9621

**Dell Publishing Co./
Trade Paperback**
113 Sylan Ave.
Englewood Cliffs, NJ
07632-2807
(415) 433-9900

Do-It-Yourself Legal Publishers
24 Commerce St., Suite 1732
Newark, NJ 07102
(201) 242-0282

Doane-Western, Inc.
8900 Manchester Rd.
St. Louis, MO 63144

Doubleday & Co., Inc.
666 5th Ave.
New York, NY 10103-4094
(212) 765-6500
(800) 223-6834

East Coast Publishing
P.O. Box 2829
Poughkeepsie, NY 12603
(914) 471-9577
(800) 327-4212

ENAAQ Publishers
P.O. Box 1375
Chicago, IL 60690
2nd address:
5226 S. Ingleside
Chicago, IL 60615
(312) 643-4247

**Executive Enterprises
Publications Co., Inc.**
22 W. 21st St.
New York, NY 10010-6904
(212) 645-7880

ExPress Publishing
P.O. Box 1639
El Cerrito, CA 94530-4639
(510) 236-5469
(800) 999-4650

Facts on File
460 Park Ave. S.
New York, NY 10016
(212) 683-2244
(800) 322-8155

Farrar, Straus, Giroux, Inc.
19 Union Square W.
New York, NY 10003
(212) 741-6900
(800) 788-6262

Fawcett Crest
201 E. 50th St.
New York, NY 10022
(800) 733-3000

Four Walls Eight Windows
39 W. 14th St., #503
New York, NY 10011
(212) 206-8965

Fred B. Rothman & Co.
10368 W. Centennial Rd.
Littleton, CO 80127-4200
(800) 457-1986

Gale Research, Inc.
835 Penobscot Bldg.
Detroit, MI 48226
(313) 961-2242
(800) 877-4253

Gambling Times
16140 Valerio St. No. B
Van Nuys, CA 91406-2916
(818) 781-9355

Government Institutes, Inc.
4 Research Plaza, Suite 200
Rockville, MD 20850
(301) 921-2355

Golden Rain Press
P.O. Box 5458
Berkeley, CA 94705

Gopher Publications, Inc.
870 Mason Rd., Suite 104-813
Katy, TX 77450
(713) 461-6700

Grand River Press
P.O. Box 1342
East Lansing, MI 48823
(517) 332-8181

Granite Publishers
2510 Martin
Willow Grove, PA 19090
(215) 659-6279

Guilford Press
72 Spring St.
New York, NY 10012
(800) 365-7006

Gulf Publishing Company
P.O. Box 2608
Houston, TX 77252-2608
(713) 520-4444
(800) 231-6275

HALT, Inc.
1319 F. St. N.W., Suite 300
Washington, DC 20004
(202) 347-9600

Harcourt Brace & Co.
6277 Sea Harbor Dr.
Orlando, FL 32887
(800) 831-7799

**Harcourt Brace
Jovanovich, Inc.**
See Harcourt Brace & Co.

Harper-Collins Canada, Ltd.
See Harper-Collins Publishers

Harper-Collins Publishers
10 E. 53rd St.
New York, NY 10022-5299
(212) 207-7000
(800) 331-3761
Ordering address:
1000 Keystone Industrial Park
Scranton, PA 18512-4621

**Harper & Row Publishing/
Trade Paperbacks**
10 E. 53rd St.
New York, NY 10022
(212) 207-7000

Henry Holt & Co.
115 West 18th St.
New York, NY 10011
(800) 247-3912

Horizon Publishers
P.O. Box 490
50 S. 500 W.
Bountiful, UT 84010
(801) 295-9451

Houghton-Mifflin
222 Berkely St.
Boston, MA 02116
(617) 272-1500
(800) 225-3362

Images Press
7 E. 17th St.
New York, NY 10003
(212) 675-3707

Interlink Press, Inc.
908 Kenfield Ave.
Los Angeles, CA 90049
(310) 472-2908

**International Self-
Counsel Press**
1704 N. State St.
Bellingham, WA 98225
(360) 676-4530
(800) 663-3007

Interweave Press, Inc.
201 E. Fourth St.
Loveland, CO 80537-5601
(970) 669-7672
(800) 272-2193

Irwin Professional Publishers
1333 Burr Ridge Pkwy.
Burr Ridge, IL 60521
(708) 789-4000
(800) 663-3961

John Wiley & Sons, Inc.
605 3rd Ave.
New York, NY 10158-0012
(212) 850-6418

Jossey-Bass Publications
350 Sansome St.
San Francisco, CA 94104
(415) 433-1767
(800) 223-2336

Joy Publishing Co.
P.O. Box 2532
Boca Raton, FL 33427
(407) 276-5879

Kent Press
P.O. Box 1169
Stamford, CT 06904-1169
(203) 358-0848

Kessinger Publishing Company
P.O. Box 160
1550 Roger's Lane
Kila, MT 59920
(406) 756-0167

Knowledge Industry Publications, Inc.
701 Westchester Ave.
White Plains, NY 10604
(914) 328-9157
(800) 800-5474

LawPrep Press, Inc.
P.O. Box 642095
San Francisco, CA 92714
(512) 459-7859
(800) 872-5273

Legal Counsel for the Elderly
601 E. St. N.W.
Washington, DC 20049
(202) 434-2120

Legal Self Help
1109 Pennsylvania Ave.
St. Cloud, FL 32769
(305) 652-5767

Legovac
P.O. Box 150340
Altamonte Springs, FL 32715
(407) 830-1380

Lexington Books
125 Spring St.
Lexington, MA 02173
(800) 235-3565

Limelight Editions
118 E. 30th St.
New York, NY 10016
(212) 532-5525

Linch Publishing
P.O. Box 75
Orlando, FL 32802
(800) 327-7055

Little, Brown & Co.
200 West St.
Waltham, MA 02514
(800) 759-0190

Longman
The Longman Building
10 Bank St.
White Plains, NY 10601
(914) 993-5000

Lyons and Burford
31 W. 21st St.
New York, NY 10010
(212) 620-9580

Macmillan Publishing Co., Inc.
200 Old Tappan Rd.
Old Tappan, NJ 07675
(800) 223-2336

Madrona Publishing Co., Inc.
P.O. Box 22667
Seattle, WA 98122
(210) 325-3973

Major Market Books
146 S. Lakeview Dr., Suite 300
Biggsboro, NJ 08026

McFarland & Company
P.O. Box 611
Jefferson, NC 28640
(910) 246-4460
(800) 253-2187

McGraw-Hill
1221 Avenue of the Americas
New York, NY 10020
(212) 512-2000
(800) 262-4729

Moyer Bell Limited
Colonial Hill/RFD 1
Mt. Kisco, NY 10549
(800) 759-4100

Mul-T-Rul Press
P.O. Box 250
Ft. Morgan, CO 80701
(303) 867-6201

**National Committee for
Citizens in Education**
1875 Connecticut Ave. N.W.,
      #150
Washington, DC 20009-5728
(202) 408-0447

**National Underwriter
Company**
505 Gest St.
Cincinnati, OH 45202
(513) 721-2140
(800) 543-0874

**Next Decade Marketing
& Advertising**
39 Old Farm Rd.
Chester, PA 07930
(908) 879-6625

Nick Lyons Books
31 W. 21st St.
New York, NY 10010
(212) 620-9580

Nolo Press
950 Parker St.
Berkeley, CA 94710
(510) 549-1976
(800) 992-6656

North Light Books
1507 Dana Ave.
Cincinnati, OH 45207
(513) 984-0717
(800) 289-0963

Northland Publishing
P.O. Box 1389
Flagstaff, AZ 86002
(520) 774-5251
(800) 346-3257

Nova Publishing Co.
1103 W. College St.
Carbondale, IL 62901
(618) 457-3521

Oasis Press/PSI Research
300 N. Valley Dr.
Grant's Pass, OR 97526
(800) 479-9464

Oceana Publications, Inc.
75 Main St.
Dobbs Ferry, NY 10522
(914) 693-8100

Outlet Book Co.
225 Park Ave. S.
New York, NY 10003
(212) 254-1600

P. Gaines Co.
P.O. Box 2253
Oak Park, IL 60303

Pantheon Books
201 E. 50th St.
New York, NY 10022
(212) 572-2838
(800) 638-6460

Penguin Books
P.O. Box 120
Bergenfield, NJ 07621
(201) 387-0600

Perigree Books
P.O. Box 506
East Rutherford, NJ 07073
(800) 223-0510

Pharos Books
(*See also* World Almanac)
200 Park Ave.
New York, NY 10166
(212) 692-3824

Pilot Books
103 Cooper St.
Babylon, NY 11702
(516) 422-2225

Pineapple Press, Inc.
P.O. Drawer 16008
Sarasota, FL 34239
(941) 335-0955
(800) 746-3275

Plain English Press
7200 Wisconsin Ave.
Bethesda, MD 20814
(301) 657-1616
(800) 453-9968

Praeger
(*See also* Greenwood Publishing
Group, Inc.)
88 Post Rd. W., Box 5007
Westport, CT 06881
(203) 226-3571

Prentice Hall
113 Sylvain Ave.
Englewood Cliffs, NJ 07632
(201) 592-2000
(800) 922-0579

Price/Stern/Sloan
11835 Olympic Blvd., 5th Fl.
Los Angeles, CA 90064
(310) 477-6100
(800) 631-8571

**Prima Publishing
& Communication**
P.O. Box 1260
Rocklin, CA 95677-1260
(916) 624-5718

Prometheus Books
59 John Glenn Dr.
Amherst, NY 14228-2197
(716) 691-0133
(800) 421-0351

**Pro Se Divorce
Group/Cobblesmith**
Patterson's Wheeltrack
Freeport, ME 04032
(207) 865-6495

ProSe Associates
9889 S. Spring Hill Dr.
Highlands Ranch, CO 80126
(303) 470-9597

Publishing Horizons, Inc.
5701 N. High St., Suite 1
Worthington, OH 43085
(614) 436-7282

Random House
400 Hahn Rd.
Westminster, MD 21157
(800) 733-3000

Reader's Digest
260 Madison Ave., 9th Fl.
New York, NY 10016
(212) 850-7007
(800) 431-1246

Royce-Baker Publishing
P.O. Box 1609
Lafayette, CA 94549
(510) 284-7684

Running Press
125 S. 22nd St.
Philadelphia, PA 19103
(800) 345-5359

Scott, Foresman and Co.
1900 E. Lake Ave.
Glenview, IL 60025
(708) 729-3000

Self-Counsel Press
1704 N. State St.
Bellingham, WA 98225
(360) 676-4530
(800) 663-3007

**Shapolsky Publishing
Company**
136 W. 22nd St.
New York, NY 10011
(212) 505-2505

Simon & Schuster, Inc.
1230 Avenue of the Americas
New York, NY 10020
(212) 698-7000
(800) 223-2348

Sourcebooks
163 Amsterdam Ave., #131
New York, NY 10023
(212) 496-1310

**Southern Illinois
University Press**
P.O. Box 3697
Carbondale, IL 62902
(618) 453-2281

Sphinx Publishing
P.O. Box 25
Clearwater, FL 34617
(813) 587-0999
(800) 226-5291

St. Martin's Press
175 Fifth Ave., Rm. 1715
New York, NY 10010
(212) 674-5151
(800) 221-7945

Staff Directories
P.O. Box 62
Mount Vernon, VA 22121
(703) 739-0900

Sterling Publishing Company
387 Park Ave. S.
New York, NY 10016-8810
(800) 367-9692

Summit Books
1230 Avenue of the Americas
New York, NY 10020
(212) 698-7501
(800) 223-2336

TAB Books/McGraw-Hill
P.O. Box 40
Blue Ridge Summit, PA
17294-0850
(717) 794-2191
(800) 233-1128

TeleTravel Network
P.O. Box 606
Northbrook, IL 60065
1200 Sherman Rd., Suite 30
Northbrook, IL 60062
(708) 564-8860

Times Books
201 E. 50th St.
New York, NY 10022
(212) 751-2600

Times Books/Random House
See Random House

Trilogy Books
50 S. Delacey Ave., Suite 201
Pasadena, CA 91105
(818) 440-0669

**U.S. Government
Printing Office**
USGPO Stop SSMR
Washington, DC 20401
(202) 512-2364

University of Hawaii Press
2840 Kolowalu St.
Honolulu, HI 96822
(800) 956-2840

University of Texas Press
P.O. Box 7819
Austin, TX 78713-7819
(512) 471-7233
(800) 252-3206

University of Washington Press
P.O. Box 50096
Seattle, WA 98145-5096
(800) 441-4115

Van Nostrand Reinhold
115 Fifth Ave.
New York, NY 10003
(212) 254-3232

Vintage Books
Div. of Random House
201 E. 50th St., 31st Fl.
New York, NY 10022
(800) 733-3000

WANT Pub. Co.
1511 K. St. N.W.
Washington, DC 20005
(202) 783-1887

Washington Book Trading Co.
P.O. Box 1676
Arlington, VA 22210
(703) 525-6873

West Publishing Co.
610 Opperman Dr.
P.O. Box 64529
Saint Paul, MN 55164-0526
(800) 328-9424

Westview Press
5500 Central Ave.
Boulder, CO 80301
(303) 444-3541
(800) 456-1995

Wiley Law Publications
7222 Commerce Center Dr.
Colorado Springs, CO 80919
(719) 548-1900
(800) 753-0655

William Morrow and Company, Inc.
Wimor Warehouse
P.O. Box 1219
29 Plymouth St.
Fairfield, NJ 07007
(201) 227-7200

Windcrest/McGraw-Hill
P.O. Box 40
Blue Ridge Summit, PA
17294-0850
(717) 794-2191
(800) 233-1128

Workman Publishers
708 Broadway
New York, NY 10003
(212) 254-5900
(800) 722-7202

Writer's Digest Books
1507 Dana Ave.
Cincinnati, OH 45207
(513) 531-2222
(800) 289-0963

Yale University Press
302 Temple St.
New Haven, CT 06520
(203) 432-0960